Civic Ground

Rhythmic Spatiality and the Communicative Movement between Architecture, Sculpture and Site

PATRICK LYNCH

She sang beyond the genius of the sea.
The water never formed to mind or voice,
Like a body wholly body, fluttering
Its empty sleeves; and yet its mimic motion
Made constant cry, caused constantly a cry,
That was not ours although we understood,
Inhuman, of the veritable ocean.

The sea was not a mask. No more was she.
The song and water were not medleyed sound
Even if what she sang was what she heard.
Since what she sang was uttered word by word.
It may be that in all her phrases stirred
The grinding water and the gasping wind;
But it was she and not the sea we heard.

For she was the maker of the song she sang.
The ever-hooded, tragic-gestured sea
Was merely a place by which she walked to sing.
Whose spirit is this? we said, because we knew
It was the spirit that we sought and knew
That we should ask this often as she sang.

If it was only the dark voice of the sea
That rose, or even colored by many waves;
If it was only the outer voice of sky
And cloud, of the sunken coral water-walled,
However clear, it would have been deep air,
The heaving speech of air, a summer sound
Repeated in a summer without end
And sound alone. But it was more than that,
More even than her voice, and ours, among
The meaningless plungings of water and the wind,
Theatrical distances, bronze shadows heaped
On high horizons, mountainous atmospheres
Of sky and sea.

        It was her voice that made
The sky acutest at its vanishing.
She measured to the hour its solitude.
She was the single artificer of the world
In which she sang. And when she sang, the sea,
Whatever self it had, became the self
That was her song, for she was the maker. Then we,
As we beheld her striding there alone,
Knew that there never was a world for her
Except the one she sang and, singing, made.

Ramon Fernandez, tell me, if you know,
Why, when the singing ended and we turned
Toward the town, tell why the glassy lights,
The lights in the fishing boats at anchor there,
As night descended, tilting in the air,
Mastered the night and portioned out the sea,
Fixing emblazoned zones and fiery poles,
Arranging, deepening, enchanting night.

Oh! Blessed rage for order, pale Ramon,
The maker's rage to order words of the sea,
Words of the fragrant portals, dimly-starred,
And of ourselves and of our origins,
In ghostlier demarcations, keener sounds.
—Wallace Stevens, *The Idea of Order at Key West*

We can only hear the rhythm that is immanent within a given form if we ourselves introduce rhythm into it. That means we must really be actively involved ourselves in order to elicit rhythm at all. Every work of art imposes its own temporality upon us, not only the transitory arts of language, music, and dance. When considering the static arts, we should remember that we also construct and read pictures, that we also have to enter into and explore the forms of architecture. These too are temporal processes. One picture may not become accessible to us as quickly as another. And this is especially true of architecture... we have to go up to a building and wander around it, both inside and out. Only in this way can we acquire a sense of what the work holds in store for us and allow it to enhance our feeling for life.
—Hans-Georg Gadamer, *The Relevance of the Beautiful and Other Essays*

... one has to be willing at some point in his reflections to turn from it to the bustling, arguing, acutely sensitive Athenian citizens, with civic sense identified with a civic religion, of whose experience the temple was an expression, and who built it not as a work of art but as a civic commemoration.... The one who sets out to theorize about the esthetic experience embodied in the Parthenon must realize in thought what the people had in common, as creators and as those who were satisfied with it, with people in our own homes and on our own streets.
—John Dewey, *Art as Experience*

There is no such thing as an absence of content, no gap between the practical and the symbolic, only progressively more explicit modes of symbolic representation.
—Peter Carl, *City as Image Versus Topography of Praxis*

"Every perception is an act of creation" as [Gerald] Edelman says. As we move about, our sense organs take samplings of the world, and from these, maps are created in the brain. There then occurs with experience a selective strengthening of those mappings that correspond to successful perceptions —successful in that they prove the most useful and powerful for the building of "reality"... "signals were going back and forth in all kinds of hidden ways (as you usually get them by the non-verbal interactions between the players) that make the whole set of sounds a unified ensemble".... The players are connected. Each player, interpreting the music individually, constantly modulates and is modulated by others.... This is Edelman's picture of the brain, as an orchestra, an ensemble, but without a conductor, an orchestra which makes its own music. When I walked back to my hotel after dinner with Gerry that evening, I found myself in a sort of rapture. It seemed to me that the moon over the Arno was the most beautiful thing I had ever seen. I had the feeling of being liberated from decades of epistemological despair—from a world of shallow, irrelevant computer analogies into one full of rich biological meaning, one which corresponded with the reality of brain and mind.
—Oliver Sacks, *On the Move*

When new factors intervene, the law must be reformulated because of new observations and new conditions. Aristotle's *causa efficiens* still belongs to the natural, prescientific worldview.... The Greeks distinguished four causes: material, formal, final, and efficient. Let's take the example of a silversmith who is going to make a bowl. Four causes must be distinguished in making it: the order (to make the bowl) is the determining factor, "what ought to be done", something final, the "for the sake of which".... The second cause is the shape of the bowl which the silversmith must have in mind as its form. This is the eidos. *Forma* is already a reinterpretation of eidos, which means (visible) shape. The final and the formal cause are interrelated. Together they determine the third cause, the material... here, the silver. The fourth cause: this is the *causa efficiens*, the production, poiesis...; this is the craftsman. The modern *causa efficiens* is no longer the same! Poiesis and praxis are not the same: making and doing. Praxis has a motivation! In the modern sense, causality presupposes a process of nature, not a poiesis.... In today's science we find the desire to have nature at one's disposal, to make it useful, to be able to calculate it in advance, to predetermine how the process of nature occurs so that I can relate it to safety.... That which can be calculated in advance and that which is measurable—only that is real.... In physics, the law of causality has a reality (*Wirklichkeit*), but even there only in a very limited way. What Aristotle said is true according to the worldview of those days: the Aristotelian concept of motion for instance... means that a body is transported from one place to another, to *its* place. Galileo abandoned notions of above and below, right and left. Physical space is homogenous. No point is more distinctive than any other. Only this conception of space makes it possible to determine locomotion. Space must be homogenous because the laws of motion must be the same everywhere. Only then can every process be calculated and measured. Nature is viewed in a very specific way to satisfy the conditions of measurability. Beings acquire the character of being mere objects and of being objectified.... Being "an object" only makes its appearance in modern natural science. The human being then becomes a "subject" in the sense of Descartes. Without these presuppositions, the expression "objective" is meaningless... Is our totally different conception of space merely subjective?... This is already a glimpse of being! A genuine insight! It's a different kind of truth than in physics, perhaps a higher one! If one sees that, then one has a free stance towards science.
—Martin Heidegger, *Zollikon Seminars: Protocols, Conversations, Letters*

9 **Preface**

11 **The Vulnerability and Re-emergence of Civic Ground: The Problem of Sculptural Form versus Sculptural Spatiality**

12 Civil and Military Architecture

20 Bacteria Navigating a Nutrient Gradient: The Schumacher-Eisenman Interview

23 The Cardboard Architecture of Peter Eisenman

23 Collisive Fields and Bricolage: Colin Rowe on Urbanism as Architectural Form

28 Architecture and Sculpture: The Eisenman-Serra Interview

30 The Harvest of a Seed: Le Corbusier and the Synthesis of the Arts

31 Sculpture versus Architecture: Serra and Judd on Eisenman and Gehry

32 Memorial to the Murdered Jews of Europe: The Eisenman-Serra Collaboration at Berlin and Rachel Whiteread's Judenplatz Holocaust Memorial at Vienna

35 *Shift* by Richard Serra

37 Rhythm and the Recuperation of Civic Ground

39 **Urban Topography, Physiognomy, Spatial Continuity and *Praxis***

40 The Topography and Physiognomy of Cologne

42 Dalibor Vesely on Topography, Physiognomy and the Continuity of References in Communicative Space

44 The Sacrifice of Space: David Leatherbarrow on Palladio's Palazzo Chiericati and the Palazzo della Ragione

46 Building as Gesture and Argument: Joseph Rykwert on Borromini's Oratory at Rome

48 Peter Carl on Topography of *Praxis*

51 **Rhythmic and Communicative Space**

52 Adolphe Appia on l'Espace Rythmique and Hellerau

56 Henri Lefebvre on Rhythmanalysis and Paris

58 Dalibor Vesely on Communicative Movement at Chartres and Würzburg

61 Peter Carl on *Praxis* as Horizons of Involvement

65   **The City Gives a Definite Direction to Nature: *Decorum*, Temporality and Urbanity**

66   Hans-Georg Gadamer on Art and Architecture as Ornament, *Decorum* and Play

70   Clare Lapraik Guest on Figural Cities and Florence

75   **Geometric and Rhythmic Spatiality in the Heidegger-Chillida Collaboration**

76   Art and Space

80   Museo Chillida-Leku and *The Wind Comb* by Eduardo Chillida at San Sebastián

90   The Kursaal by Rafael Moneo at San Sebastián

97   The Brunnenstern and *Hütte* at Todtnauberg

105   **Rhythmic Spatiality and the Communicative Movement between Site, Architecture and Sculpture at St Peter's Klippan by Sigurd Lewerentz**

147   **Álvaro Siza and Santa Maria at Marco de Canaveses**

161   **Rhythmic Spatiality and the Communicative Movement between Site, Architecture and Sculpture at Victoria Street**

162   The Problem of Civic *Decorum* and the Disunity of the Arts in Victorian London

164   The Problem of Urban Infrastructure, Civic Depth, Rhythmic Spatiality and the Disunity of Victoria Street

169   Iridescent Architecture

195   **Conclusion: The Civic Grounds for a Poetics of Architecture**

Richard Serra, *NJ-2*, Rounds: Equal
Weight, Unequal Measure, Rotate,
Gagosian Gallery, Britannia Street, London,
1 October 2016–10 March 2017.

Double Frontispiece: Adolphe Appia,
etching of stage set for *Orpheus and
Eurydice*, Act II, "The Descent into the
Underworld", 1926.

Preface

1   See Temple, Nick, "Rites of Intent: The Participatory Dimension of the City", in *Cityscapes in History: The Urban Experience*, Heléna Tóth and Katrina Gulliver ed, Surrey: Ashgate Publishing, 2014, pp 155–78 and *Renovatio Urbis: Architecture, Urbanism and Ceremony in the Rome of Julius II (The Classical Tradition in Architecture)*, London: Routledge, 2011.

2   Heidegger, Martin, *Zollikon Seminars: Protocols, Conversations, Letters*, Medard Boss ed, Evanston: Northwestern University Press, 2001, p 23.

3   "Richard Serra and Michael Craig-Martin's 50-year conversation about art", *The Guardian*, 1 October 2016. In suggesting that in his sculptural work "formal and material imagination", inform each other, Serra is surely elliptically referring to the work of Gaston Bachelard, who "defined a new concept" that "images of matter... the material imagination... [is] necessarily required for a complete philosophical study of poetic creation". Gilson, Etienne, "Foreword" in *The Poetics of Space*, Boston: Beacon Press, 1992, p ix. Serra refers at length to his problems with architects (and their lack of understanding and appreciation of sculpture, place, topography, weight etc) and to the influence of architectural space, tectonics, and the importance of phenomenological aspects of perception upon his work in *Writings/Interviews: Richard Serra*, Chicago: Chicago University Press, 1994. The influence of phenomenology upon post-war American sculptors arguably originated in the teaching and early writings of Rosalind E Krauss, and is suggested in her book *Passages in Modern Sculpture*, originally published in 1977 (Cambridge, MA: MIT Press, 2001, pp 239–40). Its continuing relevance to critical appreciation of American land art, and in particular the importance of spatiality and of Martin Heidegger's essay "The Origin of the Work of Art", is noted by Geoff Dyer in his essay about Walter De Maria's *Lightning Field* (Catron County, New Mexico, 1977), "Space in Time" in *White Sands: Experiences from the Outside World*, London: Canongate, 2016, pp 76–77. I examine below Heidegger's significant interaction with the artist Eduardo Chillida— and perhaps also surprisingly, the profound role that sculpture played in articulating his views on spatiality and temporal experience. Despite his abhorrent political views, Heidegger's influence on artists is profound; anyone seriously interested in modern sculpture cannot ignore this, I fear.

This is the third in a series of books, written over a 20-year period, which consider the architectural and urban significance of different aspects of poetics: theatricality, *mimesis*, and now rhythm.

Civic Ground is my interpretation of the civic and philosophical character of architectural poetics. The heft and urgency of my argument stems from the need to promote and to protect these values in the face of their vulnerability from formalism, cynicism and nihilistic irony.

I have attempted to reveal the persistence of an authentic tradition of poetics in imaginative creative work and critical thinking in major modern thinkers— and their interpretations of Plato and Aristotle— despite the clichés and bad faith of much twentieth-century art history, architecture and design culture.

Civic Ground concerns the public nature of artistic experience, its fundamental position in our culture, and the role that architecture, sculpture and landscape play in articulating this. "Civic" does not refer to a use class as such, ie a town hall, but to something which orients architecture towards the shared conditions of urbanity. The term "common ground" gets close to the original meaning of "civilitas", which more properly means civic order.[1] Its use in English law as common public grazing land, and its survival as "digital commons", suggests its participatory character. However, the ground itself is not simply a matter of property or of one's "rights" to use it, nor is it just a metaphor or a philosophical construction, but it is the basis and grounds for life itself. Martin Heidegger claimed that its central orienting importance for human affairs might be best described as "motive" (what Aristotle called "mythos" or plot) and wrote that: "Motive is a ground for human action.... All different grounds are themselves based on the principle of ground. All that is has a ground."[2] The term "motive" fuses together the representational and practical aspects of architecture as the expression of civic ground.

Similarly, rhythm is also a universal phenomenon, and its manifestation in culture—as festival, architectural decor, performance, sculptural spatiality etc—is one way in which the primary conditions of the natural world and the recurring social aspects of reality become sensible to us.

The traditional appreciation of rhythm in the visual arts is fragmented and disrupted, and so the location of my arguments and the instances of its possible renewal range widely across time and geography. This book is not a literature survey, nor an attempt to demonstrate a preconceived theory: it presents certain prejudices and experiences of a practicing architect, and involved my participation in a number of events and conversations.

It demands this of a reader too. It is phenomenology in the sense that writing and reading this book was and is a participatory experience. It is an example of hermeneutic enquiry in terms of an interpretation of symbolic meanings revealed in everyday life. The serious and playful wit of Sigurd Lewerentz, for example, only becomes apparent if you engage with his spaces in the ways he intended.

Unusually perhaps, interpretation in this book often began with drawings, both as memories of events and places as well as in situ observations.

My conclusions are derived from a form of *praxis* and engagement with artworks and architectural settings, situating them in their social and political and physical topography, and from my own creative attempts as a designer to situate my work in a continuum of civic culture.

My aim has been to uncover the grounds for the recuperation of civic values in architecture, and to make a case for the renewed vitality and relevance of the poetic imagination. These are obviously highly hubristic aims, but I hope that the profound significance of the contributions of the artists and architects discussed on the following pages is nonetheless useful in re-establishing its potential today. In particular, the profound influence of modern philosophy upon modern artists suggests that the ideas that informed twentieth-century visual culture still remain vital today. Coincidentally, as I write this, on 5 October 2016, Richard Serra is exhibiting a new sculpture, *NJ-2*, a few hundred yards away from Artifice's offices at London's King's Cross. Talking about *NJ-2*, and his life's work, Serra provides a coda for this book, and a fitting introduction to its thesis:

> Matter informs form... the rhythm of your body deals with time in relation to space... as the piece changes, you have to change, and either hasten your stride or turn in ways you hadn't anticipated.... Time enters into the equation of your bodily rhythms as you move through the work. It alters the time of your experience.... All our gestures, all our movements, the rhythm of our body, every time we turn, every time we take a step, every time we move, the gravitational load impinges on us.... It is a defining factor in how we know our bodily movements through space and time. And no one pays attention to that... lightness does seem to be the way the evolution of the planet is going in terms of microchips or whatever. But in terms of understanding your presence on the earth, we're all bound by weight and gravity.[3]

The Vulnerability and Re-emergence of Civic Ground: The Problem of Sculptural Form versus Sculptural Spatiality

Friendship seems to hold cities together, and
lawmakers seem to take it more seriously than justice.
—Aristotle, *Nicomachean Ethics*[1]

Do you not seek great praise, glory, and immortality
in this magnanimity of yours? Not only with pomp;
not with ostentation, nor with crowds of flatterers
will you earn real whole-hearted praise, for this can
only be won by virtue.
—Leon Battista Alberti, *On the Art of Building in
Ten Books*[2]

The narcissist has no interest in the future because,
in part, he has so little interest in the past…. In a
narcissistic society—a society that gives increasing
prominence and encouragement to narcissistic
traits—the cultural devaluation of the past reflects
not only the poverty of the prevailing ideologies,
which have lost their grip on reality and abandoned
the attempt to master it, but the poverty of the
narcissist's inner life. A society that has made
"nostalgia" a marketable commodity on the cultural
exchange quickly repudiates the suggestion that life
in the past was in any important way better than
life today.
—Christopher Lasch, *The Culture of Narcissism:
American Life in an Age of Diminishing Expectations*[3]

Civil and Military Architecture

Until the twentieth century, architectural treatises
were almost invariably concerned with "*architettura
civile*" or "*architettura civile militare*", drawing what
used to be an obvious distinction between the two.[4]
Civic architecture was primarily oriented towards an
urban context, and its architects were predominantly
concerned with the order of the city; military buildings,
by nature of their defensive role and singular purpose
could, to some degree, avoid the questions of
urbanity and "*decorum*" that ground all other types
of architecture in civic life. In particular, the closed
nature of modern military architecture finds its echo
in military parades, which are a sort of parody of
secular and religious festivals, and of everyday life.

Frontispieces to architectural treatises by Sanmicheli and Guarini.

Despite the modern tendency to associate forts
or military camps with utilitarian values, Medieval
castles and Renaissance fortifications adopted a quasi-
representational and emphatically communicative
role in the life of a city by establishing a recognisable
high point on the horizon of a town and demarcating
a clear border between urban and rural territory. This
act of fortification and definition was understood
in intellectual terms to represent some degree of
equilibrium between the cultural and natural worlds.
Furthermore, the role of *civilitas* in architecture is
closely related to notions of good government and
well-being, ideals that coalesced in Renaissance Italy
around the Humanist conception of the recuperation
of the importance of *decorum* in classical aesthetics
and philosophical thinking. The civic role of architecture
re-emerged in fifteenth-century Italian cities as a way
to unite, to accommodate and to represent abstract
concepts such as justice. This drive towards visualising
and embodying philosophical ideals was manifest
in changed attitudes towards wealth and sexual
love, with an ethos oriented towards a sense of the
appropriateness of ornament and public display in
the visual arts and in rhetoric, and in political life in
general. Architecture's civic dimension represented
an idealised and actual spatial continuity—a
balance between the intimate and representational
dimensions of city life.

This is one reason why Renaissance cities are often
described as the birthplaces of modern consciousness.
Terry Comito and Robin Evans emphasise the
gregariously physical character of this sort of society—
the embodied and carnal nature of civic life.[5]
Architects such as Michelangelo or Francesco
Borromini would not have described their architecture
in terms of "space" or "function"—as something
abstract. Architecture was a matter of rhythm and
proportion, the latter a mode of analogy of natural law
and mediation of temporal circumstances and cosmic
conditions. Geometry was a means to demonstrate
mediation in architecture, embodying the invisible
aspects of reality. Architecture coordinated and
oriented the civil aspects of law and religion within
the specific conditions of a town or city (or even a
village church). Renaissance patrons self-consciously
demanded representation of urbanity and early
modern city settings were attempts to mediate the
"intolerable strains on communal institutions".[6] The
so-called "natural states" of the Italian Republics
commingled political with religious power, and the
dominant *doxas* of church and state were often made
up of members of the same family. Renaissance
architecture therefore reflects the extremely mediated
character of society, and one very clearly sees the
theatrical character of this sort of public life in the
gestural corporeality of Michelangelo's thresholds.[7]

In general terms, Renaissance architecture
represents the tense nature of efforts to reconcile
familial loyalties—and domestic spatial typologies
—within a public realm that was made up of series of

1   Aristotle, *Nicomachean Ethics*, Joe
    Sachs trans, Newburyport: Focus
    Publishing, 2002.

2   Cited in Borsi, Franco, *Leon Battista
    Alberti: The Complete Works*, London:
    Harper and Row, 1977, p 20.

3   Lasch, Christopher, preface of *The
    Culture of Narcissism: American Life
    in an Age of Diminishing Expectations*,
    New York: WW Norton & Company,
    1991, pp xvi–xvii.

4   See for example the treatises of
    Guarino, Sanmicheli, Orsini, Fonda
    etc. Aldo Rossi made a similar point
    at the beginning of his career in
    his article "*Il concetto di tradizione
    nell'architettura neoclassica milanese*"
    ["The Concept of Tradition in Neo-
    Classical Milanese Architecture"]:
    "Despite their different origins,
    architects like Cantoni, Antonelli,
    Cagnola or Canonica represent
    among their diverse personalities
    the manifest intention of a renovation
    of architecture towards a moral and
    political conception linked to social
    life and its civic aspect", *Società*
    12, no 3, June 1956, p 482. Cited in
    Lopes, Diogo Seixas, *Melancholy and
    Architecture: On Aldo Rossi*, Zurich:
    Park Books, 2015.

5   Comito, Terry, *The Idea of the Garden
    in the Renaissance*, New Brunswick:
    Rutgers University Press, 1986;
    Evans, Robin, "Figures, Doors and
    Passages", *Translations from Drawing
    to Building and other essays*, London:
    Architectural Association Publications,
    1996; see also Brothers, Cammy,
    *Michelangelo, Drawing and the
    Invention of Architecture*, New Haven:
    Yale University Press, 2008.

6   Martines, Lauro, *Power and
    Imagination: City States in Renaissance
    Italy*, London: Pimlico, 2002, p 97;
    see also Tafuri, Manfredo, *Interpreting
    the Renaissance: Princes, Cities,
    Architects*, New Haven: Yale University
    Press, 2006.

7   Lynch, Patrick, "Only Fire Forges Iron:
    On the Architectural Drawings of
    Michelangelo", *Drawing: The Process*,
    London: Intellect Press, 2005.

Michelangelo, drawing for Porta Pia,
Rome, c 1560.

C Elam, drawing of processional route
for visiting dignitaries in Florence during
the fifteenth century showing Medici
properties, 1978.

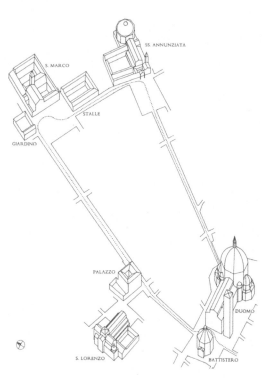

8   Marinetti, Filippo Tommaso, "The
     Founding and Manifesto of Futurism",
     Le Figaro, 20 February, 1909, cited in
     *Documents of 20th Century Art: Futurist
     Manifestos*, Robert Brain, RW Flint
     and JC Higgitt trans, Caroline Tisdall,
     Umbro Apollonio ed, New York:
     Viking Press, 1973, pp 19–24.

9   See for example Rowan Moore's
     obituary for Dame Zaha Hadid in
     which he quotes Sir Peter Cook
     from an article in *Viz*, 1978, on
     the work of OMA: "I would hate",
     he concluded, "to live with their
     buildings. I would run screaming
     from among their barrack-like
     walls and their prison-like cages: I
     would look anxiously upwards to see
     whether their absurd sculpted heads
     are going to shout slogans at me.
     So, if the office does start to build, I
     hope—despite my prejudices—that
     the viciousness is retained, the spirit
     is retained, the spirit is turned into
     awesome, upsetting flesh." Moore,
     Rowan, "Zaha Hadid, 1950–2016: an
     appreciation", *The Observer* (online),
     3 April 2016.

10 Gadamer, Hans-Georg, *The Relevance
     of the Beautiful and Other Essays*,
     Cambridge: Cambridge University
     Press, 1986, p 40.

layers of material and habitual territories, access to which was mediated by gestures as well as architectural thresholds. This network is clear in the way in which families such as the Medici consolidated their power and articulated their influence in the appropriation of parts of the city of Florence. In the creation of a series of representational *topoi* and buildings, articulated by artworks and embodied in festive movement, wealth was oriented by rhetoric, and specifically oriented by architecture towards civic virtue.

In seeing modern cities in utilitarian terms, we have extended the essential characteristics of "military architecture" into the design of modern urban architecture generally, having forgotten about its civic aspects. What we might call a "military-industrial aesthetic" has become the dominant expression of almost all urban buildings, especially so in the case of office building design, much housing and even modern universities and schools. Arguably, a process of aesthetic transference occurred at the beginning of the twentieth century whereby what was previously typical for barracks and factories only—a lack of ornament and a utilitarian appearance—became the norm for almost all buildings regardless of their use or context. We can see the influence of this thinking in the use of militaristic terms to describe design as "avant-garde", "cutting edge" or its even more aggressive cousin "bleeding edge"—often with regards to technology. This tendency originates in "The Founding and Manifesto of Futurism"

by Filippo Tommaso Marinetti, in which he declared that "we intend to exalt aggressive action, a feverish insomnia, the racer's stride, the mortal leap, the punch and the slap", and he explicitly admitted, "We will glorify war."[8] Contemporary architecture still suffers from the mistaken belief that any futuristic aesthetic must be aggressive.[9]

In contrast to this bombast, civic architecture is informed by the rhythms of civic life; one of the primary characteristics of civic ground is a tacit, latent quality of imminence. Hans-Georg Gadamer called this quality "festive quiet".[10]

When we contemplate aesthetic questions today, especially the task of creating an ecological aesthetic, we are also confronting, I believe, questions of *decorum* and ethics. Civic architecture is obviously also the expression of civic values; and this derives as much from a response to solar orientation and the rhythms of the natural world, as the expression of a building's use and its urban orientation.

In other words, the role of civic ground, and in particular its rhythmic spatial character, informs the design not only of what is now known as "the public realm", but also the physiognomy, porosity and character of buildings. This book seeks to correct the twentieth-century prejudice for militaristic design— and its revival today in parametric formalism—stating the case instead for a modern, spatial, civic architecture. In part this is a project of recovery—recovery and recuperation of ideas and an understanding of history that situates modern architecture in a continuum of social creativity. Writing in the late 1970s and then again in the early 1990s, the cultural historian Christopher Lasch describes the contempt that narcissistic societies have for history as symptomatic of "a state of restless, perpetually unsatisfied desire":

> Having trivialized the past by equating it with outmoded styles of consumption, discarded fashions and attitudes, people today resent anyone who draws on the past in a serious discussion of contemporary conditions or attempts to use the past as a standard by which to judge the present. Current critical dogma equates every such reference to the past as itself an expression of nostalgia.[11]

Lasch claims that "much of what currently goes under the name of radicalism" and involves the rejection of the past is in fact a symptom of individual and cultural narcissism. He insists that in contrast "many radical movements in the past have drawn strength and sustenance from the myth or memory of a golden age in the still more distant past."[12] Acceptance of the value of history, he contends, "by no means rests on a sentimental illusion; nor does it lead to a backward looking, reactionary paralysis of the political will". In our own discipline, however, architects continue to elide futuristic style with the idea that this somehow inevitably equates to progressive social values; equate technological advances with formal spectacle and novelty; remain seemingly unable to accept the potential of modern construction techniques; and at the same time adopt a sceptical approach towards the dangers and damage that result from the misapplication of technology to urban situations. New Urbanism seems incapable of accommodating new urban typologies; avant-garde architects refuse any political dimension to design. In both instances, the civic character of architecture suffers. The problem of narcissism that Lasch describes is a psychological and urban phenomenon, and so it is not surprising that Lasch discusses Richard Sennett's book *The Fall of Public Man* at length as both the diagnosis of and the potential antidote to the narcissistic character of American culture.[13] What is at stake in the work of Lasch and Sennett is the survival of urban culture, and this primarily involves the communal character of human identity.

Joseph Rykwert first stated over 50 years ago that "all the great civilizations... have mythical accounts of [their] origins, and rituals which guide the planner and the builder".[14] In *The Idea of a Town* he proposed an "anthropology" of architecture to counter the prevailing contemporary tendency to see urban settlement in terms of efficiency and "transport engineering":

> The rectilineal patterns of the Roman towns, which survive in the street patterns and even the country lanes of old imperial lands, from Scotland to Sudan, are often thought to be the by-product of a utilitarian surveying technique. This is not how the Romans themselves saw it: the city was organized according to divine laws.[15]

Rykwert demonstrated how "the elaborate geometrical and topographical structure of the Roman town" was not primarily the result of a picturesque or utilitarian compositional system—ie modern prejudices, but rather something "growing out of and growing around a system of custom and belief which made it a perfect vehicle for a culture and a way of life". In particular, he demonstrated that:

> [Whilst] the convention is that the Roman town was a more formal version of a military camp... the convention inverts the truth. The Roman town was not a formalized and enlarged camp. On the contrary, the Roman military camp was a diagrammatic evocation of the city of Rome, an *anamnesis* of *imperium*. The Romans did not treat the setting up of camp as a makeshift for a night's sleep: it was part of the daily military routine that no army was permitted to settle down for the night without setting up camp ceremonially.[16]

Establishing a Roman camp was essentially a rhythmic ritual. Aligning habitation with the cardinal axis of the sun grounded the architecture in the customs and habits of Rome and in the local conditions of a place; the army literally woke and slept facing the sun. Roman architecture is thus revealed to be impervious to any modern formalism that obscures the symbolic and spatial role of nature in civic architecture. In contrast to the formalistic "natural metaphors" that afflicted urban design discourse directly after the war—"images drawn from nature... a tree, a leaf, a piece of skin tissue, a hand and so on"—Rykwert claims that "the town is not really like a natural phenomenon. Rather, it is an artefact—an artefact of a curious kind, compounded by willed and random events, imperfectly controlled. If it is related to physiology at all, it is more like a dream than anything else."[17] This observation led him to question the unlimited growth of cities suggested by neo-liberal economics ("Fear of restriction often appears in the form of fear of cramping autonomous growth") and to question the invisible ideology or "conceptual framework" that "is designed to evade the issue of imposing any order of an extra-economic nature on the city".[18]

Rykwert's study was subtitled "On the Anthropology of Urban Form in Rome, Italy and the Ancient World" and it extended beyond Europe to consider the symbolic role of myth and ceremonial rites in the foundation of Chinese, Indian, Tibetan, African, South American, Greek and even Aboriginal and Sioux settlements. His work is less that of an antiquarian, as has been claimed, but concerns rather "cosmic man" and the psychological and spatial aspects of culture as they manifest themselves in human behaviour across time and in variously diverse climates, topography, and

11 Lasch, *The Culture of Narcissism*, p xvii. See Hadid's comments in her RIBA Gold Medal acceptance speech: "I have always believed in progress and in creativity's role in progress. That's why I remain critical of any traditionalism. I worry about the dominance of neo-rationalism in London's current transformation," cited in Clark, Tim, "Gold medal winner Hadid marks award with 'traditionalism' fears", *Building Design* (online), 4 February 2016.

12 Lasch, *The Culture of Narcissism*, pp xvi–xvii.

13 Sennett, Richard, *The Fall of Public Man*, New York: Knopf, 1977.

14 Rykwert, Joseph, *The Idea of a Town: The Anthropology of Urban Form in Rome, Italy and the Ancient World*, Cambridge, MA: MIT Press, 1988, p 26.

15 Rykwert, *The Idea of a Town*, p 25.

16 Rykwert, *The Idea of a Town*, p 68: "The first act was to plant the general's *vexillum* at a chosen spot. It was from the *vexillum* that the *praetorium* was paced out. On the border of the *praetorium* and the principal road a *groma* was stood to ensure that the streets were laid out at right angles. The line between the *vexillum* and the *groma* gave the surveyor the main axis of the camp... it gave the direction of the *cardo maximus* of the camp, and led to the *Porta Praetoria*, the principle of the four camp gates.... To the right of the *praetorium* was the *auguraculum*, the place where the commander sacrificed and omens were read, so the essential decisions about the future of the campaign were taken according to the will of the gods."

17 Rykwert, *The Idea of a Town*, p 24.

18 Rykwert, *The Idea of a Town*, p 24.

The Roman Forum, from the House of the Vestal Virgins to the foot of the Capitol. The north point corresponds to that of the Domus Caligulae.

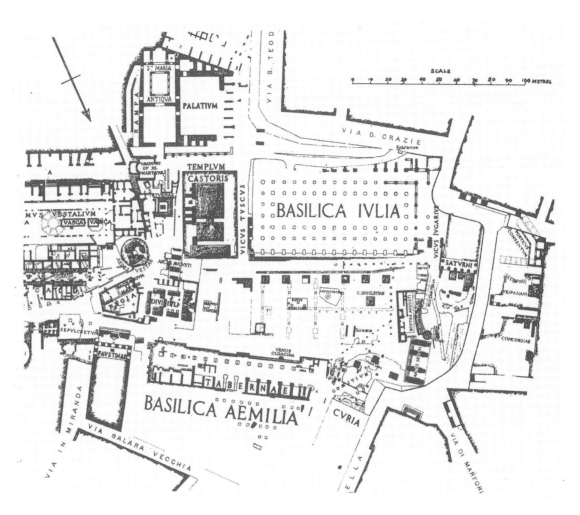

19 See "The Wobble: The Cat with Nine Lives": in discussion with Peter Eisenman, Mark Wigley claimed that "Rykwert is an antiquarian" at a graduate seminar at Columbia University School of Architecture, September 2012.

20 Rykwert, *The Idea of a Town*, p 202.

21 Quoted in Rykwert, *The Idea of a Town*, p 189.

22 Rykwert, *The Idea of a Town*, p 189.

23 See "The Cultural Significance of Architecture: In Memory of Dalibor Vesely", Emmanuel College Cambridge, 10 April 2016: "Poetics is symbolism, it's just Catholic propaganda", declared Fred Scott.

religious and everyday activities.[19] Rykwert's main *animus* is the paucity of the modern understanding of city formation, and the subsequent impoverished character of twentieth-century urbanism, in theory and in practice. He does not prescribe an easy way to recover a symbolic conception of urban form, but concludes that whilst "we have lost all certainty about the way the world works... this does not absolve us from looking for some ground of certainty in our attempts to give form to human environment".

The ancient Roman believed that "the whole universe and its meaning could be spelt out of his civic institutions", Rykwert claims.[20] Baron Haussmann, the military architect of the reconstructed "efficient" plan for Paris, asked himself rhetorically: "What municipal bonds link the two million inhabitants who crowd into Paris?... For them Paris is a great consumers' market, a vast workshop, and arena for ambition."[21] Rykwert's conclusion is that the latter tendency is not enough to establish the grounds for meaningful human habitation. However, he does not have any faith in attempts to reconstruct or to resurrect copies of traditional urban form solely in terms of style. His message is ambiguous; it is not a lament, nor is it a theory in the modern sense of a manual for reconstruction of lost artefacts or a prescription for political action. In fact

Rykwert reaches the very modern conclusion that since "the cosmologists are constantly reshaping" the world "round us" and we are "not even sure if it is expanding or contracting or is constantly renewing itself" humans today must "look for it inside ourselves: in the constitution and structure of the human person".[22]

Rykwert's criticism of capitalist "growth" and of the instrumentalist paradigm in general implies at once a rejection of both picturesque formalism and of any systematic approach towards urban design. Whilst his conclusion suggests that reflection might be a better way to think about the cosmic dimension of existence, his project primarily concerns the *polis*, not the individual psyche.

Civic life (or the life of the *polis*) cannot be reduced, Rykwert suggests, to questions about drainage or transport; in his view, urban culture transcends utilitarianism.

This view remains contentious, and the suggestion of the relevance of any legitimate survival of symbolic content in urban life remains difficult for many critics to accept.[23]

Nonetheless, the symbolic power of the public realm and of civic architecture remains strong. Beyond the world of professional architectural discourse the fundamental importance of civic ground continues

Place de la République, Paris, redesign
by TVK (Pierre Alain Trévelo and Antoine
Viger-Kohler), 2013.

to reassert itself, and architectural projects remain capable of contributing to its articulation, often without the prior permission of authorities responsible for the official formation of the urban realm. For example, our understanding of the significance of "informal settlements" remains somewhat trapped in a utilitarian interpretation of "refugee camps" as places that can be primarily defined in terms of a lack of sanitation. However, recent events in the "Jungle" refugee camp at Calais reveal the persistence of some profound aspects of human inhabitation, despite limited resources and a transient population. The creation of a Christian church by refugees was quickly followed by the erection of some ad hoc civic structures. In some cases, this initiative was supported by construction industry professionals amongst the camp population, and in others it was abetted by professional architects from Ireland. The five structures erected by Gráinne Hassett's team of volunteers can only be described in civic terms (as "a medical centre", "a women's centre" etc).[24] Their combined effect was to create a town. The aesthetic may have been provisional and the various uses defined simply by different coloured tarpaulins, but nonetheless they combined to define the camp as civic ground.[25]

Whilst this description might seem fanciful, the reaction of the British and French governments to the spontaneous formation of an informal and yet increasingly civic settlement was swift and brutally destructive. Only a few weeks after the erection of the first symbolic structures, police raids in February 2016 targeted not only the civic architecture but also its domestic hinterland.[26] In some cases the "public buildings" were torched immediately; whilst in other instances the clearing of dwellings destroyed the layers of urban depth that enabled the emergence of a recognisable "high street". The destruction of the hinterland and of the most articulate civic buildings was an explicit attack on urban order. The interdependence of both the hinterland of dwellings and the foreground of public buildings reveals their profound reciprocity. In some cases it was the hinterland that was attacked first, leading then to the isolation and ultimate end of the civic structures, and in other cases the high street itself was attacked first.

What is unusual in this instance is that a coherent urban metabolism was articulated and embodied in the formation of a recognisably permanent, civic dimension to the camp. This civic dimension was a manifestation of what Peter Carl calls "urban depth".[27] I would like to suggest that the revelation of civic ground (by its occupants' communal symbolic and practical action) led to its perception as a threat to the established political order, and ultimately to attempts at its erasure. French police were also prepared to destroy the makeshift chapel and a mosque.[28]

French public life is unusually secular for a predominantly Christian country, and its popular civic culture is largely proudly non-symbolic in any traditional sense. Nonetheless, it is the tacit dimension of civic culture that has been attacked in the recent terrorist atrocities in Paris. Bars, restaurants, publishing houses, theatres, and the street life of a modern secular city have been the targets; civic ground, and the unspoken assumption of its existence, is at stake in Paris today.

24 Gráinne Hassett, in conversation with the author, 15 March 2016. See also Siggins, Lorna, "The Irish Architect Determined to Defend the 'Jungle'", *The Irish Times* (online), 5 March 2016.

25 Robert Mull, in conversation with the author, 15 March 2016: "Walking around on duckboards, I felt as if I were in a Medieval village, without plumbing of course, but in that sense almost exactly like a Medieval village with its church, public buildings and more or less private domains facing onto streets and public spaces."

26 "Calais 'Jungle camp': clashes as authorities demolish homes", *The Guardian* (online), 1 March 2016.

27 See Carl, Peter, "Civic Depth", *Mimesis: Lynch Architects*, London: Artifice books on architecture, 2015, pp 113–134.

28 "Calais 'Jungle': Migrant church and mosque demolished", *BBC News* (online), 1 February 2015. The final destruction of the Jungle refugee camp at Calais, by French police, occurred at the end of October 2016.

Calais Women's Centre, by Gráinne Hassett et al, 2015–2016.

Photographs of the Calais Women's Centre by Gráinne Hassett, 28 February 2016, and her plan of the Calais Refugee Camp, 2015–2016. Population: 5,497. An area of homes of over 3,455 people at the bottom half of this map was subsequently demolished by the Calais Prefecture. The proto-town area held shops, restaurants, schools, mosques, churches, a theatre, a nightclub, a legal centre, a women and children's centre and vaccination and medical centres. Violent demolition commenced on 29 February 2016, days after the Court of Lille had on 23 February given an order to preserve community buildings and to initiate eviction in a planned manner over several weeks. Only 300 beds were made available to refugees. There were 445 children in the demolition area, of whom 305 were separated and unaccompanied. ©Gráinne Hassett, The Calais Builds Project.

The responses by Parisians to this attack vividly demonstrate the continuing power of civic ground to act as the setting and support for civic life. Until recently the Place de la République was a roundabout and yet its rehabilitation as a site of political *agon* cannot be clearer. It remains the place where many festivals begin and end, operating as a playground every day, and can be said to be the centre of official and unofficial political protest and action in France.[29] What has enabled its re-emergence as a site of public discourse and protest and solidarity? Partly it is the simple act of the removal of cars from what was originally common ground—it is now one of the largest open spaces in central Paris. Additionally, the civic importance of a place named after an act of political liberation cannot be underestimated even within a culture of *laïcité* and general aversion to any form of mass communication beyond sport and the pursuit of pleasure. The architects have created a pleasant enough space: areas of shade, an acknowledgement of the previous presence of a water tower in some inoffensive ponds, areas for children to play etc. What pre-exists however is not simply the memory of another more articulate civic tradition, but also its concrete presence in the sculptured figures of Marianne and the secular trinity of civic graces, *Liberté*, *Egalité* and *Fraternité*. In other words, the deep resonance of the Place de la République within the urban metabolism of Paris and the civic consciousness of Parisians was latent and arguably imminent. Attacks upon the civic virtues of the French Republic in actual terms then demanded, it seems, an actual and symbolic response. Its spontaneity and specificity points towards the abiding power of civic ground and its primary characteristics as the combined articulated power of the arts of architecture, landscape and sculpture. Their profound contribution together in the articulation of civic ground is the topic of this book.

What may have been the spontaneous recovery of a public voice in the Place de la République was possible because its spatial rehabilitation was instigated by the mayor Bertrand Delanoë. "My predecessors handed the square over to the car. We wanted to put beauty, the values of the République, and a joie de vivre at the heart of this transformation", he declared shortly after its reopening in June 2013.[30]

My aim is to reveal that the possibility of the renewal of civic architecture lies in the social and physical conditions of civic ground. Civic architecture might be said, in fact, to be the articulation of the communicative and rhythmic character of these conditions. However, these conditions are mostly obscured by the elision of aesthetic questions with social ones—as if new social conditions arise naturally from new aesthetics.

The continuing aggressive reassertion of this possibility (even its inevitability) is one of the most problematic characteristics of contemporary architectural discourse that continues to obscure and even to deny architecture's civic potential.[31] I will begin with exposing the damaging consequences of this assertion and attempt to reveal in particular the problematic consequences of neo-liberal (aesthetic) architectural theory in urbanistic terms. In contrast to this, the central role of rhythm will return as a *leitmotif*, revealing its centrality in spatiality generally, and as a primary characteristic of classical architectural theory, modern aesthetic philosophy and contemporary artistic *praxis*.

The contemporary manifestation of urbanism as window-dressing for "a great consumer market", as Haussmann saw nineteenth-century Paris, is referred to by Rykwert as "Emirates Style",[32] whereby "access to tall buildings is determined by road engineering, the traffic engineers are back in control".[33] "Emirates Style" might be seen as a sad parody of avant-garde architecture—a parody of "world class icons" erected in the hope that somehow a "world class city" might emerge despite the dominance of "road engineering" and without the urban metabolism, symbolic structure or orientation towards urban depth of serious civic design.[34] Arguably, the problems and origins of Emirates Style can be traced to the 1980s IBA projects in West Berlin of Peter Eisenman, Peter Cook, et al. It remains impossible to imagine a high street, never mind a city quarter, made up of "icon" buildings.

Similarly, despite various attempts to mimic traditional culture it is impossible to see Poundbury, UK, as anything other than a suburban car-based settlement, despite its creators' intentions to offer an alternative to this pattern of development.

My intention is to investigate the reciprocity between site, architecture and sculpture as a characteristic of civic ground. Specifically, the character of the recurring rhythmic continuity and communication between site and architecture—its disruption, or arrhythmia, and possible recuperation, is the subject of this book. This potential continuity will be investigated as a series of characteristics that can be summarised as a number of critical terms— urban topography, communicative and rhythmic spatiality, ornament, decorum, nature, second nature, representation etc—and these terms will be explored in exemplary case studies. My "method" is to look at built examples of the rhythmic continuity between architecture, site and sculpture in different contexts and at different times, looking for lessons that might account for its persistence as a mode of critical imaginative discourse and *praxis*. In other words, I proceed from theory to *praxis*, whilst keeping alive the traditional Greek idea that these terms are not exclusive and that the former is no guarantee of the success of the latter. At a couple of points I have introduced quite long footnotes in order not to interrupt the flow of the argument, whilst referring to contemporary examples today that are evidence of the misunderstanding of certain philosophical or artistic principles. My approach seeks continuity of philosophical themes across time, and is also a critique of the corruption of these themes by architects who have misconstrued their meaning. In particular, I will reveal the central importance of

29 Annabel Gray, in conversation with the author, 31 March 2016. See also "TVK: Place de la République", *domus* (online), 2 August 2013; and also Kamdar, Mira, "In Paris, a Protest Movement Awakens", *The New York Times* (online), 14 April 2016; and Mathiesen, Karl, "Peaceful Paris climate gathering descends into clashes with police", *The Guardian* (online), 29 November 2015.

30 Willsher, Kim, "Paris mayor praises beauty of revamped Place de la République", *The Guardian* (online), 16 June 2013.

31 See Schumacher, Patrik, *The Autopoiesis of Architecture Volume 1: A New Framework for Architecture*, and *Volume 2: A New Agenda for Architecture*, London: John Wiley & Sons Ltd, 2010 and 2012.

32 Rykwert, Joseph, *The Judicious Eye: Architecture Against the Other Arts*, Chicago: University of Chicago Press, 2009, p 243.

33 Joseph Rykwert in conversation with the author, "Inhabitable Models: Eric Parry, Haworth Tompkins, Lynch Architects", Common Ground, Venice Biennale of Architecture, 2012. The interview was presented as a soundtrack to a film, and considered the intellectual context in which Rykwert wrote *The Idea of a Town: The Anthropology of Urban Form in Rome, Italy and the Ancient World* in the 1950s. This was arguably the first example of an attempt to counter technological-functionalist attitudes towards "road engineering" with an appreciation of the ritualistic basis for what might more properly be called "civic design". In a discussion with Mark Wigley at a graduate seminar at Colombia University a few weeks after the Biennale opened in September 2012, Eisenman asked himself aloud, presumably rhetorically, "Why did Colin Rowe ask me to attack Rykwert?" ("The Wobble", graduate seminar at Columbia University School of Architecture, Peter Eisenman and Mark Wigley, September 2012.) Eisenman was angry and amazed that "phenomenology" had reappeared at the Biennale, something which he and Wigley "thought we had killed off" ("they took your *alma mater*, your old mother, Cambridge University, and corrupted her" etc). Whilst it is not wholly accurate to describe Rykwert's work as "phenomenology", it is an attempt to create a more profound discourse for architecture than narrow technical functionalism or pseudo-intellectual formalism. This study is inspired by such endeavours also, and by the sense that if one took seriously the question of sculpture and architecture, and more generally examined the relationships between philosophy and architecture, one might arrive at somewhat different conclusions than the literalism of Eisenman and Rowe.

34 See for example "Dubai: World-class Infrastructure and a Global Hub for Trade, Transport and Tourism", *Articles, Economic Development, Forbes Custom* (online) and Mayo, Anthony, Nitin Nohria, Umaimah Mendhro and Johnathan Cromwell, "Sheikh Mohammed and the Making of 'Dubai, Inc.'", HBS Case Collection, Harvard Business School website, last updated August 2010.

35 Gadamer, "Art as Play Symbol and Festival", *The Relevance of the Beautiful*, pp 44–45; see also Dewey, John, *Art as Experience*, New York: Perigee Books, 2005, pp 14–15, pp 153–157, pp 165–193.

36 On the one hand, this is the basis of an augment that Heidegger articulates as earth/world = conditions/possibilities (which is what one might also call the ethical basis for any artistic or practical "commission"); which is why it is possible for him to claim that "the city gives a direction to nature" (I will investigate the historical basis for this claim in some detail below: it is interesting to note that orientation is implied in the notion of a commission, and that it shares a common etymological ground with "missile"). On the other hand, we now find ourselves in a condition of committing to "nature" as a way to orient our cities with regards to natural conditions, ecology, ethical and sustainable architecture and food production etc.

37 Gadamer, "Hermeneutics as Practical Philosophy", *The Relevance of the Beautiful*, p 90. William Blake reminds us that, "Energy is eternal delight!"

38 *Praxis* in this sense should not be confused with "action", as it is in much contemporary political thought; *praxis* is also a mode of contemplation.

39 Gadamer, Hans-Georg, *Truth and Method*, London: Sheed and Ward, 1993, pp 124–125.

40 See Harman, Graham, et al, "Is there an Object Oriented Architecture?" for The Architecture Exchange, London, May–June 2013. NB: Harman is now a professor of architectural theory at Sci-Arc, Los Angeles.

41 Gadamer, *Truth and Method*, p 315: "the prior knowledge involved in a techne cannot be called 'theoretical', especially since experience is automatically acquired in using this knowledge. For, as knowledge, it is always related to practical application, and even if recalcitrant material does not always obey the person who has learnt his craft, Aristotle can still rightly quote the words of the poet: 'Techne love tyche (luck) and tyche loves techne.' This means that the person who has been taught his trade will have the most luck."

42 Gadamer, *Truth and Method*, p 316.

eurhythmia in Greek aesthetics—in dance, poetry and architecture—as a form of measure, and as the pause in movement that makes it communicative.

Gadamer believed that rhythm plays a central role in revealing the participatory character of artworks, and that this establishes the grounds for the continuous "relevance of the beautiful":

> The autonomous temporality of the artwork is illustrated particularly well by our experience of rhythm. What a remarkable phenomenon rhythm is! Psychological research tells us that rhythm is a factor in our hearing and understanding. If we produce a series of sounds or notes repeated at regular intervals, we find that the listener cannot help introducing rhythm into the series. But where precisely is this rhythm? Is it to be found in the objective and physical temporal relations between the sounds, in the wavelengths, frequencies, and so on? Or is it in the mind of the listener? It is clearly inadequate to conceive the matter in terms of such a crude set of alternatives. It is as true to say that we … perceive it there. Of course, our example of the rhythm to be perceived within a monotonous series is not an example drawn from art. Nevertheless, it shows that we can only hear the rhythm that is immanent within a given form if we ourselves introduce the rhythm into it. That means we must really be actively involved ourselves in order to elicit the rhythm at all. Every work of art imposes its own temporality upon us, not only the transitory arts of language, music, and dance. When considering the static arts, we should remember that we also construct and read pictures, that we also have to enter into and explore the forms of architecture. These too are temporal processes. One picture may not become accessible to us as quickly as another. And this is especially true of architecture. Our contemporary forms of technical reproduction have so deceived us, that when we actually stand before one of the great architectural monuments of human culture for the first time, we are apt to experience a certain disappointment. They do not look as "painterly" as they seem from the photographic reproductions that are so familiar to us. In fact, this feeling of disappointment only shows that we still have to go beyond the purely artistic quality of the building considered as an image and actually approach it as architectural art in its own right. To do that, we have to go up to a building and wander around it, both inside and out. Only in this way can we acquire a sense of what the work holds in store for us and allow it to enrich our feeling for life.[35]

I would like to suggest that the rhythmic character of the typical situations that one finds in buildings, and in urban settings generally (as rooms), is accompanied also by the rhythmic character of architectural facades and thresholds (as niches, windows, doorways etc). Both enable the hinterland of building interiors and of civic territories to coexist in the rhythm of city life, animated by both social occasion and analogues of myth, tradition, and the effects of weather, the seasons, natural and second nature etc.

Gadamer foregrounds the organic nature of humanity whilst emphasising "a decisive difference between animal and human being. The way of life of human beings is not so fixed by nature as is that of other living beings". He makes it clear that "animals too have *praxis* and *bios*… a way of life", whilst emphasising the role that the horizon of language plays in reason; the role this plays in choice defines humanity, just as natural conditions define the basis for freedom as "freedom from".[36] I write as a practising architect, not just as a theoretician; whilst I am concerned with the philosophical importance of civic ground as the site of human self-consciousness and action, my work is primarily oriented towards *praxis*. It is my belief that civic ground reveals the poetic nature of practical life and the practical character of poetics; the contribution they make together to the revelation of the full potential of civic life points to the shared character of creativity and the civic nature of the architectural imagination. *Praxis* is central to human life, since practice is "the mode of behaviour of that which is living in the broadest sense", Gadamer claims:

> Practice, as the character of being alive, stands between activity and situatedness. As such it is not confined to human beings, who alone are active on the basis of free choice (*prohairesis*). Practice means instead the articulation of life (*energia*) of anything alive, to which corresponds a life, a way of life, a life that is led in a certain way (*bios*).[37]

Praxis is thus an ethos (way of life) with energy and orientation.[38]

The character of *praxis* is closely related to both practical everyday life and to festive time. A participant in an ancient Greek festival was called a "*theoros*" Gadamer reminds us, and he defines theory as "true participation, not something active but something passive (*pathos*), namely being totally involved in and carried away by what one sees".[39] Modern theory does not define itself in terms of passive participation, but rather as productive knowledge. In the discipline of architectural education, the goal of theory is most often the desire to assert the dominance of reason; it is ordinarily manifest in systematic architecture and in its attempted autonomy from human situations and ecology.[40] Theory has become simultaneously divorced from practical life and somehow imbued with a spirit of automatic production—it is as if theory can stand in for experience and craft in assuring the success of an act of imagination. The character of this production is curiously sealed off from the traditional relationship between skill and luck that typifies the classical concept of creativity,[41] and also from the traditional character of artistic work as a kind of "self knowledge".[42]

Yet even contemporary architects and theorists otherwise convinced by its autonomy are beginning to question the limits of the possibility of systematic architecture, and do so by invoking notions of topography.[43] A sense of the deprived quality of abstract space leads those otherwise concerned with the autonomy of systematic or "parametric" architecture towards attempts to resituate their computational abstractions in concrete situations, albeit in ones in which "depth" and "landscape" become formalist metaphors.

Bacteria Navigating a Nutrient Gradient: The Schumacher-Eisenman Interview

An amusing, if also somewhat bemusing example of this type of confused systematic attitude towards theory and practice was published in 2013 in *Log* magazine. In discussion with Peter Eisenman, Patrik Schumacher declares:

> Each point in the urban field of our master-plan is embedded in a sequence of transformation that modulates building height, block size, grid density and directionality. Each block is also located within a typological morphing series. So urban dwellers and visitors can navigate the field according to all these gradients, like bacteria are navigating a nutrition gradient.[44]

Eisenman responds, suggesting that he has also recently become increasingly concerned with variety and locale:

> Give me any collage of initially unrelated elements and I can generate connections, resonances, invent correlations. I reject the pure interruption, the pure discontinuity, collage. That doesn't mean I'm not craving for as much versatility and diversity within this coherent texture.

However, despite referring to "texture", their primary design intent is "systems", "rules" and "aesthetic sensibility", attempting to combine "intuitive knowledge" with "order"—understood as self-consistent system, like apodictic geometry, ie a pile of rubbish has an order, as does improvisation—in an attempt to "simulate natural processes" and only then to allow these metaphoric and mechanistic "natural processes" to approach life. Schumacher admits to Eisenman, rather bizarrely—since they have both just professed little respect for Peter Zumthor (apparently he is not "critical" like "Rem")—that:

> I criticize your work to some extent because I think you're a great innovator on the level of concept and process—reflecting process and making it productive—but when I look at your work I feel that you could have benefitted from reflecting the

phenomenological dimension better.... It needs to acquire a sense of phenomenological presence that comes with attention to materiality and light. I think we sense our environment not only visually, but with the whole body where we feel lightness, heaviness, and that's the way we orient and navigate space. I feel sometimes, and this may be harsh, that you don't do that, that the environments you create don't have the force required to truly stimulate and you don't give your structures the material power and force that compels our attention and trust in them as forces to be reckoned with; you don't deliver sufficient presence. It's not substantial enough to draw you in. Your works are like stage sets; it doesn't give me the sense of reality that would compel me to pay attention to its ordering suggestions. Plaster and sheet rock cannot compete with concrete, steel, stone. Even the material magic of carbon fibre compels attention. So it's not heaviness, it's character that comes with material performances and specific affordances; the different characteristic presences and levels of force to draw you in and propel you. These are mediated via phenomenology, ie via visual, tactile, acoustic as well as proprioception and vestibular perception etc. Initially I'm always going by my intuitions and by what I am feeling, asking why I am attracted to this, why I am exhilarated here; and then I am trying to analyze what it is that works and what doesn't work intuitively. This way I can rationally validate or critique my aesthetic reactions. But there is a caution to be observed: the architect needs to distinguish and assess the difference between one's professional sensibilities as designers, the way we read and evaluate buildings as expert connoisseurs versus how the ordinary users of the buildings would experience them. The purpose must be to construct successful, innovative, productive spaces for users who are in the midst of their high performance pursuits: spatial orders and spaces that communicate and frame communication on a new level of complexity and intensity.

Schumacher seems to sense that there might be something else missing in a diagrammatic approach to architecture, which he approaches—as it were, from above (topography looks like a gradient graph when seen from above)—as the problem not only of the meaning of space, but also the problem of meaning understood as experience.[45] The problem remains for him not one of culture—or of wit or talent or rhetoric—but of how to relate abstract measurements and digital information to the lived world of a room, situated somewhere in a city. Except he doesn't start with a room, but with systems, and so his comments are at once poignant and sometimes unintentionally humorous:

> I found a way to integrate the semantic layer, the meaning layer, into the digital design model. I get the meaning layer as another correlated subsystem

43 See Autonomous Architecture exhibition as part of Common Ground, Venice Biennale of Architecture 2012, Pier Vittorio Aureli, Peter Eisenman, et al.

44 "I Am Trying to Imagine a Radical Free Market Urbanism: Conversation between Peter Eisenman and Patrik Schumacher", New York 2013, *Log 28*, Anyone Corporation, summer 2013. All quotes from Eisenman and Schumacher in this section are from the *Log* article cited above. The *Log* essay shows that Schumacher's comments at the World Architecture Festival in November 2016—in which he called for an end to state-owned public space and an end to the funding of affordable housing via taxation on new development—were the demonstration of a long-held "radical free-market" neo-liberal political attitude, not a sudden thought experiment.

45 Ie bringing him close, somewhat unwillingly perhaps, to Borromini's intentions, wit, and sense of *decorum* in play at the Roman Oratory—see below.

46 "I Am Trying to Imagine a Radical Free Market Urbanism". Schumacher seems to be unwittingly imitating the *Landscape Urbanism Bullshit Generator* website. See http://www.ruderal.com/bullshit/bullshit.htm.

47 "I Am Trying to Imagine a Radical Free Market Urbanism". As before, all quotes from Eisenman and Schumacher in this section are from the *Log* article, cited above.

48 See Giedion, Sigfried, *Space, Time and Architecture: The Growth of a New Tradition*, Cambridge, MA: Harvard University Press, 1951.

49 See "The Wobble", and *Chora L Works: Jacques Derrida and Peter Eisenman*, Kipnis, Jeffrey and Thomas Lesser eds, New York: Monacelli Press, 1997.

50 Ansari, Iman, "Interview: Peter Eisenman", *The Architectural Review*, 26 April 2013: "Through my psychoanalysis sessions I realised that what was wrong with my architecture was that it wasn't from the ground, from inside the unconscious, beneath the surface. So the first evidence of this occurs in Cannaregio where for the first time I do a project that is totally in the ground. And it's not only in the ground, it's also urban. But it's also not real. It's conceptual; and uses Corbusier's unbuilt hospital project as an initial context. This is in 1978."

51 Kimmelman, Michael, "The Craving for Public Squares", *The New York Review of Books* (online), 7 April 2016.

in my multi-system parametric model. The signifying relation is another correlation within the logic of associative modeling. Specifically, I'm taking agent-based crowd modeling as this meaning layer and program agents to be responsive to designed environmental clues in their behavior; their behavior is modulated by architectural articulation. Any feature of the environment might modulate their behavior, and thus becomes an effective sign or communication. That's the signifying relation proper for architecture. In the end the meaning of the space is what takes place within it, that's what it should be communicating. The designated, designed space is a framing communication that invites potential participants to share a certain particular communicative situation. The meaning is the use, the social function. I can bring that social function into the model by crowd modeling and by scripting individual actors' behavioral rules relative to spatial distinctions. Agents might come into a space and slow down as they move from a marble floor onto a carpet, gather around a central position that they're invited to gather around by a territorializing ceiling feature. These are not key-frame animations, they are literally programmed agents that move autonomously according to stochastic rules that change in dependency to spatial markers, thresholds, gradients etc. The agents are scripted, modulate their behavior relative to selected stimuli, which are the features of the model, the designer. So I can say carpet means "slow down and orient towards others" (private places), hard surface means "move independently and ignore other agents" (public spaces). That's operationalized, parametric semiology.[46]

Despite his perhaps deliberately oxymoronic phrase "autopoiesis" (from *poiesis*, to make), what Schumacher is trying to explain—the rhythmic character of *decorum* and the occasion for spontaneity and recognition in urban situations—might be better called "practical poetics". Whilst aspects of a city are systematic—drainage, traffic, IT etc, the question facing architects today is: how can one absorb these systems into buildings and places? I argue that this is only possible via imagination, because one cannot derive *decorum* from systems. City life mirrors human creativity generally in this regard, since making in general, and poetry in particular, are anything but systematic or automatic.[47]

Schumacher's attempts to engage systematic thinking with specificity are hampered by the fact that his thinking is derived from the legacy of modern architectural theory. In the twentieth century, critics typically discussed design in terms of its distinct aspects—the clichés of space, function and form—rather than as the manifestation of a particular commission. Even if some modern architectural theorists attempted to try to recombine these atomised parts into a theoretical whole, this task has

not been helped, I suggest, by accepting definitions of architecture that are not conducive to the tradition of "rhythmic spatiality"—of which architecture is the most stable representation.[48]

In contrast to modern theory in general—of which architectural theory is symptomatic—the traditional relationship between culture and life (*theoria*) is built upwards from natural conditions and from embodied experience of the world, towards the more articulate realm of concepts and symbols. Modern theory in contrast—and most contemporary architecture—works downwards, attempting to embed "forms" in the quality-less *res extensa* of the Cartesian universe.

For example, the term "common ground" is seen as deeply problematic by Peter Eisenman, even though he agreed to participate in David Chipperfield's Biennale at Venice in 2012 with this title. In fact, "ground" itself is a highly problematic notion for Eisenman in "epistemological terms". He has regularly referred to its broken status in post-nineteenth-century metaphysics as the justification for his inability to engage with ground as the basis of architectural presence.[49] His elision of ground as the basis for representation with epistemology is curious, and symptomatic of a misunderstanding of ground as the foundation of ontological experience. Ground is not simply a linguistic construct, and its revelation as something common is a political and spatial act.

One can see the problem of common ground not as a philosophical problem of selfhood or of certainty (what Eisenman calls "tradition" or "traditional metaphysics"), but as an actual architectural question. In contrast to Eisenman's "aesthetic" problems (which are arguably largely questions of self-representation for him), a recent example of the ontological and spatial relevance of civic ground can be found in the example of the creation of a public square, another informal settlement, and its transformation into a place.[50]

Michael Kimmelman writes about the project by Palestinian architect Sandi Hilal at the Fawwar refugee camp in the West Bank to create the first permanent spatial structure there since its formation in 1974.[51] Initially, camp inhabitants were suspicious of the architects' attempts to create a public space, anxious that this would signify the semi-permanent nature of their inhabitation and thus endorse Israel's occupation of the Gaza Strip and the Palestinian homelands. Kimmelman writes:

> For Palestinian refugees, the creation of any urban amenity, by implying normalcy and permanence, undermines their fundamental self-image, even after several generations have passed, as temporary occupants of the camps who preserve the right of return to Israel. Moreover, in refugee camps, public and private do not really exist as they do elsewhere. There is, strictly speaking, no private property in the camps. Refugees do not own their homes. Streets are not municipal properties, as they are in cities, because refugees are not citizens of their host

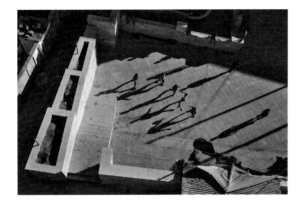

countries, and the camp is not really a city. The legal notion of a refugee camp, according to the United Nations, is a temporary site for displaced, stateless individuals, not a civic body.

Specifically, the camp leaders were concerned with the visibility of women in public space. Yet it was their wives' insistence upon the need for a public space that persuaded the men to allow the project to proceed. Its success lies, Kimmerman claims, in the fact that:

> The square has given children a place to play other than crowded streets. Mothers who rarely felt free to leave their homes to socialize in public now meet there to talk and weave, selling what they make in the square, an enterprise that is entirely new in the community and that one of the mothers told me "gives us self-esteem and a sense of worth, like the men have". "For me", another mother said, "the radical change is that men here now look at women in a public square as a normal phenomenon. I can bring my kids. I can meet my friends here. We are in our homes all the time. We need to get out. We want to be free. Here, in the public square, we feel free."

The square is made of stone and defined into thirds by a wall behind which the women trade. It has been used as an external classroom and the addition of draped fabric transforms the space into a civic room. Its success seems to lie less in any explicit attempt to address questions of representation, and one can

applaud its architectural character; the themes of embodiment and materiality are nicely handled. But its great contribution to the lives of the camp occupants is primarily spatial, and by this I mean its social and material significance as the backdrop for the daily, seasonal and ritualistic rhythms of a "city". In this way, the formation of a civic ground establishes the primary conditions of urbanity.

One cannot distinguish between function and form, or between meaning and pragmatics in communicative architecture, and the use of these terms in modern architectural theory is confusing and misleading; it leads to the diminishing of architecture's primary civic role and in its contribution to city life. The problems with a formalist approach will be investigated in some detail in this book, as its influence is profound and continues to dominate academic life in North America, especially at graduate level on non-professional Masters courses. In discussing historical and modern examples alongside exemplary contemporary projects and projects built with scarce resources, my intention is to reveal the continuity of thematic content across cultures and across "epochs". In doing so I hope to undermine the assumption that there is a legitimate theoretical approach to architecture that asserts its autonomy from and derides popular culture. In particular, my intention is to demonstrate that the idea that there is an academic or theoretical architecture in conflict with practical design is specious. My approach is to reveal the weakness of systematic and formalist theoretical approaches towards architecture, in philosophical and artistic terms.

52 Ansari, Iman, "Eisenman's
    Evolution: Architecture, Syntax, and
    New Subjectivity: Interview with Peter
    Eisenman", *Architecture Daily* (online),
    13 September 2013; Brillembourg,
    Carlos, "Peter Eisenman by Carlos
    Brillembourg", *Bomb Magazine*
    (online), no 117, fall 2011.

53 Ansari, "Eisenman's Evolution:
    Architecture, Syntax, and
    New Subjectivity".

54 Brillembourg, Carlos, "Peter
    Eisenman by Carlos Brillembourg",
    Bomb Magazine 94, winter 2006.

55 Rowe, Colin, *The Architecture of Good
    Intentions*, London: Academy Edition,
    1994, pp 28–29.

56 Rowe, *The Architecture of Good
    Intentions*, p 49.

57 Rowe, *The Architecture of Good
    Intentions*, pp 52–65.

The Cardboard Architecture of Peter Eisenman

Certain contemporary architects seem to have an antagonistic relationship with sculptors (particularly in America) one that is founded on a misunderstanding of the spatial aspects of sculpture in favour of "sculptural form". This problem, I suggest, profoundly effects the quality of American architecture and, as a consequence, the cities where it is built.

It is instructive to consider the example of a recent attempt by an architect to re-establish a working relationship with a sculptor—albeit in the deprived context of Peter Eisenman's formalistic and pseudo-philosophical discourse—if only to see how problematic such collaborations can be.

Contemporary collaborations between architects and sculptors are often fraught with misunderstanding and not a little aggression from both sides. Indeed, claiming kinship with sculpture is almost a cliché for a certain sort of architect, presumably because one influence of "sculptural form" has been to create rivalry, jealousy and also the need to be taken seriously as an "artist".[52]

However, his particular view of architecture as an art form disregards the traditional notions of craft and poetics in favour of conceptualism and formalism—which led to tension in his working relationship with Richard Serra.

Eisenman is emphatic that:

> If there is a debate in architecture today, the lasting debate is between architecture as a conceptual, cultural, and intellectual enterprise, and architecture as a phenomenological enterprise—that is, the experience of the subject in architecture, the experience of materiality, of light, of color, of space, etc. I have always been on the side opposed to phenomenology. I'm not interested in Peter Zumthor's work or people who spend their time worrying about the details or the grain of wood on one side or the color of the material on the surface, etc. I couldn't care less. That having been said, it is still necessary to build. But the whole notion of the idea of "cardboard architecture" meant that the materiality of the work was important as an "anti-material" statement. Probably the most important work I did in the conceptualist realm was the cardboard architecture houses. Pictures of House II, for instance, were taken without sunlight so you have no shadows, and no reveals or things like this, and in fact one of the pictures we took of House II was in a French magazine that said it was a "model of House II". So I achieved what I wanted to achieve, which was to lessen the difference between the built form and the model. I was always trying to say "built model" as the conceptual reality of architecture. So when you see these houses and you visit them you realize that they were very didactic and very important exercises—each one had a different thematic—but they were concerned not

with meaning in the social sense of the word or the cultural sense, but in the "architectural meaning". What meaning they had and what role they played in the critical culture of architecture as it evolved over time. So while the work was interested in syntax and grammar, it was interesting to see what the analogical relationships were between language and architecture. And of course that's when I get into working with Jacques Derrida.[53]

I believe that his interest in analogy has been hampered by a formalist conception of language, and is, as a consequence, quite superficial. Arguably, Eisenman changes what he says about his work depending upon the audience, and after the 2012 Venice Biennale he has begun to temper his statements about the supposedly autonomous nature of architecture in favour of a quasi-sculptural approach. For example, when interviewed by Carlos Brillembourg for *Bomb Magazine* he claimed that:

> The energy of Terragni permeated my early work; House I is certainly Terragni, but House II is much more influenced by, say, Rosalind Krauss' writing on contemporary art at the time and the idea of sculpture in the expanded field and the work of minimalist sculptors Robert Morris and Sol LeWitt. By House II, Krauss and I were working closely—she eventually wrote "Notes on the Index" in *October* 3 and 4, which became key to House IV.[54]

Brillembourg then asked "What about Donald Judd?", to which Eisenman claimed, "We did a project with him, and one with Michael Heizer. By then I had put the Terragni book aside and was working on my own project, which was more influenced by conceptual art, by colour field painting, by Krauss's, Michael Fried's, and Clement Greenberg's writings."

Collisive Fields and Bricolage:
Colin Rowe on Urbanism as Architectural Form

Peter Eisenman is arguably the most prominent exponent of this sort of confused attitude towards architecture as sculpture, although I'd also suggest that the formalist tendencies of Eisenman, Jeffrey Kipnis and Greg Lynn et al derive from Colin Rowe's emphasis upon the urban form of Rome and his notion of "collage city". This might initially seem a perverse assertion, since Rowe was also concerned in *The Architecture of Good Intentions* with utopia and metaphysics as much as with form.[55] However, both of these themes derive from his thesis that architecture expresses "cultural concepts", that buildings operate as a "theatre of prophecy".[56] Against this idealism and literalism, Rowe used the example of gestalt diagrams to try to articulate the need for backgrounds for prominent "built objects", what he called the "predicament of texture".[57] I will return to the problematic nature of these seductive visual

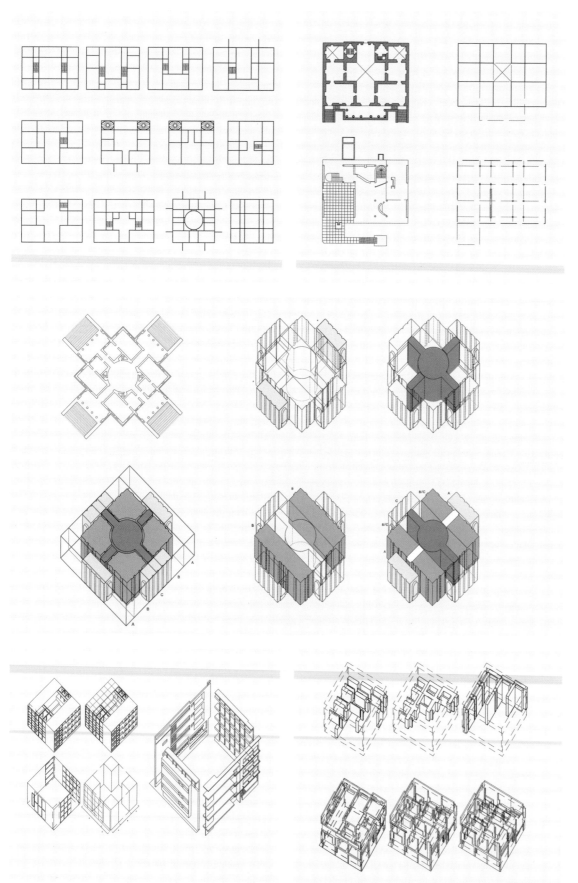

Left: "Schematized plans of eleven of Palladio's villas", from Rudolf Wittkower's *Architectural Principles in the Age of Humanism* (redrawn by Lynch Architects).

Right: Plan drawings of Palladio's Villa Foscari/La Malcontenta and Le Corbusier's Villa Stein, from Colin Rowe's *The Mathematics of the Ideal Villa* (redrawn by Lynch Architects).

Opposite: Drawings of Zurich (left) and Wiesbaden (right) from Colin Rowe's studio at Cornell University.

"Ideal and virtual diagrams of Rotonda. Spatial layerings", from Peter Eisenman's *Palladio Virtuel* (redrawn by Lynch Architects).

Left: "Casa del Fascio. Axonometric diagram showing the four-tower palazzo conception, which gives rise to a tripartite A-B-A, solid-void-solid, rhythm", from Peter Eisenman's *Giuseppe Terragni Transformations, Decompositions, Critiques* (redrawn by Lynch Architects).

Right: Axonometric diagrams of House II by Peter Eisenman (redrawn by Lynch Architects).

58 Dalibor Vesely acknowledges a debt to Rowe in the introduction to his book, but reminds us in it of the problem with "Gestalt" theories of architecture: "The nature of vision manifests itself in its most elementary form as a tendency to experience reality in terms of visual patterns and identifiable configurations, a tendency conventionally described as eidetic vision or Gestalt. Unfortunately, many interpret Gestalt principles as if they were a law establishing the formal identity of objects or object-like structures, forgetting that Gestalt is always situated in the intentionality of our life and therefore closely linked with the meaning of some potential or actual action." Vesely, Dalibor, *Architecture in the Age of Divided Representation: The Question of Creativity in the Shadow of Production*, Cambridge, MA: MIT Press, 2004, p 84.

59 James Stirling being Rowe's other very famous student. Unlike Eisenman, Stirling latterly wrote little, but his impatience with systematic architecture is clear in his essays in "The Black Notebook" (see Crinson, Mark ed, *James Stirling: Early Unpublished Writings on Architecture*, London: Routledge, 2009) and they took very different approaches towards the role of history in design (see Maxwell, Robert, "Situating Stirling", *The Architectural Review*, 30 March 2011.

60 Eisenman, Peter, *The Formal Basis of Modern Architecture*, PhD Dissertation, Cambridge University, 1963; Facsimile published by Lars Muller, 2006.

61 Eisenman, *The Formal Basis of Modern Architecture*, p 31.

62 Eisenman, *The Formal Basis of Modern Architecture*, p 30.

63 Eisenman, *The Formal Basis of Modern Architecture*, p 29.

64 See Wilson, Colin St John, "Albert Speer and the Fear of Freedom", *Architectural Reflections*, Oxford: Oxford University Press, 1992.

65 The mistranslation of philosophical terms, and also Beaux Arts themes, by Anglo-Saxon theorists, is part of the problem that afflicts our discipline today, eg, "*genre*" did not mean "type" for Durand etc.

66 See Vesely, Dalibor, "Architecture and the Conflict of Representation", *AA Files* 8, 1985.

67 Rowe, Colin, *The Mathematics of the Ideal Villa and Other Essays*, Cambridge, MA: MIT Press, (1947) 1987.

68 Rowe, "Transparency: Literal and Phenomenal", *The Mathematics of the Ideal Villa and Other Essays*.

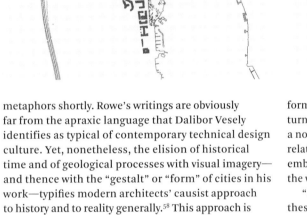

metaphors shortly. Rowe's writings are obviously far from the apraxic language that Dalibor Vesely identifies as typical of contemporary technical design culture. Yet, nonetheless, the elision of historical time and of geological processes with visual imagery—and thence with the "gestalt" or "form" of cities in his work—typifies modern architects' causist approach to history and to reality generally.[58] This approach is exemplified by the theoretical and built work of his student Peter Eisenman.[59]

Eisenman's PhD, "The Formal Basis of Modern Architecture", was supervised by Colin Rowe at Cambridge University and completed in 1963.[60] He declares in the introduction that "a specific situation, by its relative nature, limits us to relative ends".[61] Instead, Eisenman claims, what matters is "form", and "total external order is our absolute".[62] The term "formal" is used in an attempt to limit and to control "individual expression", which Eisenman accepts as "legitimate", but which needs to be controlled for the sake of "the comprehensibility of the environment as a whole".[63] It is perhaps no surprise that it is Terragni's architecture that is seen by Eisenman as the means by which individualism can be subjugated to absolute (formalist) order—as, arguably, fascism arose as a response to nineteenth-century Romantic individualism.[64] Whilst Eisenman categorises "generic form in its Platonic sense", no mention is made of Plato's understanding of Cosmos, geometry or analogy. The influence of Rowe's art history studies at the Warburg Institute coincided in Eisenman's dissertation with Rowe's attempts to create a historical legitimacy for modern architecture based upon geometry and proportion understood as form. Neither are historically or philosophically precise.[65] Plato sees *eidos*—often wrongly translated as

form, when it more closely means ideas (which in turn is not the Kantian idea of a concept, but rather a noetic symbol)—embodied in certain geometric relationships as analogous of the relative degree of embodiment (of, for example, an individual soul in the world-soul).[66]

"Formal" is perhaps the most pernicious of these mistranslations, as it corrupts the language that we use so that the meaning of formal loses its connotations of "correct", "proper" and "appropriate". The result is that the *decorum* of a specific situation—that is implicit in any discussion of the formal aspects of architecture—is forgotten in favour of abstractions. Whilst Colin Rowe's description of the arrangement of spatial dimensions in the plan of Le Corbusier's and Palladio's villas is rhythmic in "The Mathematics of the Ideal Villa",[67] and his essay "Transparency: Literal and Phenomenal" is evidence of an interest in experience in architecture, the overriding emphasis in his writing is upon composition as metaphor.[68]

Arguably, Rowe was the first English-speaking architect to adopt the critical perspectives of the German School of Erwin Panofsky and Rudolf Wittkower. It was his graduate work with Wittkower at the Warburg Institute in London that led to Rowe's "ambiguous article, which has received too much extensive/obsessive attention", "The Mathematics of the Ideal Villa", published in *The Architectural Review* in 1947. Rowe famously compared Palladio's villas with those of Le Corbusier, suggesting that they shared geometric and rhythmic similarities largely based on the prevalence of certain compositional figures such as squares and "golden rectangles". This method evolved from Wittkower's own analysis of Palladio's plans as pure types, which were eventually published in 1949

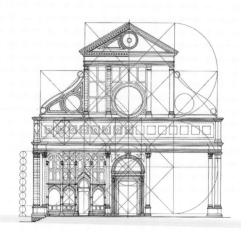

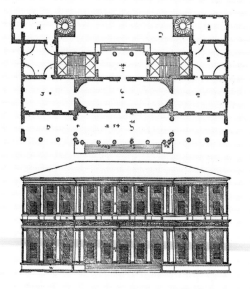

Left: Analysis of proportions and
"lineaments" in the facade of Alberti's
Santa Maria Novella, Florence, 1470,
from *On Alberti and the Art of Building*
by Robert Tavernor.

Right: Plan and facade drawings of
Palladio's Palazzo Chiericati, Vicenza,
1680, from Palladio's *The Four Books
of Architecture*.

69 Wittkower, Rudolf, *Architectural
    Principles in the Age of Humanism*,
    2nd edition, New Jersey: John Wiley &
    Sons, 1998.

70 Rowe, Colin, "Excursus on Contessa
    Priuli-Bon", *AA Files* 72, 2016, p 71.

71 Palladio's patrons included the poet
    Gian Giorgio Trissino, who urged him
    to travel to Rome and introduced him
    to the noblemen of the Veneto.

72 Alberti, Leon Battista, *On the Art of
    Building in Ten Books*, Joseph Rykwert,
    Neil Leach, Robert Tavernor trans,
    Cambridge, MA: MIT Press, 1988; see
    also Borsi, *Leon Battista Alberti: The
    Complete Works*.

73 "Palladianism" is perhaps the
    inevitable result of the relatively
    ill-educated nature of most architects
    from the sixteenth century onwards.
    Palladio provided almost the only
    education that generations of
    gentleman architects received
    outside of their Grand Tour—hence
    the success of his work as a model
    for a large number of country
    houses in Britain and America in the
    eighteenth and nineteenth centuries.
    See Tavernor, Robert, *Palladio and
    Palladianism*, London: Thames &
    Hudson, 1991. Sadly, Alberti's work,
    which emphasised analogy, was much
    less easy to understand and to copy.

74 See Tavernor, Robert, "Beauty in
    Art and Building", *On Alberti and
    the Art of Building*, New Haven: Yale
    University Press, 1998, pp 39–48:
    on the unorthodox proportions of
    the upper storeys of the facade of
    Palazzo Rucellai at Florence, their
    relationship with the Stoa and the
    point at which one encounters the
    building in the streetscape.

75 See Tavernor, Robert, "Concinnitas in
    the architectural theory and practice
    of Leon Battista Alberti", unpublished
    PhD thesis, Cambridge University,
    1985 (and Tavernor, *On Alberti and the
    Art of Building*).

76 Formalism is perhaps a series of
    attempted mechanistic short cuts to
    architectural glory. It seems suited to
    certain political situations, working
    perhaps best to glorify particularly
    autocratic regimes: "Do you not seek
    great praise, glory, and immortality
    in this magnanimity of yours? Not
    only with pomp: not with ostentation,
    nor with crowds of flatterers will you

in *Architectural Principles in the Age of Humanism*.[69]
According to Rowe, however, "Wittkower didn't like
the article... Rudy saw it as lacking in scholarship and
frivolous."[70] In suggesting that architecture could
be analysed, like music, in terms of "composition",
they were both responding to Palladio's method of
publishing plans and elevations of his buildings
(in *The Four Books of Architecture*, self-published in
Venice in 1570), without any drawn information about
their context, de-situated and seemingly autonomous.
Wittkower elides music and Pythagorean mathematics,
something which he claims Palladio applied to
architecture following Leon Battista Alberti's example.
Wittkower's argument is based on his claim that Palladio
was a Humanist, despite the fact that unlike Alberti—
a graduate of Padua University, Professor of Rhetoric at
Florence, Papal Envoy etc—Palladio was not university
educated and had little theoretical knowledge of the
Medieval curriculum nor Renaissance Neo-Platonism.[71]

In contrast to Alberti's *Ten Books*,[72] Palladio produced
a profoundly simplified form of architectural theory,
which in turn was exceptionally influential on those
architects similarly lacking a Neo-Platonic Humanist
education.[73] Palladio's work emphasises Alberti's theory
of "lineaments", whereby the proportions and ratios of
parts of a building's plan resemble a bodily whole, and
enable one to project appropriate sectional drawings.
Alberti's work emphasised the study of relationships,
and his method of analysis of existing buildings was
tempered, in terms of its relevance to design, by
the corrective role of "perspective" upon the ratios
of facades and specifically their civic presence when
experienced within a city context. Recent scholarship
has revealed that Alberti's architectural theory was
tempered by a pragmatic and situated approach
to composition and his buildings' proportions do
not precisely adhere to the principles that he sets

out in his books.[74] Alberti's theory of *concinnitas*—
harmony or congruity of parts—was interpreted by
Wittkower as analogous of musical relationships
that can be expressed in simple diagrammatic plans;
this abstraction inevitably isolates architecture
(and geometry) from its cultural and symbolic roles.[75]
In particular, the role that architecture played in civic
life and its traditional relationship with virtue has
been largely lost today as a result of the dominance
of this sort of formalist analysis.[76]

Despite its attraction as a way to teach "principles"
of analysis, Wittkower's approach was first distorted
by Rowe, and then deformed by his student Peter
Eisenman, into a theory of composition. In particular,
the role that ornament plays in the *decorum* of
urban buildings was largely cast off and ignored in
the "formal" analysis of buildings as plans, and yet
Alberti was sensitive to advising his readers, whom he
knew would be patrons as much as artists, to exercise
prudence and to acknowledge the civic dimension
of their work.[77] Palladio is careful to refer his readers
to this too, urging that "an edifice may be esteemed
commodious, when every part or member stands in
its due place and fit situation, neither above or below
its dignity and use; or when the *loggia's* [sic] halls,
chambers, cellars and granaries are conveniently
disposed, and in their proper places."[78]

Arguably, what was being studied by Rowe and
Eisenman wasn't buildings, but Palladio's drawings
of his buildings—drawing attention away from their
tectonic and civic reality. Palladio's self-promotional
treatise was an attempt to dignify his edifices,
and in order to do so he sought to emphasise their
independence from use, situation, topography, tradition,
urbanity, *decorum* etc.[79] In studying Palladio's projects
as an abstract combination of grids, and extrapolating
from this that Le Corbusier and Terragni's architecture

earn real whole-hearted praise, for this can only be won by virtue." Leon Battista Alberti, cited by Borsi, *Leon Battista Alberti: The Complete Works,* p 20.

77 See Alberti, "Ornament to Private Buildings", *On the Art of Building in Ten Books,* (411, 162–175v), pp 298–319.

78 Ware, Isaac, *The Four Books of Andrea Palladio's Architecture,* dedicated to Lord Burlington, 1738; New York: Dover Publications, 1965, p 1.

79 Arguably, Palladio goes some way towards beginning the process of distancing his work from its context, which Wittkower, in attempting to overcome aesthetic appreciation, pushes further towards abstraction by emphasising its quasi-Pythagorean character. We will see how Palladio's work is grounded in the life of Verona below, and see how Alberti's work, filtered via Palladio's reading of Vitruvius, is also profoundly urban.

80 Goldberger, Paul, "The Museum That Theory Built", *The New York Times,* 5 November 1989. See also Langdon, David, "AD Classics: Wexner Center for the Arts/Peter Eisenman", *archdaily,* 17 October 2014.

81 See Rowe, Colin, "Cornell Studio Projects and Theses", *As I was Saying: Recollections and Miscellaneous Essays,* vol 3, Cambridge, MA: MIT Press, 1995.

82 Rowe, Colin and Fred Koetter, *Collage City,* Cambridge, MA: MIT Press, 1978, pp 106–107. Rowe's student projects formed the basis of international design charrettes such as "Roma Interrotta" in 1978, whereby eminent architects took parts of the city and proposed urban redesign without commissions or reference to patrons or clients. The participating architects were Piero Sartogo, Costantino Dardi, Antoine Grumbach, James Stirling, Paolo Portoghesi, Romaldo Giurgola, Venturi and Rauch, Colin Rowe, Michael Graves, Rob Krier, Aldo Rossi and Léon Krier. The competition and all 12 entries are examined in detail in *Architectural Design,* Profile 20, no 3-4, 1979, which was guest edited by Michael Graves.

83 See Rowe, "Ideas, Talent, Poetics: A Problem of Manifesto", *As I was Saying: Recollections and Miscellaneous Essays,* vol 2.

84 Rowe, *Collage City,* p 106.

85 Rowe, *Collage City,* p 106.

86 Rowe, *Collage City,* p 107.

can similarly be reduced to this, it is perhaps no surprise to find that the dominant characteristic of design teaching derived (as an unintended consequence) from Wittkower's historical studies is an architecture based on the manipulation of grids.

The success of this approach, in Eisenman's and his students' buildings, is questionable. The Wexner Centre for the Arts at Ohio State University, 1989, was memorably described by Paul Goldberg as "the museum that theory built".[80] The collision of city block grids with distorted typological fragments recalls very strongly Rowe's design students' urban scale projects at Cornell University, albeit in a more frantically "deconstructivist" rather than neo-classical mode of post-modernist "historicity". At the heart of their endeavours, both drawn and written, lies a superabundance of historical quotation and words, and a love of superfluidity and restless flow at the expense of the civic values that informed Renaissance architecture. Arguably, architects and critics today are still reeling from their disorienting effects.

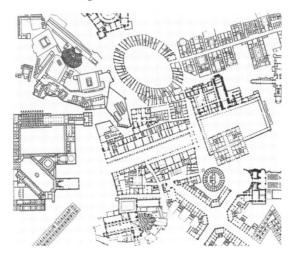

Hans Kollhoff and David Griffin, *City of Composite Presence,* drawing of historical typologies assembled to form a conceivable urban texture, from *Collage City* by Colin Rowe and Fred Koetter.

In particular, it is the elision of formalistic building analysis with formalistic city analysis that is most damaging. Rowe's *Collage City* exhibits a formalist approach to architectural urbanism that ignores the social forces that shaped the architecture of the past. His appreciation of neo-classical town planning principles, and his fondness for the picturesque tradition, created in his Cornell students' projects an eclectic mixture of fragments,[81] which he called, after Levi-Strauss, "bricolage".[82] The site of this eclecticism was not the modern city as we encounter it as architects working for private or commercial or institutional clients, but an academic view of the historical city as a formal system. Rowe's city was one filtered through a transformation of the Nolli Plan of Rome (1748) into the figure-field dialectic imported from gestalt psychology; hence the predominance of the term "analysis". This formalist reading of cities tended to ignore the

intentionality of the various agents who paid for and made the civic monuments and dwellings that make up a city; everything is talent and/or ideas.[83] There is an unresolved conflict in Rowe's work, between the life of the nineteenth-century city depicted so brilliantly in *The Architecture of Good Intentions* and his theory of design, in which, arguably, there is no mediation, no economy and no representation beyond form. For example, in *Collage City* Rome is described with fizzing verbal brio as:

> a collision of palaces... an anthology of closed compositions and ad hoc stuff in-between which is simultaneously a dialectic of ideal types plus a dialectic of ideal types with empirical context... something of the bricolage mentality at its most lavish.[84]

Rowe's exuberant descriptions disguise rather than explain the life of the city, and his desire to impose verbal order—of a sort—upon what he sees as "a traffic jam of intentions" reveals also a certain relish in using visual metaphors to illustrate generalisations. Rowe's prose flits between the universal and the particular, like a low-flying pilot turning verbal stunts. Rowe's prose strains to lift up the city so that it becomes a record of ideals, emancipating it as "some sort of model which might be envisaged in contrast to the disastrous urbanism of social engineering and total design". He claims that whilst it is "products of a specific topography and two particular but not wholly separate cultures" (imperial and Catholic), Rome is actually "a style of argument which is not lacking in universality". Unlike many of his contemporaries, Rowe's universality of form was not propelled by science, efficiency or technology, but instead visual metaphors that elide history with quasi-natural processes. Rowe's views of cities resemble at once a parachutist's (he was in the Parachute Regiment in the Second World War), and a Baedeker guide (plans and history and novels) and his imagery recalls film stills, time-lapse photography and speeded up sections of a disaster movie:

> The physique and politics of Rome provide perhaps the most graphic example of collisive [sic] fields and interstitial debris, there are the calmer versions of equivalent interests, which are not hard to find.[85]

Rowe claims—somewhat *ex-cathedra*—that his flippant description of "the politics of bricolage" that characterises "the Rome-London Model" is sufficient that it "may, of course, perfectly well be expanded to provide comparable interpretations of a Houston or a Los Angeles. It is simply a question of a frame of mind with which one visits places".[86] The use of the phrase "a Houston" reveals that Rowe has no interest in the actual Houston in Texas, beyond its capacity to reveal the efficacy of his methodology, which he summarised with breathtaking bathos as "a frame of mind". The uninteresting parts of cities, to a formalist "frame of

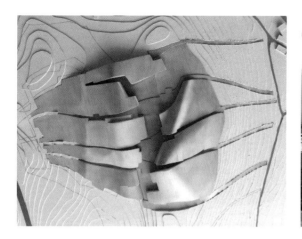

City of Culture, Santiago de Compostela
by Peter Eisenman, 2010, model
photograph (left) and photograph from
carpark (right).

mind", are dismissed as "interstitial debris", leading
to the tendency of American architects to concern
themselves with replicating or simulating the effects of
imaginary "collisive fields" [sic] .[87]

Similarly, Peter Eisenman uses almost the same
visual metaphor to attempt to ground his City
of Culture outside Santiago de Compostela in a
plausible imitation of public topography as geology.
Unfortunately, it is only a visual metaphor, not an
actual city. In William JR Curtis's view the project is
in fact a copy of an artwork:

> Eisenman's (competition) presentation was
> accompanied by computer drawings which
> gave the impression that the project had been
> "generated" by scanning the structure of the old
> city then distorting it in a fractured geometry. The
> plan shape of the vast new "city" was also traced
> to the shape of a shell, the emblem of Saint James
> and of the pilgrimage route. There was in turn an
> overlaid grid (a customary Eisenman device). The
> complex thus combined several geometrical systems
> and emerged as a sort of palimpsest, supposedly
> filtering the natural surroundings into the artificial
> world of the architecture. Eisenman's project for
> Galicia summed up several years of research into
> fragmentation, striation, and interstitial space. Folds,
> of course, were very much in fashion at the time and
> Eisenman was forever sexing up his dossiers with
> a little French theory, for example quotations from
> Deleuze on *Le Pli* (The Fold). Some of his followers
> in turn introduced a pseudo-scientific badinage
> concerning strings and algorithmic transformations.
> Behind the smokescreen of pretentious theorising,
> Eisenman is in fact a formalist who raids sources
> and manipulates forms for their own sake, leaving
> aside the problem of content. For all the promotional
> chatter, the City of Culture in Galicia seems to have
> been inspired fairly directly by an example in the
> realm of land art: Grande Cretto in Gibellina, Sicily
> (1985–1989) designed by Alberto Burri as a memorial
> to the earthquake of 1968. This takes the form of a
> solidified "map" of the destroyed city made from
> concrete and rubble, with folding shapes, incised

streets, and the striations of a distorted grid laid
out across the landscape. 11 years later Eisenman's
project for the City of Culture is less than half
constructed and the original budget of a little over
100 million euros has more than quadrupled; the
programme has also continued to change, with talk
now of a major centre of contemporary art. There is
enough already built to get some idea of how things
may look, and one section is even open to the public.
The project promoted for its topographical sensitivity
in fact required the complete decapitation of *Monte
Gaias* and the removal of millions of cubic metres
of soil.[88]

Eisenman's formalistic attitudes towards city-scale
buildings reveal the profound problems that arise
when pseudo-philosophical metaphors become
confused with pseudo-artistic manoeuvres. This
confusion of architecture with sculpture (and of
sculpture as "form") is in fact a sort of running battle
between American architects and sculptors, particularly
obvious in the rancour between Peter Eisenman and
Richard Serra that first manifested 35 years ago.

Architecture and Sculpture:
The Eisenman-Serra Interview

> When sculpture enters the realm of the non-
> institution, when it leaves the gallery or museum
> to occupy the same space and place as architecture,
> when it redefines space and place in terms of
> sculptural necessities, architects become annoyed.
> Not only is their concept of space being changed, but
> for the most part it is being criticized. The criticism
> can come into effect only when architectural scale,
> methods, materials, and procedures are being
> used. Comparisons are provoked. Every language
> has a structure about which nothing critical in
> that language can be said. To criticize a language
> there must be a second language dealing with the
> structure of the first but possessing a new structure.
> —Richard Serra (in an interview with Peter
> Eisenman), *Perspecta 19*, 1982

87 See Cooper Union dormitory block
    Manhattan designed by Ohlhausen
    DuBois Architects, whose "form" is
    based upon the observation that the
    grid of Alphabet City "collides", with
    the Lower Manhattan Grid, which
    commences at this point—all of
    which is supposed to be significant
    and a useful reason to design the
    building. Sunlight, views, *decorum*,
    use: all of these design principles
    are subjugated to the "formal
    manipulation" of a series of cubes
    and grids, which is only contextual
    in the sense that this is the design
    methodology taught by Eisenman,
    his ex-students and his associates
    to the second year architecture
    students at Cooper Union. See John
    Hejduk, "Centralized Relief upon
    a Tableau", in John Hejduk's *Mask
    of Medusa Works 1947–1983*, New
    York: Rizzoli, 1985, pp 66–67, cited in
    Jasper, Michael, "Thinking Through
    the Architecture Studio: Two Models
    of Research", *Artifact*, vol 3, no 2,
    2014, p 3.1: "The architect starts with
    the abstract world, and due to the
    nature of his work, works towards the
    real world. The significant architect
    is one who, when finished with a
    work, is as close to that original as he
    could possibly be". Jasper compares
    and contrasts Hejduk's studio
    teaching at Cooper Union between
    1964 and 2000, and Rowe's at Cornell
    1963–1988: the former was typified
    by "the pedagogical use of exemplary
    or abstract problems... removed from
    real implementation or function",
    the latter also by "grid collisions,
    and the use of figure/ground as the
    predominant realm of representation
    and investigation... conceptualising
    the city as a (single) gestalt.... A
    limited number of design problems:
    figure, field, pattern texture, edge,
    axis", pp 3.7–3.9. In both cases,
    design is taught without reference
    to use or ecology. See also Jasper,
    Michael "Embracing Ambiguity in the
    Teaching Practices of Peter Eisenman
    and Colin Rowe", *Nordes Design
    Ecologies*, no 6, 2015.

88 See Curtis, William JR, "Galicia,
    Spain—Peter Eisenman fails to
    translate a seductive proposal into a
    successful City of Culture for Spain",
    The Architectural Review (online), 22
    September 2010. The project also
    bears some resemblance to Michael
    Heizer's mile-long earth work *The City*
    (see Kimmelman, Michael, "Michael
    Heizer's Big Work and Long View",
    The New York Times (online),
    13 May 2015).

Memorial to the Murdered Jews of
Europe, Berlin, by Peter Eisenman (and
originally also Richard Serra), 2005.

89 Serra, Richard, *Richard Serra: Writings,
Interviews*, Chicago: University of
Chicago Press, 1994, pp 141–142.
Serra's observation is very insightful
and he is right to suggest that
architects continue to use outdated
artistic conventions. In the twentieth
century, a number of modernist
architects incorporated sculptures
on pedestals within their buildings,
long after sculptors themselves had
begun to abandon this way of working,
and Penelope Curtis investigates
this tendency in *Patio and Pavilion:
The Place of Sculpture in Modern
Architecture*, London: Ridinghouse
and the J Paul Getty Museum, 2007.
She also considers the work of
sculptors such as Dan Graham, whose
work is "semi-architectural", and
architects such as Frank Gehry whose
buildings are "semi-sculptural". My
interest is slightly different, and
following conversation with Curtis
I decided to take Serra's assertion
that "the biggest break in the history
of sculpture in the twentieth century
occurred when the pedestal was
removed" as the basis for a discussion
about what is particular about modern
sculpture—which according to Serra
is its "site-specific" character. It
seems to me that that is something
that sculpture shares, or could
share with architecture. Arguably, as
sculptors became more interested
in specificity, architects became
more interested in serialisation
and autonomy, mistaking this for
"sculptural form", which confirms
Serra's belief that "architects are
openly reactionary in their adaptation
of watered-down artistic conventions."

90 Serra, *Richard Serra: Writings,
Interviews*, p 142.

91 Serra, *Richard Serra: Writings,
Interviews*, p 154.

92 Saunders, Frances Stonor,
"Modern Art was CIA Weapon",
The Independent on Sunday, 22
October 1995.

93 Kammen, Michael, *Visual Shock*, New
York: First Vintage Books Edition,
2007, p 238. See also Hopkins, David,
After Modern Art: 1945–2000, Oxford:
Oxford University Press, 2000, p 159.

94 Hopkins, *After Modern Art: 1945–2000*,
p 142. (See his letter to Viktor
Nekrasov, 20 December 1932, in
Oppositions 23, 1981, p 133).

Richard Serra was invited by Peter Eisenman in 1981 to discuss the relationship between sculpture and architecture, in an interview that was published in *Perspecta*, the journal of the Yale School of Architecture, the next year. Serra established immediately his distaste for postmodernist architecture and, in particular, the ways in which architects appropriate sculptures in aid of a supposed "humanist project":

> The biggest break in the history of sculpture in the twentieth century occurred when the pedestal was removed... the need architects feel today to repress the history of sculpture since Rodin is based upon their desire to represent questionable symbolic values under the guise of questionable humanism. The fact of the matter is that symbolic values have become synonymous with advertisements... trying to convince people that placing a contraposto figure atop a column serves humanistic needs.[89]

Serra continued his attack asking if "Charles Moore's Piazza d'Italia in New Orleans, for instance", isn't just "a little condescending?" He claimed that "one reason architects consume and use traditional sculpture is to control and domesticate art", continuing, "architects are openly reactionary in their adaptation of watered-down artistic conventions. Their continual misuse of art as ornamentation, decoration, and garnish denies the inventions of the past."[90] He attacked also Michael Grave's "Portlandia logo for the Portland building" and what he called "Johnson/Burgee's 'Golden Boy' for the AT&T Building", concluding the interview with the observation that "postmodernists also believe in the future: the future of AT&T and corporate America".[91] Arguably the symbolic advertising content of capitalist America had evolved by the time it reached Bilbao,

by which point it was freedom and creativity that were being celebrated, just as in Berlin the IBA projects promoted these values towards the Soviet Bloc. Presumably Serra was not aware in 1982 of the CIA's tacit financial support of Abstract Expressionism and its support for Jackson Pollock?[92] Nonetheless, his attack upon architects was not simply political, but artistic. On the one hand Serra repeats the Kantian view that "to deprive art of its uselessness is to make it other than art", and on the other hand his disdain for ornament mirrors modernist architects' misunderstanding of the communicative depth that can be articulated in architecture. Certainly, the fate of the *Tilted Arc* sculpture in Manhattan—which was originally commissioned by the United States General Services Administration Arts-in-Architecture programme for the Foley Federal Plaza in front of the Jacob K Javits Federal Building, installed in 1981 and then removed in 1989 after a public controversy—reveals something of the hubris of his disavowal of the ornamental or communicative aspects of sculpture—its civic spatial role.[93]

Serra is at loggerheads with Eisenman throughout most of the interview, but for the most part their differences are superficial and personal (Eisenman talks about Pollock's works being "not representations" but "expressions of his feelings... pulsations"; Serra replies, "I have great difficulty with spurious psychological interpretations"). Both subscribe to the view that art is best when useless, except that Eisenman seems to think that architecture is also best when useless. Serra believes that "the internal necessities and motivations" of "sculpture and painting" have the "potential to alter the construction, function, and meaning of architecture" and he claims that "Le Corbusier understood this" potential in his Soviet projects.[94]

The Harvest of a Seed:
Le Corbusier and the Synthesis of the Arts

Le Corbusier was quite willing to jump on the
bandwagon of Constructivism in an attempt to win
work in Russia.[95] However, his dedication to artistic
integration, to the "plastic incident", is clear in his
work from the 1950s. He declares in the introduction
of volume six of *Oeuvre Complete*, published in 1957,
that whilst "in our century it is not permitted in
the eyes of the 'organizers of work' to be a man of
different arts—one must be specialized", what he
aspires to is the "act of unity" of a "poetic incident".
In this unity, "architecture, sculpture, painting, that
is to say one volume, form, colour and rhythm are
incommensurable or synchronous—synchronous
and symphonic".[96] This highly ambiguous phrase
was written when Le Corbusier was "in his seventieth
year", and is the "harvest" of a "seed" that had been
planted "50 years ago", he claims, for which he had only
recently been able to find "expression". Le Corbusier
worked as a writer or painter each working morning,
and he worked as a stained glass artist at Ronchamp.[97]
In the same way, Le Corbusier acted as a textile
artist at the Palais de Justice building at Chandigarh,
commissioning and collaborating with the Mill Owners'
Cooperative upon several massive hanging tapestries,
amplifying the use and *decorum* of the building through
ornamental artwork. Le Corbusier's attitude towards
representation remained highly figurative, both in
terms of spatial typology (altars, porticos, kitchens,
cloisters etc), and in sculptural terms (bull's horns,
shell roofs etc).

Palace of Assembly, Chandigarh, India, by Le Corbusier, 1963.

Le Corbusier's architecture is undoubtedly a form of
ornament, where the figural elements are embedded
in geometric armatures; his comparisons between his
paintings and architectural plans (*Modulor*) are not
strictly formal, as Colin Rowe imagined, but analogical.[98]
Peter Carl demonstrates this in the opening argument
in his essay "Architecture and Time: A Prolegomena",
stating of Le Corbusier's "comprehensiveness of the algebra
of signs", "in so far as this code is possessed of content, it
resides in the 'marriage of the human and cosmic orders',
for which the *Modulor* provides the paradigm".[99]

Door of Legislative Assembly, Chandigarh, India, by Le Corbusier, 1963.

Carl goes on to demonstrate that Le Corbusier's "whole
enterprise" is summarised in this declaration from his
Le poème de l'angle droit:

> This for Urb(anism)
> architecture
> painting
> for dialogue
> for exegesis
> essay (writing)[100]

Furthermore, Carl shows that "proportion" relates
these "categories" in a way that makes sense of
Le Corbusier's assertion that "music is like architecture,
is time and space. Music and architecture alike are a form
of measurement".[101] He does so by referring us back to
the origins of architectural discourse (of Vitruvius) in
rhetoric (Cicero):

> In this discussion of *ornatus* (and notably, the
> section on *numerus*, "rhythmic utterance" recalling
> both ritual speech and the presence of "discourse"
> and "ratio" in *logos*), Cicero remarks that good
> oratory must have *utilitas*, *dignitas*, and
> *venustas* (beauty).[102]

Le Corbusier was attempting to articulate the unity or
"harmony" of the arts that are combined together in
architecture via analogue, as geometry, and in rhythm.
For Le Corbusier, ornament is the articulation of spatial
rhythm as geometry.[103] He struggled to recover the
analogical significance of proportion from the purely
aesthetic use to which it had descended. There are
roughly four layers to Le Corbusier's "geometric play",
Carl contends:

> A geometric figure, by virtue of participation in
> "golden" ratios offers a paradigmatic sequence
> of relations (implicitly recovering Neo-Platonic
> harmonic hierarchies but displaced from
> Pythagorean harmonics to a logarithmic visual

95 See Starr, Frederick, "Le Corbusier
    and the USSR: New Documentation",
    Cahiers du monde russe et soviétique,
    vol 21, no 21-22, 1980, pp 209-221;
    and Cohen, JL, *Le Corbusier and the
    Mystique of the USSR: Theories and
    Projects for Moscow 1928-1936*,
    New Jersey: Princeton University
    Press, 1992.

96 Le Corbusier, *Oeuvre Complete*, vol 6,
    Boston: Birkhäuser, 1957, pp 8-9.

97 Peter Carl notes that Le Corbusier was
    not at all the first to "revive" this art—
    its revival begins in the nineteenth
    century—eg the cathedral at Christ
    Church Oxford—and continues
    unabated through arts and crafts to
    folk like Leger. His early watercolours
    from *Voyage en Orient* are full of
    Ruskinian attention to the synthesis
    of stone carved and coloured, mosaic,
    fresco; and he went through the
    stages of painting via Expressionism
    to Cubism. The early Purist buildings
    were white articulated with colour,
    but Pessac was seen to be an urban
    scheme articulated through paint (on
    the exterior). In the late 1920s, his
    painting shifts from the "harmony"
    of the still lifes to figural (and
    more mystical) themes; that is to
    say, situational. Admittedly, these
    were situations in an emblematic
    space—like those illustrating Michael
    Maier's *Atalanta Fugiens*—but the
    insight corresponded to what he was
    trying to do with the architecture:
    create settings in which these
    relationships and their meanings
    (according to him—as in the *Le poème
    de l'angle droit*) became evident (the
    emblematic approach makes these
    situations easier to reconcile with
    the generally ornamental order, as
    below). The *synthese des arts* text in
    volume six is important, to which the
    porte molitor exhibition proposal also
    belongs; these and Ronchamp are all
    happening at the same time, and that
    building and Chandigarh are the most
    explicit iconographically in his oeuvre.
    Otherwise, he is quite aniconic, and
    it was not until well after his death
    that people began to wake up to what
    he was doing. The iconographic
    work was explicit in Ronchamp and
    Chandigarh and otherwise conveyed
    in photos and in his paintings/
    graphic work. What is constant is
    the reciprocity of a structured spatial
    field and situational requirements—a
    basis for all metaphoric or thematic
    development. Email to the author,
    29 August 2013.

98 Rowe, Colin, "The Mathematics of the
    Ideal Villa: Palladio and Le Corbusier
    Compared", *The Architectural Review*,
    March 1947 (published also in Rowe,
    *The Mathematics of the Ideal Villa and
    Other Essays*).

99 Carl, Peter, "Architecture and Time:
    A Prolegomena", *AA Files* 22, 1991, p 50.

100 Carl, "Architecture and Time", p 49.

Site-specific artworks by Donald Judd at Marfa, Texas showing their integration into interiors and landscapes.

101 Carl, "Architecture and Time", p 48.

102 Carl, Peter, "Ornament and Time: A Prolegomena", *AA Files* 23, 1992, p 50.

103 See pp 15–16 of the *Le poème de l'angle droit* by Le Corbusier, where he moves from his head in a stone to a stone inscribed with the golden ratio geometry to the "dance" of the earth, moon, sun, to the annual day-night cycles—solstice/equinox, in which golden-section geometry is cast as mediation between opposites embodied materially.

104 Paraphrased from an email discussion with the author, 29 August 2013.

105 McGuirk, Justin, "The Matter of Time", *ICON*, no 26, August 2005.

106 McGuirk, "The Matter of Time": "It is nearly 40 years since Serra started leaning steel slabs against each other like playing cards. Far from the very basic power of those early works, The Matter of Time has a fluency, you might even say a facility. Serra has mastered his material, and as far as he is concerned materials give form. That is why the building rankles him. Standing in the middle of the spiral piece, he looks up at the arcing horizon and the way it frames Gehry's elaborate ceiling. 'Is that real?' he asks, pointing at the ceiling. 'As architecture it's junk.' He is confident; he knows that his works are doing exactly what they appear to be doing, whereas the building is mostly hollow and ornamental—in short, that the building is bluffing. Serra describes the piece at the end of the hall as the installation's ballast, and in a way the whole ensemble is the building's ballast. The museum needed content, and now it has it. Serra looks up again. 'I don't think of my piece as a container for the superfluousness of the architecture,' he says. 'It ain't a trash can.'" Throughout his career, Gehry has produced objects which might be called "Design Art". Rather predictably, he thinks "the lines are kind of blurry" between sculpture and architecture (interview with Deborah McLeod, *Gagosian Quarterly*, September–October 2016, pp 99–100).

107 Judd, Donald, "Specific Objects", *Complete Writings 1959–1975*, Nova Scotia: Nova Scotia College of Art and Design Press, 2005, p 181.

108 See Davidovici, Irina, "Marfa, Texas: Art and Exile", *Scroope: Cambridge Architecture Journal*, no 15, 2003.

109 Judd, Donald, "Nie Wieder Krieg", *Donald Judd: Architecture*, Peter Noever ed, Berlin: Cantz Verlag, 2003.

110 Judd, "Nie Wieder Krieg".

cone he called "visual acoustics"). Secondly this is given dimensional significance through correlation with a putative human standard (reinterpreting *Vitruvian* man via a London bobby). Thirdly, a geometric armature contains within it the potential for figuration according to standard ornamental procedures (his buildings are effectively enlarged portions of ornament) and as deployed in his paintings (for which the Cubist 2D/3D fluctuation is essential). The basic role of ornament is to mediate between the primordial natural conditions and human history. Finally, certain geometric armatures contain "arguments" that can be deployed architecturally to locate key settings, walls, columns, *promenades architecturales* etc—for example the double square with slipped third square (mediation of the *coincidentia oppositorum*) that constructs the *Modulor* and underlay the plan of the chapel at Ronchamp.[104]

Le Corbusier's insistence upon the power of art to transform architecture was a valid point for Serra to make, even if it is somewhat weakened by Serra's insistence upon the "uselessness" of art, and his refusal to accept the orientation that "ornamentation" provides both art and architecture.

Sculpture versus Architecture:
Serra and Judd on Eisenman and Gehry

Writing in 2005, Justin McGuirk suggested that: "If Gehry shows us how to do architecture as sculpture, then Serra has returned the favour by showing us sculpture as building."[105] However, in an interview with McGuirk Serra is contemptuous of Gehry's Guggenheim Bilbao, stating, "As architecture, it's junk."[106]

A passionate line of criticism of modern architecture came directly from sculptors, who saw architects' attempts to usurp their discipline as specious and immoral. Donald Judd developed from philosopher to art critic to artist, and then towards architecture and finally polemic. Judd's 1964 essay "Specific Objects" rails against Yves Klein's blue-daubed female bodies, fabricating against this spectacle a case for considering perception itself to be the subject

of modern art.[107] When challenged by the "art world" to justify himself, Judd produced a series of cubic sculptures that draw attention to the specific tectonic character of each object—in other words, exposing to public scrutiny the fallacy that objects lack specificity. Judd cites the influence of *The Phenomenology of Perception* by Maurice Merleau-Ponty upon his thinking and art, and although "Specific Objects" work well as experiential sculptures and as a provocative essay, the repetition of this approach at Marfa in Texas revealed the limits of an object-based approach to place making.[108]

Arguably, Judd's most insightful contribution to architectural criticism is his essay "Nie Wieder Krieg" written just before the First Gulf War in 1991 and his death three years later.[109] Discussing the effects of "the war machine" upon culture generally, he sees American foreign policy as imperial and colonial, as a way of "opening up markets" for exploitation. American architects are complicit in this process of invasion, he declared, as the destruction of cities creates perfect opportunities for international modern architecture. Judd is belligerently damning of those architects who present their work as art, and in fact of the whole economy of the art world. Long before Richard Serra's memorable phrase "the wafer thin junk culture of the Guggenheim", Judd decries the "horrifying design of Frank Gehry's museum of design for Vitra. These buildings make a joke of art, of culture, of the community, and of the whole society", he declares. Judd goes on to suggest, however, that the design is a symptom of a general problem:

> The consequence of a fake economy, which is a war economy, is a fake society. One consequence of this is fake art and architecture…. The art museum becomes exquisitely pointless, a fake for fakes, a double fake, the inner sanctum of a fake society.[110]

Such damning dismissal of the work of this architect and of a whole culture is touched with righteous indignation and a sort of despair (and is not dissimilar to the critique of Henri Lefebvre, which we will look at in some detail below). Beyond aesthetic or personal moral distaste for the complicit nature of architecture, what is at stake in Judd's despair? I believe that this despair derives from what he sees as the powerlessness of architects and artists, and that the search for autonomy in "specific objects", or the anonymity of "collisive fields", are two sides of the same problem—the problem of imaginative agency in "creative" work today. This is ultimately not an ontological problem—although we each have to try to resolve our feelings of powerlessness in the face of the world—but an ethical problem, a problem of civic culture generally.

It was somewhat naïve of Serra and Judd (and Heizer and Smithson), to say the least, to suggest that this condition might be challenged by an authentic encounter with "place" mediated by artworks. Yet this is exactly what they advocated in experience of their large, external sculptures. This work did not resolve the problem of "our persistent inability to make decent cities", of course—and the prevalence of what James Wines called "the turd in the piazza" makes one wonder if sculptures are not supposed to stand in not only for "public art" but also for "public life" itself.[111] The encounter of architecture with sculpture in the 1970s and 1980s—and the confrontations between architects and sculptors—generated some friction, though, and opened up the possibility of "site-specific architecture", if only as a throwaway comment in a conversation.

Serra's most effective, and critical, attack upon architecture is informed by Land art. Eisenman continues to use phrases that he had presumably ingested from neo-classical misreadings of Vitruvius via Rowe, viz "it seems that you ultimately reject this idea of dis-equilibrium in your work and that you reject it because it implies formalist notions of balance, symmetry, and, finally, composition"; and "is there a notion of scale specificity that is not anthropomorphic, not related to man, but related to the intrinsic being of sculpture?"[112] In contrast, Serra rejects formalist descriptions of sculpture, and instead replies specifically: "I use gravity as a building principle. I am not particularly interested in dis-equilibrium"; "I don't think it's related to the intrinsic being of sculpture. I think that it's related to site and context."[113] In particular, Serra is keen to challenge architecture through sculpture, and he uses the exemplar sculpture offers of both scale and context to attack both the theory and practice of formalism generally:

> You can't build a work in one context, indiscriminately place it in another, and expect the scale relation to remain. Scale is dependent on context. Portable objects moved from one place to another most often fail for this reason. Henry Moore's work is the most glaring example of this site-adjusted folly. An iron deer on the proverbial front lawn has more contextual significance. Architects suffer from the same studio syndrome. They work out of their offices, terrace the landscape, and place their buildings into a carved site. As a result, the studio-designed then site adjusted buildings look like blown-up cardboard models.[114]

Sculpture challenges architecture as a mode of *praxis*, Serra suggests, by being "site-specific". It also challenges what architects call "context", and "contextualist architects" generally (Eisenman claims that Serra criticises "specifically Robert Venturi"—in fact he doesn't mention Venturi):

> For "contextualists" to build site-specific means to analyse the context and the content of an indigenous cultural situation, then to conclude that what's needed is to maintain the status quo. That's how they seek meaning. They give a great deal of priority to the person who laid down the first rock as well as the last person who put up a signboard.[115]

Eisenman's response to this accusation is to accept it and to propose that "there could be site-specific architecture that is critical, that attempts something other than an affirmation that everything pre-existing on the site is good". He then suggests that "Piranesi's recreations and Palladio's redrawings were inventions and not so much concerned with what had actually been on a site". In doing so, he immediately distances himself from the problems of "critical site-specific architecture" in favour of fictional and formalistic abstractions of architectural language. Eisenman seems to have instigated the interview with Serra because he felt genuine "interest" in his work. However, he cannot cope with the challenge that Serra makes to formalism.

Furniture design and architecture by Donald Judd at Marfa, Texas.

Memorial to the Murdered Jews of Europe: The Eisenman-Serra Collaboration at Berlin and Rachel Whiteread's Judenplatz Holocaust Memorial at Vienna

Superficially, Serra and Eisenman's Holocaust Memorial is heavily indebted, at least formally, to Serra's early work, in particular *Shift*, 1970–1972.[116] However, Shift is a situational and a geometric construction not a formal one. Serra describes it very precisely as a way in which "looking back across the valley, images and thoughts are remembered which were initiated by the consciousness of having experienced them". Eisenman and Serra's response to the broken nature of Berlin, in Memorial to the Murdered Jews of Europe, refers

111 Wines, James, *De-Architecture*, New York: Rizzoli International, 1987.

112 Eisenman, *The Formal Basis of Modern Architecture*.

113 Serra, *Richard Serra: Writings, Interviews*, p 145.

114 Serra, *Richard Serra: Writings, Interviews*, pp 145–146. Serra continues however to declare that "There are exceptions: the work of Le Corbusier, Wright, Kahn, Gehry…". Presumably, at this point Gehry was still friendly with the Venice Beach crowd that included Robert Irwin, et al. For a description of this scene see Weschler, Lawrence, *Seeing is forgetting the name of the thing one sees*, Berkeley: University of California Press, 1982.

115 Serra, *Richard Serra: Writings, Interviews*, p 147.

116 Serra left the project unexpectedly in 1998 before a winner was announced. See Andrews, Edmund L, "Serra Quits Berlin's Holocaust Memorial Project", *The New York Times* (online), 4 June 1998.

Memorial to the Murdered Jews of
Europe, Berlin, by Peter Eisenman (and
Richard Serra), 2005, showing a plaque
explaining what visitors cannot do there,
and people ignoring this nonetheless.

117 See von Buttlar, Adrian, *Neues
Museum Berlin: Architectural Guide*,
Berlin: Deutscher Kunstverlag 2010,
in which he describes how close
Frank Gehry came to winning the
competition to refurbish the museum,
with a scheme that certain members
of the jury thought might replicate the
"commercial success" of the Bilbao
Guggenheim. Gehry's proposals
contained elements with formal
similarities to his projects in Spain and
elsewhere, which are often considered
to possess rhythm. My aim is to situate
this quality as an aspect of spatiality,
not as a description of shapes.

118 Adorno, Theodor, "Cultural Criticism
and Society", 1951: *"Kulturkritik
findet sich der letzten Stufe der
Dialektik von Kultur und Barbarei
gegenüber: nach Auschwitz ein Gedicht
zu schreiben, ist barbarisch, und
das frißt auch die Erkenntnis an, die
ausspricht, warum es unmöglich ward,
heute Gedichte zu schreibe."*

us to its historical situation via disorientation, ie
as one walks through it one experiences fear, as one's
companions temporarily disappear.

Despite its formal abstraction, the work is
illustrative of a predetermined position, an emotional
response to a somewhat hokey metaphor ("Berlin is
broken") and an emotionally manipulative experience
("your loved ones disappear"). Serra dropped out
of the collaboration before winning the competition,
presumably before the pragmatic aspects of the
project became so unbearably demanding, leaving
Eisenman to try to incorporate disabled entrances
into a project that is at once a monument and also
a small museum. The functional architectural
elements struggle to continue the formal language
of the "stelai" columns, but fail to reconcile the site-
specific aspects of the design within a convincing
architectural setting. There is no rhythmical
communication between the practical and the poetic
aspects of the project, and one is left wondering if
this is a failure of design, or whether it fails as art,
or in fact, it simply fails as both.

This is in stark contrast to the immediate context
of *Unter den Linden*, *Brandenburger Tor* and *Tiergarten*.
Boulevard , city gate and park manage to both define and
allude to a typical and an actual city. Whilst Eisenman's
memorial structure has a powerfully morbid presence,
it fails to offer the freedom of the neighbouring park,
or of a typical civic square. In fact, security guards
stop spontaneous games and the typical activities that
constitute the public life of an urban space.

The project seems to be a metaphor, but its meaning
is confusing; are the "stelai" tombs or people? Is the site
a representation of a graveyard, or sacred ground? Or a
representation of a city? It is impossible to participate
with the structure, nor to make any other reading of the
artwork than a literal one (stelai = tombs).

In contrast, the reconstructed colonnade that
winds around David Chipperfield's imaginative
reconstruction of the Neues Museum recovers the
rhythm of central Berlin, albeit interrupted and
scarred by evidence of the city's ignoble past.[117] Part
of the problem that Eisenman's project poses is the
impossibility of forgetting, in this context, Theodor
Adorno's statement—usually mistranslated—that there
should be "no poetry after Auschwitz".[118] Eisenman's
memorial has a peculiar sort of haunting quality,
but it is neither particularly communicative nor a
mundane city square; it neither offers a "time out of
time" experience, like a graveyard or a festive space, nor
is it capable of transformation, like most other parts of
most cities.

Arguably, Daniel Libeskind's Jewish Museum
had already provided for Berlin spaces both within
and around its galleries that act as series of powerful
memorials of absences—and it achieved this in making
a critique of the Humanist conventions of museum
culture and of neo-classical architecture without
claiming to be sculpture. Crucially, it acts as a critique
of semiotic and visual formalism and achieves this in
spatial terms.

In contrast, Rachel Whiteread's Judenplatz
Holocaust Memorial, opened in Vienna in 2000,
succeeds as a public sculpture and as part of a city for
a number of reasons. Firstly, the solid concrete block is
situated in a city space that was traditionally the centre
of Jewish life in the city, and which is used everyday
as a route, and so one's encounter with it—and its
power—is not dependent upon its disconnection
from city life. Secondly, since the memorial sits in
front of, and tacitly defines the forecourt of, the
Viennese Jewish Museum (whose cafe acts also
as an informal community centre); it is part of the
everyday experience of Jewish and non-Jewish life

Judenplatz Holocaust Memorial, Vienna,
by Rachel Whiteread, 2000.

119 Lessing, Gotthold Ephraim, *Nathan the Wise: A dramatic poem in five acts*, Leo Markun trans and ed, Kansas: Haldeman-Julius Co, 1926. See also his essay of 1766, *Laocoon: An essay upon the limits of painting and poetry: With remarks illustrative of various points in the history of ancient art*, Ellen Frothingham trans, Boston: Little Brown, 1904. In this essay Lessing criticises the trend to accept Horace's *ut pictura poesis* (as painting, so poetry) as definitive also for literature: "In other words, he objected to trying to write poetry using the same devices as one would in painting. Instead, poetry and painting each has its character (the former is extended in time; the latter is extended in space). This is related to Lessing's turn from French classicism to Aristotelian *mimesis*." "Gotthold Ephraim Lessing", *Wikipedia*, accessed 7 October 2014.

120 Serra, Richard, "Shift", *Richard Serra: Writings, Interviews*, pp 11–12.

121 Serra, Richard, "Shift", *Richard Serra: Writings, Interviews*, p 13. It is debatable whether he actually meant to praise Copernicus!

122 Serra seems to have been referring to Thomas Kuhn's *The Copernican Revolution*, originally published by Harvard in 1957, which introduced the phrase "paradigm shift".

123 Smithson, Robert, "The Topography of the Mind", *Robert Smithson: The Complete Writings*, Jack Flam ed, Berkeley: The University of California Press, 1979.

in Vienna. Thirdly, the intellectual, material and figurative content of the artwork brilliantly conveys both the scale of a single room, and represents the absence of a multitude. It also operates as a poetic image that resonates with Jewish cultural and religious metaphors—a room of books, an impenetrable ark, the world petrified in unreadable and unspeakable words.

Eisenman attempts in his memorial to represent the terrible nature of loss, the loss of a multitude of human figures, reified as stones, and, arguably, objectified as guilt. It is as if Germans and Germany can never be forgiven, can never recover, even if the city of Berlin belies this. Whiteread's memorial resonates because it is a fragment of what is lost, leaving visitors' imaginations to occupy the silence—a typical room that has been suddenly brought forward from the domestic into the civic realm. The major achievement of the sculpture resides in the way that the civic depth of the site is revealed. The simultaneous presence and absence of human voices resides in a petrified image of devastated Jewish *Mittel European* culture—a memento mori that succeeds through the figurative character and scale of a room. One's hands are drawn to touch the books, and the implacable withdrawn resistance of the concrete somehow manages to evoke its opposite, burnt books, burning hands. This mimetic inversion occurs on the "outside" of a room that one cannot enter, whose interior is paradoxically suddenly all around you in the city. The Judenplatz Holocaust Memorial faces a nineteenth-century bronze statue of the playwright Gotthold Ephraim Lessing, which is seated on a granite plinth approximately the same height as the Holocaust Memorial. Lessing's attempts to reveal the equality of Judaism, Christianity and Islam, in his play *Nathan the Wise*, 1779, led to his commemoration in Judenplatz, and his continued rebuke to chauvinism helps to situate Whiteread's work in an urban and cultural continuum.[119] The situation of Jewish culture in Berlin and Vienna is of course very different, but the condition of urban depth is typical; in the former it is occluded by the artwork, in the latter, revealed.

Shift by Richard Serra

In contrast to his collaboration with Eisenman in Berlin, Serra insists plausibly that *Shift* was made as a discovery:

> We discovered that two people walking the distance of the field opposite one another, attempting to keep each other in view despite the curvature of the land, would mutually determine a topographical definition of the space. The boundary of the work became the maximum distance two people could occupy and still keep each other in view. The horizon of the work was established by the possibility of maintaining this viewpoint... a dialectic between one's perception of the place

in totality and one's relation to the field as walked. The result is a way of measuring oneself against the indeterminacy of the land.[120]

In contrast to what Serra calls "the machinery of Renaissance space" (by which he means perspective I presume) that "depends on measurements remaining fixed and immutable, these steps relate to a continually shifting horizon, and as measurements they are totally transitive... the line, as a visual element, per step, becomes a transitive verb". In other words, in contrast to a picturesque or formalist approach to sculpture and to spatiality generally—and revealing also their causal link—*Shift* makes a case for a phenomenological approach to sculptural spatiality.

Due to the role memory plays in one's experience of place, "the work does not concern itself with centering", Serra concludes. Rather, whilst there are two vaguely symmetrical forms created by the walls, your experience of them as you walk on them is not of things; instead, "this alignment contracts the intervals of space—not as drawing (or linear configuration) but as volume (as space contained)". As a result of participation in the artwork, which is a way of participating with the site (hence "site-specific" artwork), "the expanse of the work allows one to perceive and locate a multiplicity of centres". He concludes that the work "shifts" perception from objects to the spaces described by figures walking on them, and so its name refers to how it is perceived cognitively, not what it looks like metaphorically. Cognition is involved, however; not simply visual perception, but also a geometric experience of something described by one's involvement with the site, and with someone else there:

> Similar elevations—elevations equal in height—in an open field, on a flat floor, shift both horizontally and vertically in relation to one's locomotion. Because of this, the centre, or the question of centering, is dislocated from the physical centre of the work and found in a moving centre. Hats off Galileo.[121]

As well as a critique of perspectival space, Serra reveals in the last line of his description of the artwork—itself a critical part of one's experience of it—what can only be described as literally a cosmic dimension to *Shift*. One's perception of it echoes the elliptical orbit of planets.

Not only did Copernicus (Serra mistakes him for Galileo) "shift" the centre of the cosmos from the Earth to the Sun, he also set in motion a new mental image of the place of mankind on Earth in relation to tradition, the Church etc.[122] Perception was shown to be a construction that could alter with knowledge, and through action. Serra's friend Robert Smithson refers to this as "the topography of the mind" whereby mental processes occur like tectonic shifts, rock falls etc.[123] Land art reproduces the processes of the mind, not by imitating the appearance of mental topography as a visual metaphor, but by offering

Left and top right: Richard Serra, *Shift*,
1970, King City, Ontario.

Bottom right: sketch, Patrick Lynch.

Left: Disabled entrance with cleaner's equipment at Memorial to the Murdered Jews of Europe in Berlin by Peter Eisenman (and Richard Serra), 2005.

Right: Roman floor mosaic of the Late Republic showing fortified labyrinth, from *The Idea of a Town* by Joseph Rykwert.

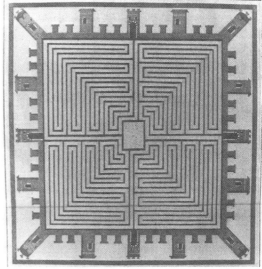

124 This is a failure of imagination I suggest, and arguably derives from an obsession with formal patterns over actions, ie, is a direct result, I would argue, of Eisenman's formalistic theoretical position, which arguably exaggerates and distorts Rowe's own work.

125 *Shift* is located in King City, Ontario, Canada about 50 kilometres north of Toronto. The work was commissioned in 1970 by art collector Roger Davidson and installed on his family property.

126 Leatherbarrow, David, *Architecture Oriented Otherwise*, New Jersey: Princeton University Press, 2009, p 11.

127 Heidegger was influenced a great deal by the concept of *Umwelt* developed by Jakob von Uexküll, Tim Ingold claims in "Point, Line, Counterpoint: From Environment to Fluid Space", *Being Alive: Essays on Movement, Knowledge and Description*, London: Routledge, 2011, p 81. For von Uexküll "every creature is equivalent to a melody in counterpoint", and it seems that Gilles Deleuze may have also been aware of this metaphor when he claimed that to improvise is "to join with the world or meld with it. One ventures home on the thread of a tune." (Cited by Ingold, "Point, Line, Counterpoint", p 84). In contrast, my thesis is that it is the rhythm of situations that structures one's movement each day, and that architecture supports, enables and re-presents the rhythmic character of situations in its physiognomy and spatial order.

128 See Sennett, *The Fall of Public Man*.

experiences in which perception shifts, making one aware of the gravity of thought and its contingency dependent upon situations.

Rhythm and the Recuperation of Civic Ground

Rhythm is of course ubiquitous—it is present in all aspects of life. Whilst it is possible to say that the Jewish memorial in Berlin is rhythmic in the sense that there is a formally rhythmic composition of blocks, it is cut off from the actual rhythms of life of the city—its institutions and everyday life—its civic depth. What one might call the rhythms of city life include the possibility for spontaneity and also for highly structured representation.

Despite his attempts to elide architecture with sculpture, Eisenman's memorial in Berlin isn't a gallery piece, it's part of the city. One can't help but think that the need for a private police force to control the space—to have to constantly tell children and teenagers off for walking on the blocks—reveals that something is fundamentally lacking in the project; what is lacking is any civic imagination and anticipation of how the work of art might work in its site as an articulate example of civic ground.[124] Eisenman's gridded blocks in Berlin are a visually arresting example of repetition standing in for a sort of civic rhythm—if only as a cliché for order—and yet one cannot help but notice the disjunctions between the monument and the life of the city, manifest also in the unwanted and slightly embarrassing presence of cleaners' equipment and the unresolved urban presence of disabled entrances etc. One of the ironies of Eisenman's "Formalist" design method—in contrast to the rhythmic character of civic architecture—is that it seemingly inevitably results in inarticulate "formlessness". In other words, rhythmic spatiality is not simply picturesque asymmetry, but an existential aspect of our encounter with reality, mediated by architecture and artworks.

In *Shift,* Serra succeeds in revealing that the "grounds of being" are at once bodily and imaginative. Despite being in a field in the middle of the countryside, it is communicative in the sense that it throws the participant beyond themselves into the world. In experiential and geometric terms, its centre is displaced.[125] In his book *Architecture Oriented Otherwise*, David Leatherbarrow describes what he calls "aliocentric architecture":

Always a matter of degree, the individuality of a building, like that of a person, is measured by its participation in shared conditions. With this observation in mind, one can also say that the disintegration of urban order is the precondition for the building's objectlike independence. More positively, the dependence assumed in both sharing and privation suggests that the building is codetermined by conditions that are not of its own making. This means that the definition of a location involves a corresponding act of dislocation, a centering of the building outside itself. Orientation is nothing other than the acknowledgement of this *ecstasis* or *allocentricity*.[126]

I'd like to suggest that "*ecstasis*" is an aspect of the civic potential of imagination, experienced as spatial rhythm. Rhythm establishes the possibility of communicative reference between site, architecture and sculpture as an innate and latent aspect of the encounter between the imagination and the world.[127] My aim in this book is to offer a critical framework to discuss the potential for the renewal of civic ground—what might be called, hubristically, "the Rebirth of Public Man"—and the grounds thereon for the renewal of a practical poetics of civic architecture.[128] What follows is a description of the central role that rhythmic spatiality plays in urban architecture, concluding with the specific example of Victoria Street in London's Westminster; and in particular, my collaborative efforts with artists and landscape architects to recover the tradition of civic ground there.

Urban Topography, Physiognomy, Spatial Continuity and *Praxis*

To situate means also to communicate.
—Dalibor Vesely, *Architecture in the Age of
Divided Representation*

The Topography and Physiognomy of Cologne

Whilst it might seem an odd juxtaposition with Cologne, Victoria Street is arguably a direct and also indirect result of the effect of the aerial bombardment of cities during the Second World War. Even those parts of European cities not affected by extensive bombing were routinely subject to whole-scale redevelopment after the War, largely motivated by a combination of architectural dogma inspired by an enthusiasm for the motor car and a dislike of streets, and developers' zeal for profit. In both cases, the Victorian ideal of the high street was regularly sacrificed in favour of ground plans comprised of car parks or service zones. New building types disrupted the traditional urban metabolism of cites, destroying the layered character of hinterland and foreground and obscuring, if not obliterating, the reciprocity and hierarchy of civic domestic and representational buildings (the physiognomy and topography of urban settings). In traditional cities, even in nineteenth-century parts of them, the relationships between high street and background city quarters maintained and in some cases even represented aspects of civic depth, and this depth is often an expression of the topography of urban settings and the effects of technology upon them. The relationship of a cathedral on a hill to the mercantile river sat below it is a mode of *decorum* one finds in Roman and Medieval cities such as Porto, and in early industrial cities such as Liverpool.[1] In contrast, the modernist city is characterised by buildings disconnected from the topography of the city, and as a consequence it is usually very difficult to orient oneself in such places (Stuttgart, Birmingham etc). An attitude of partial demolition predominated in cities where only parts of them were destroyed by war, creating the opportunity for further "site-clearance" and the instigation of "mega-blocks". In London, this led to the creation of the Barbican and then the Brunswick Centre, and also to the strange juxtaposition of the slab blocks of Victoria Street adjacent to the stone facades and quads of Westminster Abbey and Whitehall.[2]

In cities that were almost totally destroyed, the question was whether to start afresh (Coventry) or to try to renew the existing urban structure (Cologne)—albeit with modern building techniques in combination with careful restoration of the most beautiful and important civic monuments (Coventry and Cologne Cathedrals). This process involved concrete judgements in response to finances and to the customs of a place, public witness, participation and democratic processes. At Cologne, the approach of architects and planners after the war was to maintain and to resurrect the Roman and Medieval street pattern, yet to rebuild the domestic and mercantile city blocks as modern buildings. The result offers us a powerful insight into the importance of urban topography, and its positive benefits for modern architecture that seeks to recover the communicative aspects of cities.

Arriving at Cologne by train for the first time is a thrilling and satisfying experience of strangely familiar orientation and discovery. The station forecourt opens directly onto the long south facade of Cologne Cathedral, turning the ticket hall into one of the most memorable rooms in Europe. One is struck by the realisation that this is, despite the station's unimpressive decor, perhaps even deliberately anonymous. Raised directly above this, on a stepped stone plinth, the Cathedral is strangely porous and accessible. Wandering through the Cathedral with luggage, one is without any feeling of impropriety, as if the Cathedral is simply another, albeit extraordinary, part of a city.

View of Cologne Cathedral from the Romano-Germanic Museum.

The Cathedral is largely surrounded by modern buildings four to six storeys tall, all of which were constructed after the Second World War, laid out in an almost perfect simulation of the bombed Medieval city centre. Cologne retains not only the formal characteristics of its *Altstadt*, but also its character—despite the modern detailing of the buildings. These are obviously modern buildings, and whilst they respect the rhythm and scale of the old city (the "mass and bulk" that planners refer to remains intact)—the architectural expression varies depending upon the use of a building and the talent of the architect. What is impressive is that the essential characteristics of a Medieval city remain recognisable, the structure of spaces and the main civic buildings exist still, albeit in different guises. The town hall is now concrete.

However, beyond what are arguably superficial differences, the spatial and political relationships that the domestic and civic architecture of Cologne has with its religious buildings and institutions is continuous, if not completely unchanged. The rhythm of Cologne's urban spaces remains consistent despite huge and sudden destruction, and massive changes to

1   If one stands on the traffic island crossing between the Adelphi Hotel and Renshaw Street in Liverpool and looks around 360 degrees, the view encompasses St George's Hall, Palazzo Adelphi, the Victoria Tower of the University of Liverpool and then the Catholic Metropolitan and Anglican cathedrals on the skyline above, and Jacob Epstein's sculpture of a merchant sailor on the facade of George Henry Lee's department store.

2   Such was the enthusiasm for renewal after the war that even sensitive architects like Leslie Martin were caught up in the mania for destruction, and his Westminster master plan project of 1964 has recently been re-examined in *Demolishing Whitehall: Leslie Martin, Harold Martin and the Architecture of White Heat* by Adam Sharr and Stephen Thornton (Ashgate Publishing, 2013). James Dunnett describes Martin's "proposed Government precinct", which "was to be largely traffic-free thanks to a proposed tunnel alongside the Thames [and] would have stretched westwards from the Houses of Parliament all the way to Central Hall and north to south between the 'gateways' spanning the ends of Whitehall and Millbank. The Middlesex Guildhall (present Supreme Court) and the whole of its block were to be removed.... The grandeur of the conception was certainly breathtaking (and its hinted-at extension northwards to the British Museum even more so), and you cannot help feeling that Martin, the former practical-minded architect to the LCC, must well have known he was giving a hostage to fortune: it would have required the determined backing of a politician of major calibre to see it through, and in the event, commissioned by one government (Conservative) and delivered to another (Labour), it got not much more than lip service. Martin was seen by many to have exceeded his brief, and indeed the forms he proposed for the major office component are so prescriptive that it is hard to see how they could ever have constituted (as claimed and required) no more than guidance to whichever architect was actually commissioned to carry them out. They were an architectural solution in themselves, and the Grand Gallery concept could not have worked unless the whole of the Foreign Office, the Great George Street and Bridge Street buildings and Richmond Terrace were demolished." Dunnett, James, "Let's Demolish Whitehall", *The Architectural Review* (online), 26 February 2014.

Postcard showing the destroyed inner city
of Cologne in 1945.

Left: Cologne Cathedral from the south
with retail, office and apartment buildings
from the 1950s.

Right: Kolumba Museum at Cologne by
Peter Zumthor, 2007.

3   Vesely, Dalibor, *Architecture in the
Age of Divided Representation: The
Question of Creativity in the Shadow
of Production*, Cambridge, MA: MIT
Press, 2004, p 45.

the appearance of the architecture. Whilst this mélange
of old and new might not satisfy conservationists on
the one hand, nor a modernist attitude towards urban
regeneration on the other, the juxtaposition of modest
background buildings and civic monuments works well
as a recognisable human habitat. The achievements of
many generations—centuries of thinking—are not only
legible still, and largely intact, but also open to change
and capable of accepting new architecture.

This capacity to accept new parts into a whole derives
from and is a characteristic of the rhythmic qualities
of urban space there. These spaces are animated by
the rhythms of typical situations and the diurnal and
seasonal rhythms of use that are accommodated—

markets, annual festivals and carnivals, weekly events
etc. It is clear at Cologne that "the prominence of
certain buildings or spaces helps us to move from a
random sequence of experiences to a more structured
vision of a situational pattern", and that orientation
occurs seemingly naturally and without a great deal
of effort.[3]

It is this legibility and coherence perhaps that made
it almost inevitable that the terrible events of New
Year's Eve 2016 occurred exactly between the train
station and the Cathedral; the structure of the city
is so clear that, to anyone wishing to disrupt the civic
culture of Cologne, its civic ground is the obvious
place to disturb.

Cologne Cathedral is a reliquary or frame for things and events, with a cold stone, attending, waiting presence that is transformed by use and music. It is hard to think of another building and place that has endured and absorbed so much. Architecture there is geometry and rhythm articulated by sculpture. Painting hardly comes into it: even the stained glass at Cologne relies upon weather to fully become articulate.

Dalibor Vesely on Topography, Physiognomy and the Continuity of References in Communicative Space

Arguably, a building's relation to its sculptures is like a city's relation to its buildings; all are spatial settings, which are more or less connected as rhythm. The more interesting thing, perhaps, is not that buildings are like sculptures, but that both operate spatially and it is this that makes a good building like a decent city quarter: that is homely and uncanny, for work and pleasure, renewing and consoling at once.

Reading a map of the city of Cologne on the train corresponds somewhat gracefully with one's corporeal experience of it in a satisfying manner, and "the relationship between the given reality and its representation is mediated and communicated" by the architecture of the city itself. In many modern cities a degree of anomie and dislocation typify one's first encounter with them, yet in other places very quickly one gains a "sense of reality asserting itself, very often against our will". It is not so much "intellectual curiosity" as the "situational conditions of everyday life" and the "spatial characteristics of the natural world in which we live" that orient us, Dalibor Vesely claims.[4] What is often overlooked, Vesely suggests, is the crucial role that representation plays in orientation. Whilst the typology of buildings and spaces is important to one's orientation when looking at a map of a city, "it is not just the visible appearance or surface of things but the visible manifestation of the whole topography of the actual space in which it is possible to recognize the physiognomy as well as their place and purpose", Vesely insists.[5] This is true as much for a room as for a city, I suggest, since a city is made up of a series of internal and external rooms.

Physiognomy is an aspect of specificity to be sure, yet Vesely is insistent that spatiality is also territorial and temporal:

> The topology, orientation, and physiognomy of space constitute a unity: the visible aspects of space, its physiognomy, depend on orientation; and orientation depends on the topological character of the surrounding world. This sequence of relationships and dependencies brings us closer to understanding the phenomenon of continuity in its identifiable manifestations.[6]

Vesely elaborates upon an observation by Maurice Merleau-Ponty that "what counts for the orientation of

the spectacle is not my body as it in fact is, as a thing in objective space, but as a system of possible actions, a virtual body with its phenomenal 'place' defined by its task and situation".[7] His elaboration of this point leads to a startling conclusion:

> The concept of "virtual body", defined by its tasks and situation, refers to the creative formation of space in terms not only of its topography (as a situated place), or its orientation, but also its physiognomy. Only with these aspects of architectural space in mind can we understand the deepest levels of space as it is constituted in the domain of given natural conditions and human spontaneity. On this level, spatiality is primarily dependent not on the position of the human body, but on the continuity between the actual and possible structures of the surrounding world to which the human body belongs... the horizon of all of our experiences that cannot be fully thematized in fact defines a world in which space is only a dimension. In this context it would be more appropriate to speak about the spatiality of the world so that structure, topography, and orientation of space could receive their proper ontological meaning. There is no ultimate origin or ground of space, for the same reason that there is no ultimate ground of the world. Instead there is a continuum of references mediating between the more articulated and explicit forms of space and its implicit deep structure.[8]

The "continuum of references" includes the physiognomic characteristics of a city, eg "the prominence of certain buildings or spaces", but Vesely is clear that "the nature of space depends on the continuity of reference to deeper structures of the human world" and that "these structures are in a certain sense related to the earth as a primary reference (*arché*)... the integrity of space is reflected in the coherence of human experience."[9] What is also suggested is that the "creative formation of space" reveals an aspect of "embodied memory" and "creativity" that is common both to the designer and inhabitant of cities: "Each project rests on a network of communication that involves the silent language of craftsmanship and skills, drawings, sketches, and other visual representations... and instructions."[10]

It is more precise, Vesely claims, to describe this creative aspect of spatiality as "ontological",[11] as it involves "openness to what is given in the conditions of our existence".[12] Vesely describes this as "pre-reflective experience", as something that sportsmen and craftsmen experience when in tune with their work or game, and he suggests that the "unity and order" that is revealed in situations has a number of consequences for designers also. Primarily, pre-reflective experience (in contrast to modern theory), "overlaps considerably with the classical notion of practical life (*praxis*)". A clue to this lies in the fact that whilst "we may be able to produce

4   Vesely, *Architecture in the Age of Divided Representation*, p 44.

5   Vesely, *Architecture in the Age of Divided Representation*, p 52. The example that Vesely gives to illustrate and to prove this point is a space station in zero gravity conditions, citing an astronaut: "it is as though your mind won't recognize the situation you are in until it sees it pretty close to the right orientation and then all of a sudden you get these transformations made in your mind that tell you exactly where you are". Vesely, *Architecture in the Age of Divided Representation*, p 54.

6   Vesely, *Architecture in the Age of Divided Representation*, p 52.

7   Vesely, *Architecture in the Age of Divided Representation*, p 48. Vesely is citing Merleau-Ponty's *Phenomenology of Perception*, Colin Smith trans, London: Routledge, 1962, p 250.

8   Vesely, *Architecture in the Age of Divided Representation*, pp 48–49.

9   Vesely, *Architecture in the Age of Divided Representation*, pp 51–52.

10   Vesely, *Architecture in the Age of Divided Representation*, p 44.

11   Vesely, *Architecture in the Age of Divided Representation*, p 81.

12   Vesely, *Architecture in the Age of Divided Representation*, pp 82–83.

13   Vesely, *Architecture in the Age of Divided Representation*, p 83.

14   See de Certeau, Michel, *The Practice of Everyday Life*, University of California Press, 2011.

15   de Certeau, Michel, *The Practice of Everyday Life*, p 56. Vesely is citing Kisiel, T, "Aphasiology, Phenomenology, Structuralism", *Language and Language Disturbances*, Pittsburgh: Duquesne University Press, 1974, p 217.

16   Vesely, *Architecture in the Age of Divided Representation*, p 81.

17   Vesely, *Architecture in the Age of Divided Representation*, p 56. Vesely is citing Merleau-Ponty, *Phenomenology of Perception*, p 136.

18   Vesely, *Architecture in the Age of Divided Representation*, p 83.

19   See Carl, Peter, "Death and the Model", forthcoming: "If actual three-dimensionality is responsible for this quirk of the nomenclature, it is not obvious why the CAD representation is always called a model, since it is a collection of algorithms organising data pertaining to length, orientation, parameters, Bezier splines, types of connectedness etc (a mathematical model). Architects tend to succumb

to a digital autism in this milieu, enthralled with geometric processing, unlike the digital practitioners in video games or films who work fluidly between sketches, several kinds of maquette and material from actual settings."

20 In contrast to the obviously systematic language used by Eisenman and Schumacher, attempts to create a "universal language" of typology (semiotics, historicism etc) treat architecture, independent of context, as if it were a branch of grammar. The relevance of language to architecture is and is also not obvious—when language becomes systematic, the assumption is that meaning is similarly systematic. Vesely's work addresses this phenomenon as an aspect of spatiality and at the same time as a problem of creativity. Spatial creativity reveals the role that language plays in structuring reality— which, despite architects' misguided efforts, resists systematisation.

21 Vesely, *Architecture in the Age of Divided Representation*, p 57. Vesely is citing Sacks, Oliver, *A Leg to Stand On*, Touchstone: New York, 1984, pp 144–150.

22 Rhythm's etymological origin is the Greek, *eurhythmia*.

23 See Schumacher, Patrik, *The Autopoiesis of Architecture: A New Framework for Architecture*, London: Academy Editions, John Wiley and Sons, 2011. Schumacher describes his desire for a "radical autonomy and ultra-stable demarcation of the domain of architecture within society" (p 26) and describes the basis of the "origin of the discipline in the Renaissance" as "autonomization" (p 81). Whilst this obsession with autonomy might explain why the work of Zaha Hadid architects is curiously similar regardless of location, climate, programme and culture, ie air-conditioned with fully sealed walls, such special pleading doesn't extricate it from an ethical, philosophical or a political critique.

24 Vitruvius, *Ten Books on Architecture*, 1.2.3, Ingrid D Rowland and Thomas Noble Howe eds, Cambridge: Cambridge University Press, 2001. See Pollitt, JJ, *The Ancient View of Greek Art*, New Haven: Yale University Press, 1974, pp 144–148. See also McEwan, Indra Kagis, *Vitruvius: Writing the Body of Architecture*, Cambridge, MA: MIT Press, 2003, pp 200–203.

25 Vitruvius, *Ten Books on Architecture*, 6.2.5.

a drawing or play a piece of music with great skill", we "are not always able to explain how we do it. The same is true for other skills and indeed for much of everyday life."[13] *Praxis*, therefore, is not something unique to "the professions" or to specialist sportsmen or women, but is an intrinsic aspect of everyday life (as the Jesuit Michel de Certeau suggests).[14] Other aspects of pre-reflective experience will be examined in some detail below, including the essential role that movement plays in spatiality and in comprehension, and in particular we will examine the "resonance" between embodiment and articulation, which typifies architectural space.

Vesely provocatively compares the "language" of brain-injured sufferers of *apraxia* to the "intelligent arc" that Merleau-Ponty refers to, which "projects round us our past and future, our human setting, our physical and moral situation which results in our being situated in all these respects."[15] In contrast to *praxis*, which moves from a pre-reflective to a reflective ontology (akin to a footballer or craftsman's "synaesthetic" immersion in play or work), apraxics' use of language becomes, Vesely suggests (citing Kisiel),[16] "akin to the highly technical univocal language of science which, having been disengaged from its original hold on life-world structures, can now be employed only mechanically according to the rules of the game like cards or chess."[17] Whilst the former are "more focused on the tactile domain" and are involved in the world via movement, apraxics are distanced from phenomena in a manner that suggests similarities with modern notions of theory and perspective generally. Although we are "largely unaware of the richness of articulation and the potential meaning of what is shaped by spontaneous movement, communication with other people, objects and tasks, taken together, common situations can best be described as the latent world, to be understood", Vesely contends, "only under certain conditions".[18]

By implication, the systematic language of most architectural theory and systematic design methodologies might be said to exhibit characteristics of "mental blindness".[19] Similarly, systematic approaches to architectural design fail to acknowledge the fundamentally spatial character of architecture and the essentially situated nature of representation.[20] The continuity of references that characterise architectural experience, Vesely suggests, articulates the situational character of human "tasks" and "motility" in general.

Rhythm is revealed as central to spatiality in the example of the role that music played in Dr Oliver Sacks' recovery from "a serious inability to coordinate the movement of his leg with the rest of his body". Vesely recounts Sacks' account of his recuperation from injury as an example of the situated and spatial character of corporeal experience generally, and how this is often most clearly revealed when disturbed. Sacks was not responding to therapy until he was "eventually exposed to the sound of music", and this "enabled him to regain the ability to walk normally in a very short time". Vesely surmises that: "What is surprising is not

that music, generated by movement, could contribute to the coordination of movement but that the source of movement and change was in the situation and not in the brain or in the body of the patient."[21]

Rhythm is pattern in sound or images or things, and also in words and movements. It is the outward manifestation of time organised into sequences, and these can relate to the cycle of the year as seasonal time, as well as its division into festive events.[22] It is rhythm—and dance and music and architecture as manifestations of this—that situates movement into a coherent structure in which gestures can become meaningful. Rhythm enables bodily movement to recover its coherence; the continuity of references that structure reality, and enable us to participate with it, is ordered by rhythm. However, whilst rhythm is situated movement (and rhythm has content through the structure of references of a situation), situation is not something that most contemporary architectural thinkers concern themselves with.

Attempts to define architecture as a theoretical discipline tend to describe it as something that is independent of context and situation.[23] In other words, and whilst it might be impolite to suggest this, contemporary architectural theory appears be an extreme parody of what Vesely refers to, apropos *apraxia* and *aphasia*, as "mental blindness to the external environment". Mental blindness, however, at least according to Merleau-Ponty and Kurt Goldstein, is not terminal. "Mental blindness can be partly cured", Vesely suggests, and the antidote "has much to do with a change of environment". As the example of music and Sack's leg reveals, the rhythmic continuity of a situation helps to mediate between fundamental conditions and particular situations.

Rhythm is something that characterises architecture, our bodies, the natural world and social life in general. If we have forgotten its central role in architecture and in culture generally, this is because rhythm is something common to all, an aspect of the background to our lives which is largely unremarked upon and taken for granted. Nonetheless, its importance was recognised by Greek philosophers as an essential aspect of geometry and measurement, poetry and visual composition, mathematics, dance and architecture. Similarly, Vitruvius recognised the relationship between rhythm and harmony:

> *Eurhythmia* is a beautiful appearance and a fitting aspect of the parts in compositions. This is achieved when the parts of a work have a height suitable to their width, a width suitable to their length; in short, when all the parts are commensurate with one another (*ad summam omnia respondent suae symetria*).[24]

Eurhythmia is a matter of pleasing proportion—or what Ingrid Rowland terms "shapeliness"; *symmetria* being commensurate parts.[25]

Vitruvius then offers an analogy of the human body as a doorway to suggest the vital role that poise and gesture play in composition, and the intrinsic relationship perception has with *symmetria*. He noted that "appearances can be deceptive. Optical illusion and distortion must be taken into account by an architect, and he must make additions and subtractions in his work, based on his own intuition, in order to achieve the proper effect".[26] JJ Pollitt emphasises that the purpose of distortion is not caprice, but rather, Vitruvius "points out that it is sometimes necessary to alter the real, measurable proportions of parts of a building to compensate for the distortion caused them by our vision. When the measurable proportions are altered to suit the decor of the temple, the 'appearance of *eurhythmia*' results."[27] The "proper effect" is determined not by abstract measures alone, although "it is necessary to first establish a theoretical system for the relationship of parts". Nor, as Pollitt somewhat confusingly suggests, should *eurhythmia* be "understood subjectively" since "proportions are altered to suit the decor of a temple".[28]

Rhythm is not only something plastic, then ("shapeliness"), but it is also communicative of appropriateness, scale and situation. It is clear from Vitruvius's emphasis upon the importance of rhythm that architectural proportion and symmetry are not things that can be considered as autonomous, assessed independently of human situations, but a matter of correspondence, perception and appropriateness: "a theoretical system for the relationship of parts, from which adjustment can be made without hesitant uncertainty... so that the appearance of being well formed should be beyond doubt to all viewers".[29]

The Sacrifice of Space:
David Leatherbarrow on Palladio's Palazzo Chiericati and the Palazzo della Ragione

David Leatherbarrow's description of the "portico" of Palladio's Palazzo Chiericati at Vicenza situates it exactly in the civic topography of the sixteenth-century town and suggests that its status as both grand entrance and public short cut derives from this contingency. Leatherbarrow describes how the location of the project on the edge of the town led to complex negotiations between the authorities and Chiericati, who argued in his petition to build a colonnade beyond the limit of his property that "the 'portico' would not only offer him 'greater convenience' (greater depth for his *salone* and associated loggias) but the entire city too (the covered walk)".[30]

Leatherbarrow notes that in his treatise Palladio argued that ancient precedent provided a model for donations to the public good: "Porticos should be arranged around squares... their purpose is to enable people to escape the showers, snow, and discomfort caused by wind or sun."[31] The inconvenience of the marginal site led to the "difficulty of assimilating Palazzo Chiericati into the typology of arcaded urban palazzo" when the base of the building meets a site that slopes and does so via a colonnade that is also open to

the town. An upper loggia and *salone* afford good views over a river and the countryside beyond, making the building appear as both a palazzo and a villa, ie as both urban and individualistic.

Colonnades, Leatherbarrow observes, "typically suppress the individuality of the buildings they join", however Palladio's colonnade is also clearly part of the facade of the house, and "shows how the house is disjointed from the town". His "aim", Leatherbarrow suggests, was to emphasise "the room above—an emblem of the house", giving this "greater prominence, without detaching it entirely from the running length of the colonnade. Both details bind the house to the sidewalk and therefore the public realm."[32] If one only studied Palladio's drawings, which famously do not show doors or any information about his sites, one might be misled into assuming that his architecture is primarily concerned with the autonomy of geometric figures freed from any context. As we have seen from this brief example, Palladio's projects are far from being examples of some theoretically autonomous art—and the architect's skill lies in resolving the tension between the inhabitant's needs and the civility of their setting.[33] Both are manifest in terms of rooms, internal and external, and reconciled and articulated by rhythmic spatial qualities that articulate a strong sense of public and domestic *decorum*—of body and world.[34]

Palazzo Chiericati, Vicenza by Palladio, 1680.

26 Vitruvius, *Ten Books on Architecture* 6.2.5.

27 Pollitt, *The Ancient View of Greek Art*, p 148.

28 Pollitt, *The Ancient View of Greek Art*, p 148.

29 Vitruvius, *Ten Books on Architecture*, 6.2.5.

30 Leatherbarrow, David, "The Sacrifice of Space", *Common Ground: A Critical Reader*, David Chipperfield, Kieran Long and Shumi Bose eds, 13th International Architecture Exhibition, La Biennale di Venezia: Marsilio, 2012, p 30.

31 Leatherbarrow, "The Sacrifice of Space", p 30.

32 Leatherbarrow, "The Sacrifice of Space", p 32.

33 Palazzo della Ragione is also known as the Basilica, revealing that this type is capable of a variety of uses, analogical as well as programmatic.

34 "The metaphor with which I have been concerned is more extended—a double one—in that it involves three terms: a body is like a building and the building in turn is like the world", Rykwert, Joseph, *The Dancing Column: On Order in Architecture*, Cambridge, MA: MIT Press, 1999, p 373.

Palazzo della Ragione, Vicenza,
by Palladio, 1614.

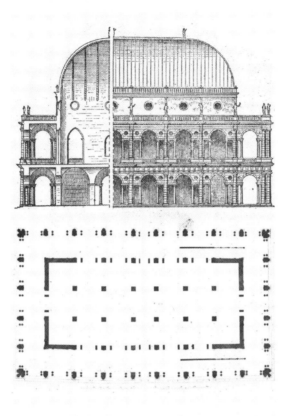

At the Palazzo della Ragione at Vicenza, Palladio applied a decorative ornamental facade to a collection of Medieval structures, creating an urban loggia distinguished by a rhythm of arches whose inter-colonnation is adjusted to relate to the openings in the older structures behind it. Far from seeking autonomy, Palladio skilfully accommodates the existence of previous structures into a coherent and civic architectural rhythm that is capable of acknowledging and accepting different programmes (town hall, shops etc) as well as mediating the extreme topography of the site. The "town hall" acts as a face to the hinterland of the town and the "region" of Vicenza. In doing so, a new/old urban facade appears, one that situates the civic depth of the site. This "depth" involves the rhythms of local agriculture, trade, government, festivals etc with civic life in general. Palladio's facade situates the topography of the civic situation in relation to use, custom, habit, ornament and *decorum*.

Building as Gesture and Argument:
Joseph Rykwert on Borromini's Oratory at Rome

The prominent role of mediation and of the human figure in Borromini's buildings reveals his debt to Michelangelo. The Oratory of St Philip Neri at Rome sits beside the chapel of St Maria in Vallicella on Piazza della Chiesa Nuova, whose travertine facade was finished by Fausto Rughesi in 1605. Joseph Rykwert describes how "when Borromini took over in 1637, his main problem was how to provide an exterior for a hall in which the new kind of literary-musical devotions (now called '*oratorio*' after the congregation which devised them), were to be held".[35] Rykwert describes this problem as a "rhetorical" one. He claims that Borromini makes a joke about the presence of a figure in the brick facade, with open arms welcoming you into the Oratory. It might be better to describe this as an example of wit, as it is a deeply serious and respectful gesture. Brick was appropriate, Borromini claims, since:

> The Oratory is the child of the church... it was resolved that the facade of the Oratory should be, as the daughter of the Church facade, smaller, less ornate, and of inferior material.... Where the church was of travertine it was resolved to make it of brick. Where the first is of Corinthian order, the other should only have a skeleton of a good order, and only indicate the members and the parts of architecture, not ornament and perfect them.[36]

The Oratory's facade to the piazza steps forwards, as it were, and the upper level steps back like a torso with extended arms. A small balcony sits between these two extremes of projection and withdrawal. This balcony sits in front of the library situated at the first floor. What appears at first to be a church facade, sat somewhat oddly beside the church next door, is in fact not the entry to a chapel, but the decorated face of what Rykwert calls a "new building type". The curves and swells of the facade do not describe a single volume within, but rather create a spatial threshold between the various levels within the building and the square that it faces. The library balcony at first floor emphasises the entrance, whilst projecting the interior of the building outwards onto the piazza. Rykwert suggests that "he makes his joke in order to sharpen the passer-by's awareness of his metaphor, as the masters of rhetoric suggested. He could, of course, only operate at this level of complexity because he is indeed invoking a commonplace—or *topos*, to use a rhetorical term."[37]

In fact, it is more precise to say that the building is two pairings: library over oratory and, for the monks, *sala di ricreazione* over the refectory (these latter are both oval). These are respectively *contemplativa* above and *attiva* below. St Philip Neri was famous for having an enlarged chest, from an enlarged heart, and this source of heat/warmth was thought of as being obviously analogous to the flaming heart of Christian symbolism. The facade faces south, catching the sun, and the *topos* about chest and arms is an embodiment of St Philip Neri himself (Borromini also speaks of being able to see the early Christian church of San Pancrazio on the Gianicolo from this balcony). In the *sala di ricreazione* there is a huge oval hearth—a marble tent in fact—which is paired with the pulpit for readings whilst dining in the refectory below. There is a famous engraving by Khunrath of what he calls a "lab-oratory" featuring just such a tented fireplace on the left and musical instruments in the foreground. It appears, therefore, that Borromini was playing with this transformational power of heat and music, and St Philip Neri's curative powers.

Facade of Chiesa Nuova Santa Maria in Vallicella, Rome by Fausto Rughesi et al, 1606 (right) and the Oratory of St Philip Neri, Rome by Borromini, 1650 (left).

Rykwert calls this rhetorical architecture "gesture" and "argument", noting, in agreement with Aristotle, that whilst "the architect's life must be... the poetic life... he will inevitably have recourse to rhetoric" if only "to convince his client and his public that he is doing something worthwhile". Rykwert stresses that what Aristotle calls "the contemplative life" (*bios theoretikos*) in his *Nicomachean Ethics* was "always complementary to *bios poietikos*, *bios praktikos*, a life of making or of political activity. The good life relied upon their constant interaction." The "theoretical" aspects of architecture reside therefore with ethical orientation towards the idea of a "good life", and designing architecture is considered by Aristotle to be an exemplary mode of "practical wisdom" (*phronesis*).[38] Rhetoric plays a key role in the formation of civic values, Aristotle believed, as a way of orienting public life towards truth and justice. This orientation was seen to be capable of manifestation, in Renaissance architectural theory (following Vitruvius), via the *decorum* of buildings, and specifically not only in their appearance per se, but in the spatial relationships that can be established by the communicative depth of facades as thresholds.

As the example of Borromini's St Philip Neri Oratory demonstrates, the *decorum* of a threshold is also a matter of the way in which the experience of the interior is expressed on a facade, and expresses not only

35 Rykwert, Joseph, "Building as Gesture, Building as Argument", *Thesis: Medium Architektur: Zur Krise der Vermittlung*, Weimar: Bauhaus-Universität Weimar, 2003.

36 Rykwert is citing Borromini from Borromini, Francesco and Virgilio Spada of the Oratory, *Borromini's Book: The "Full Relation of the Building" of the Roman Oratory*, Wetherby, West Yorkshire: Oblong Creative Ltd, 2010.

37 Rykwert, "Building as Gesture, Building as Argument". For a fuller description of the role of rhetoric in Humanist culture see Grassi, Ernesto, *Rhetoric as Philosophy: The Humanist Tradition*, Illinois, 2001: for a demonstration of the importance of rhetoric in logical thought see the description of the importance of the analogy of "the time before the Muses" for Plato's argument (in *Phaedrus*) that "true rhetoric" is not *episteme* because it is musical, ie, *rhythmical*, leading to the belief (in late Medieval) culture, that "Philosophy itself becomes possible only on the basis of metaphors, on the basis of the ingenuity which supplies the foundation of every rational, derivative process" (p 34).

38 "We may return to the good which is the object of our search. What is it? The question must be asked because good seems to vary with the art or pursuit in which it appears. It is one thing in medicine and another in strategy, and so in the other branches of human skill. We must enquire, then, what is the good which is the end common to all of them? Shall we say it is for the sake of which everything else is done? In medicine this is health, in military science victory, in architecture a building and so on—different ends in different arts; every consciously directed activity has an end for the sake of which everything that it does is done. This end may be described as its good. Consequently, if there be some one thing which is the end of all things consciously done, this will be a doable good; or, if there be more than one end, then it will be all of these." Aristotle, *Nicomachean Ethics*, 10 vols, JAK Thomson trans, London: Penguin, 1965, book i: chpt 7, pp 35-36. Aristotle describes *Phronesis*, or practical wisdom (Thomson also calls this "sagacity" in his references) in book vi: chpt 5, p 177, noting that: "Practical wisdom is a rational faculty exercised for the attainment of truth in things that are humanly good or bad. This accounts for the reputation of Pericles and other men of like practical genius. Such men have the power of seeing what is good for themselves and for humanity; and we assign that character also to men who display an aptitude for governing a household or a state".

Above: Facade drawing of Borromini's the
Oratory of St Philip Neri, Rome, 1650 (left)
and Rughesi's Chiesa Nuova Santa Maria,
Vallicella, 1606 (right).

Left: Facade drawing of Borromini's the
Oratory of St Philip Neri, Rome, 1650.

Right: Khunrath etching (probably by
Vriedeman de Vries) of what he calls a "lab-
oratory" from *Amphitheatrum Sapientiae
Aeternae*, Hamburg 1595, showing a tent
(before which Khunrath prays) similar
to that in the *sala di ricreazione* of the
Oratory of St Philip Neri as well as music
and a hearth, combining the principal
reciprocities of the *salae di ricreazione* and
refectory, as well as the library and oratory.

39   Borromini, Francesco and Virgilio
     Spada of the Oratory, *Borromini's
     Book: The "Full Relation of the
     Building" of the Roman Oratory.*

40   Blunt, Anthony, *Borromini*, Cambridge,
     MA: Harvard University Press, 1979, p 89.

outward beauty but communicates also relationships between the inner and outer characteristics of a situation. More generally, a literate building project for a villa, for example, will manifest not only aspects of the "*vita contemplativa*", or the pleasure of country life (*otium*), but also a degree of distance from and acknowledgement of the negotiations (*negotium*) of city life. *Decorum* is not simply then a matter of an individual building's style or form, but something that orients it within the continuity of reality that we call urbanity, the theoretical and practical basis for city life and politics generally.

In very simple terms, the oratory chapel in Rome is a room focused upon an altar, decorated with a painting set within an oval left within the cross-webbing of the vaulted ceiling, created for several kinds of performances and housing and making explicit the co-fraternity of the lay and consecrated Oratarians. Something of the inner life of a traditional Medieval cloister appears coincidentally with a typical Renaissance *Scuole* or Guild Room. The entry is centred on the facade and leads to the oratory and to the centre of the cortile. This cortile was supposed to have housed the fountain at Monte Giordano, and its long corridor was described by Borromini as the longest street in Rome.[39]

In order to reconcile the perfected inner realm of the cloister garden—a square of grass fringed with a colonnade—with the extrovert face of the oratory towards the piazza, the architect had to adjust the inter-colonnation of the vestibule columns. Or rather, in order to dignify both situations with appropriate geometric *decorum*, the last column of the entrance loggia thickens and is absorbed into the wall of the chapel. The tension between the three specific spatial rhythms of the facade, the chapel and the cortile is resolved and disguised by the placement of a bust of St Philip Neri at this point, forming a niche and a significant threshold between the inner and outer

world of the complex.[40] At this moment the particular and special character of the Oratarian mission—as both active and worldly, and at the same time declamatory, musical and contemplative—are brought together at their intersection between *monasticum* and city, in a gesture of subtle and significant symbolism. The role of sculpture and architecture here is irreconcilably site-specific, and the background and physiognomic aspects of the city remain in concert.

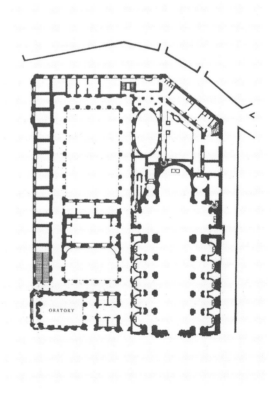

Ground plan of the Oratory of St Philip Neri

Peter Carl on Topography of *Praxis*

In contrast to this harmonious situation, in the modern city "the deep background of language and conditions that give it life must be rediscovered", Vesely claims. The modern city is comparable to how, "in amnesic aphasia, the discontinuity between the possible and actual reality of words, between their concrete and abstract meanings, destroys the physiognomic qualities of experience, perception and language". He concludes that "the loss of physiognomic qualities is directly related to the loss of categorical background, affecting language and perception." From this analysis of "mental blindness" we can see why contemporary architects' emphasis upon "sculptural form" has two dire consequences: not only do "icon" buildings lack figural or figurative physiognomic presence, ie *decorum*, they also destroy the background aspects of urbanity. I will discuss below some of the reasons for this development, and its origins in architectural modernism, but at this point it is worth noting David Leatherbarrow's observation that whilst twentieth-century architects such as Maxwell Fry and Jane Drew "suggested that art could compensate for the cultural sterility of functionally determined buildings":

> The widely celebrated architects of our time no longer *insert* art into functional solutions, but use it to drape or cover them; yet here too sculptural form is essentially compensation for the inadequacy of functionalist solutions.[41]

An almost ubiquitous acceptance of "sculptural form" by architects has had a seriously negative effect upon recent buildings and urban design, and contributes to what Peter Carl wryly calls "our current persistent inability to make decent cities".[42] Part of the difficulties that architects have with civic design today is the result of looking at existing cities as "built form", as the manifestation of a concept, rather than the result of negotiation and exchange.[43] This often—if not usually, in fact—leads architects to propose superficially complicated sculptural forms in response to complex situations. This tendency has a long and ignoble history and its origins lie not only in "mental blindness" or "ontological blindness", but also in insecurity about the contingent nature of architecture as *praxis*. Similarly, the obvious fact that cities are not "projects" does not deter architects from claiming that they are.[44]

Attempts to make architecture an academic subject led, in the twentieth century, to phrases such as "built form" being used to denote "the embodiment of cultural ideas", usually considered manifest in that other chimera "city image".[45] Peter Carl contends that looking at city plan forms as images leads architects then to think of the "city as concept".[46] Our use of confused terminology leads to confused notions of what cities and architects are for, "most evident in the profligate use of such terminology as 'aesthetics', 'ideology', 'technology', 'commerce' or 'space'", Carl

claims.[47] These terms obscure what he calls the "tensional network of analogies" that "arises from within the practical domain of concrete and metaphoric relationships" that constitute city life, and these "methodologies" and "generalisations of concepts" tend to "flatten the difficulty of reality" inducing "an ontological blindness".[48] Carl does not believe in the Hegelian distinction between "matter and spirit", nor the subsequent functionalist-symbolic dichotomy that arises from this distortion of reality: he asserts instead that "there is no such thing as an absence of content, no gap between the practical and the symbolic, only progressively more explicit modes of symbolic representation". The problem of the city, therefore, is not a question of the form or image of the city, or one of methodology, but of recognition that "no universal exists in separation apart from its particulars".[49] Carl proposes that Aristotle's description of situational knowledge (in his *Metaphysics)* is the basis of *praxis* in *Nicomachean Ethics*. What enables one to move between the universal and particular, Carl calls "typicality of *praxis*". *Praxis* cannot be reduced to materialism, nor to tectonics (materiality), nor to the variously pseudo-scientific modes of formalism that are really the search for a new style of architecture based upon information (semiotic postmodernism and digital parametricism are curiously alike in this way).[50] Carl's ambition for "*praxis*" as a conceptual basis for architectural meaning is clear in this passage:

> I want to emphasise that the measures of a *techne* are only partially determined by questions of fabrication; rather, the key to these measures are the customary postures or gestures, distances, groupings, the distinctions and hierarchies of human situations. For example, discourse is customarily face-to-face; dining is customarily inflected towards the manners of host/guest and involves the often elaborate symbolism of food preparation... the house is customarily the institution which is most consistently present in architectural and urban representation. The paradigmatic dimensions of this typicality are also the basis (in the Ancient Near East) of larger "symbolism", since what is always present in such situations is the exchange between the given conditions and historical possibilities. There is an arbitrary element in any symbol; and a symbol is less illuminated by looking at its intrinsic qualities (a mountain, for example) than by looking at its modes of use (eg, as throne base, or in poetry), which are culturally specific.[51]

Carl's work is concerned with the latent conditions of urbanity that constitute the grounds for *praxis*, and he acknowledges that architectural *praxis* provides encounters that architectural theory cannot, "the sorts of opportunities which only reality throws up".[52]

Carl's term "culturally specific" resonates with the expression "site-specific" which Richard Serra uses

41 Leatherbarrow, David, *Architecture Oriented Otherwise*, Princeton: Princeton University Press, 2009, p 48.

42 Carl, Peter, "City-image Versus Topography of Praxis", *Cambridge Archaeology Journal*, October 2000, p 328.

43 "Civic Design" is the name of the department of "Town Planning" at Liverpool University, and it is where the architecture students used to receive their undergraduate urbanism lectures.

44 See "The City as Project: A Research project at TU Delft", and Pier Vittorio Aureli ed, *The City as Project*, Berlin: Ruby Press, 2014: "The city is often depicted as a sort of self-organising chaos. This collection of essays, edited by Aureli, makes the case for the opposite hypothesis: The city is always the result of political intention, often in the form of specific architectural projects." Whilst the argument with Schumacher's notion of the city as automatic is clear, it is worth noting that Aureli exhibited alongside Eisenman and Kipnis at Venice in 2012 as *The Piranesi Variations*. The theme was autonomy in architecture, a reprise of the motif of Aureli, Pier Vittorio, *The Possibility of an Absolute Architecture*, Cambridge, MA: MIT Press, 2011. In terms of practical poetics, the problems begin in the very first sentence: "This book proposes to reconsider architectural form in light of a unitary interpretation of architecture and the city"; and ultimately lie in the impossibility of "an absolute architecture", (p ix). Pier Vittorio Aureli is struggling with the legacy of political philosopher Mario Tronti and his ideal of *Autonomia Operaia*. Tronti attempted to reconcile the ideas of Karl Marx and the Nazi legal theorist and judge Carl Schmitt; and Aureli attempts to link teleological politics and "political theology" to the autonomy of architecture advocated by Rossi in his categories of type and place. "Struggle" is the correct term for this effort, I suggest, with all of its associations with absolutism in twentieth-century thought.

45 See Lynch, Kevin, *The Image of the City*, Harvard–MIT Joint Center for Urban Studies, Cambridge, MA: MIT Press, 1960. This interesting and evocative book sits somewhat on the threshold between systematic and hermeneutic readings of cities I suggest: at once open to the importance of analogy in architecture, whilst restricted by an overarching emphasis upon city as "image"—as opposed to city as quotidian and civic life.

46 Carl, "City-image versus Topography of Praxis".

to describe his sculpture, and with Donald Judd's provocative term "specific objects", but of course is significantly different. What is meant by "contextualism" is at stake, and also the problem of formalism per se. The method of this study is to examine the language that has been traditionally used to discuss sculpture and architecture (*eurhythmia, analogia* etc).[53] Partly this involves the reconstruction of terms such as "space" and "rhythm", and it ultimately leads me to examine the possibility of their recuperation as ways to bring architecture closer to life, and specifically to city life. For Dalibor Vesely, the simultaneous loss of background and articulated urbanity in contemporary architecture raises some very complex questions about *decorum* in buildings, and their potential to communicate in the modern city:

> The example of the highly developed space of a Medieval cathedral brings to the fore a number of important but difficult questions. What is the nature of the relationship between the verbal articulation of the program, painting, sculpture, and the body of architecture? Are the more articulated possibilities of expression anticipated or prefigured in architecture, or is architecture only a passive receptacle for the more expressive possibilities of sculpture, painting and the spoken or written word? Is there anything in architecture that can be seen literally, or metaphorically as a form of language or text?[54]

I aim to try to address these questions by discussing sculpture and architecture in terms of what these disciplines have in common: spatiality, rhythm and site. Rhythm is not simply a primary aspect of physical movement but also of communicative space. Dalibor Vesely's term "communicative movement" hints at the power of architecture to articulate the conditions of life that are common to all. The horizon of engagement that is established in typical situations is matched by a degree of inarticulate structure, the rhythm of light and architectonics, all of which set up the possibility for spontaneity and participation. Urban topography contributes powerfully to the communication between architecture, site and sculpture, and its recovery re-establishes the possibility for a civic ground.

47 See Baumgarten, Alexander Gottlieb, *Aesthetica*, 1750: "Baumgarten appropriated the word aesthetics, which had always meant sensation, to mean taste or 'sense' of beauty. In so doing, he gave the word a different significance, thereby inventing its modern usage. The word had been used differently since the time of the ancient Greeks to mean the ability to receive stimulation from one or more of the five bodily senses. In his *Metaphysics*, § 451, Baumgarten defined taste in its wider meaning, as the ability to judge according to the senses, instead of according to the intellect. Such a judgment of taste is based on feelings of pleasure or displeasure. A science of aesthetics would be, for Baumgarten, a deduction of the rules or principles of artistic or natural beauty from individual 'taste'." In 1897, Leo Tolstoy, in his *What is Art?*, criticised Baumgarten's book on aesthetics. Tolstoy opposed "Baumgarten's trinity—Good, Truth and Beauty...." Tolstoy asserted that "these words not only have no definite meaning, but they hinder us from giving any definite meaning to existing art...." Baumgarten, he said, claimed that there are three ways to know perfection: "Beauty is the perfect (the absolute) perceived by the senses. Truth is the perfect perceived by reason. The good is the perfect attained by the moral will." Tolstoy, however, contradicted Baumgarten's theory and claimed that good, truth and beauty have nothing in common and may even oppose each other: "The arbitrary uniting of these three concepts served as a basis for the astonishing theory according to which the difference between good art, conveying good feelings, and bad art, conveying wicked feelings, was totally obliterated, and one of the lowest manifestations of art, art for mere pleasure... came to be regarded as the highest art. And art became, not the important thing it was intended to be, but the empty amusement of idle people." Tolstoy, *What is Art?* vii, 1897.

48 Carl, "City-image versus Topography of Praxis".

49 Carl, "City-image versus Topography of Praxis", p 334. (Carl is of course citing Aristotle, *Metaphysics*, 1040b26.)

50 See Schumacher, *The Autopoiesis of Architecture: A New Framework for Architecture* and Aureli, *The Possibility of an Absolute Architecture*.

51 Carl, "City-image versus Topography of Praxis", p 332.

52 Peter Carl, email to the author, 24 June 2013: "these are indeed the sorts of opportunities which only reality throws up. The opportunity presents itself to do a complete life cycle... La Tourette's cells are little churches". Correspondence concerned the example of a catafalque being used as a bed in the chapel of a convent that my practice have designed in London, in order for it to comply with disabled access regulations ("Similarly, it would be possible to place a bed at ground floor, to provide accommodation if the lift were ever broken. We could detail the chapel for example to accommodate a piece of furniture that could also become a bed, as it is highly likely that this item would also be used as a catafalque to support coffins". Patrick Lynch, email to Ben Dixon at Islington Planning Department, 24 June 2013.)

53 Weschler, Lawrence, *Seeing is Forgetting the Name of the Thing one Sees: A Life of Contemporary Artist Robert Irwin*, Berkeley: University of California Press, 1982. There is a story about an attempt to bring the best minds together to discuss the possibility of collaboration between architecture and sculpture. As introductions were being made, each architect in turn described themselves as "an artist". The only actual artist present was Robert Irwin, and he got up and left, "leaving the artists to it". Subsequently, Irwin became "the architect" for the Dia Foundation's rural collection. The Dia felt that architects were unable to behave appropriately, that only an artist could deal appropriately with the site and with the artworks. Similarly, when Richard Serra's sculptures were installed in the Bilbao branch of the Guggenheim, Serra was aggrieved at the poor quality of the building. See McGuirk, Justin, "The Matter of Time", *ICON*, no 26, August 2005.

54 Vesely, *Architecture in the Age of Divided Representation*, p 68.

Rhythmic and Communicative Space

Designs for various stage sets by Adolphe
Appia, depicting drama situated within
allusions to civic topography and archaic,
archetypical thresholds characterised by
a spatial dialectic of earth (darkness,
matter, city) and sky (light, orientation,
horizon).

Adolphe Appia on l'Espace Rythmique and Hellerau

An ornament, a decoration, a piece of sculpture set
up in a chosen place are representative in the same
sense that, say, the church where they are found is
itself representative.
—Hans Georg Gadamer, *Truth and Method*

Arguably, the birth of the term "space" occurred
simultaneously with the idea of rhythmic space. This
may be because "space" became an important aspect
of human culture whilst human events were still
entwined with natural conditions, even if for Mallarmé
space appeared as a gulf or void, as death amidst a
shipwreck—the wreckage of traditional society wrought
by the violence of industrial capitalism.[1] For El Lissitzky
"space" is whiteness, a tabula rasa of post-revolutionary
possibility upon which architects might project their
axonometric visions of buildings that are optimistic
about their potential to transform the flotsam of
the broken world into paradise. For Adolphe Appia,
however, space was essentially musical—"*l'espace
rythmique*". "Without changing my basic orientation",
Appia claimed, "eurhythmics freed me from too rigid
a tradition, and in particular from the decorative
romanticism of Wagner", for whom he had designed
stage sets.[2]

Space was not only musical but also theatrical for
Appia, and he is emphatic that space is not abstract:

I shall call this *corporeal space*, which becomes
living space once the body animates it.... Whereas
earlier, in the case of Wagner, I had based my
designs on the performer, now lacking a score, I
thought I could begin with space itself, but I failed
miserably. Finally I understood! If I lacked a score,
I at least had the living body.... This conclusion
liberated me.... Wherever the pencil touched the
paper it evoked the naked body, the naked limbs.
The active role of light developed naturally from
a spatial arrangement, which demanded it, and
everything thereby took on the *appearance of
expectancy*: the nature of space made the presence
of the body indispensable....[3]

Crucial to his conception of space was the rhythmic
character of light as much as the "eurhythmic
movements" that Appia learnt about from Émile
Jaques-Dalcroze, his patron at Hellerau, as well of
course as the music of Wagner, for whom he had
created earlier stage sets. "Apollo was not only the god
of music; he was also the god of light!", Appia declared
in his essay "Eurhythmics and Light" in 1912.[4]

His setting for *Orpheus and Eurydice*, Act II, "The
Descent into the Underworld", created in Hellerau in
collaboration with Jaques-Dalcroze in 1912 consisted of
a staircase down which Orpheus "gradually descended...
bringing the light with him as he was opposed by, then
gradually subdued, the Furies".[5]

1 See Carl, Peter, "Convivimus Ergo
   Sumus", *Phenomenology and
   Architecture*, Henriette Steiner and
   Maximillian Sternberg eds, London:
   Routledge, 2015.

2 Appia, Adolphe, *Texts on Theatre*,
   Richard C Beacham ed, London:
   Routledge, 1993, p 76. Appia's term
   "eurhythmics" means, loosely
   speaking, rhythmic theatre, which
   distinguishes it from Vitruvius's
   eurhythmy, ie "shapeliness". As
   outlined above, direction, *decorum*
   and orientation is implied by
   Vitruvius's use of the phrase, and
   light and "*mythos*" (or plot) situates
   Appia's theatrical spaces also.

3 Appia, *Texts on Theatre*, p 74.

4 Appia, *Texts on Theatre*, p 94 (Appia
   is citing his friend Houston Stewart
   Chamberlain's *Richard Wagner*,
   1896, p 196).

5 Appia, *Texts on Theatre*, p 97.

Left: Stage set for *Orpheus and Eurydice*, Act II, "The Descent into the Underworld", Adolphe Appia 1926 (see also frontispiece and image opposite top left).

Right: *Festspielhaus stage*, Hellerau, Adolphe Appia, 1910.

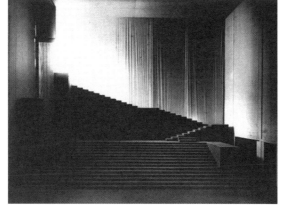 

Left: Caspar David Friedrich, *Junotempel in Agrigent*, 1828–1830.

Right: JMW Turner, *Ulysses Deriding Polyphemus*, 1829.

6   Wiedmann, August, *Romantic Art Theories*, London: Gresham Books, 1986, pp 82–83.

7   Wiedmann, *Romantic Art Theories*, p 12. Wiedmann claims that for many eighteenth-century observers of Romanticism, and in particular Fichte's notion that "Within leads the Mysterious Way!" was "nothing more than Protestantism *in extremis*, the hubris of the subject before the Fall" (p 68). On the other hand, a Romantic poet was usually a "passionately religious poet" (such as Shelley), and "the backward-looking Christian Romanticism of the Nazarenes" was emphatically Catholic (p 77). Regardless of denomination, Romanticism was at once a search for and acceptance of "cosmic harmony and conflict of the elements" (p 83), Wiedmann claims; and this was fundamentally anti-urban, against "rational-scientific culture" (p 13) and "in favour of humble and rustic life" (p 12). Whilst their sense of "horror before an imminent Wasteland", and "dread of a disenchanted world" led to many to seek in "cultic" art refuge from modernity, it is also worth noting that in Schelling's *System of Transcendental Idealism*, "Genuine art always combined *natural* necessity and *ideal* purpose" (p 74).

Whilst Appia's later work at Hellerau may have superficially overcome what he saw as his earlier "decorative Romanticism", it retains a primordial sense of "clearing" and of earth/sky. In fact, his spatial settings retained a strongly communicative quality, and spatial rhythms articulated both the content and action of an opera—although the eurhythmic performances were less opera than ballet—emphasising a rhythmic order, needless to say. This spatial exegesis was powerfully atmospheric, turning "thousands of electric light bulbs", secreted behind gauze, into a lambent threshold between human and divine realms, whilst maintaining a strongly situational and human scale. A sort of grand if not quite civic—although the fêtes at the theatre were meant to be part of a festival cycle for the town—quality of emotion was invoked but remained somewhat abstract and inarticulate. This ambiguity is akin to the resacralising tendencies of Romantic painters whereby light symbolised God-in-nature, and a sort of Germano-Hellenic mythic *topos*.

What saves Appia's stage sets from becoming pure signs, in the manner of Leni Riefenstahl's theatres of light at Nuremberg—although there exist obvious similarities, not only in the Wagnerian ecstasy of mood but also their common dramatic exaggeration—is the combination of dramatic and real time, of the movement of actors across naturalistic terrain, in recognisably symbolic versions of real situations. These topographic thresholds are primitive and earthy, and exhibit a mute resistance to the fleeting action upon them, both abstract and figural—settings for real bodies as Appia suggests. It is this carnal quality and the articulation of temporality (by artificial light that imitates natural light) that grounds Appia's rhythmic spaces in common experience.

The question they pose, however, is "how do these rhythms contribute to the creation of a communicative spatial realm?" In part they are examples of twentieth-century primitivism, with its roots in Romanticism, what August Wiedmann calls "the mythopoetic instinct" that is present in Turner's *Ulysses Deriding Polyphemus*.[6] This "mythopoetic instinct" led not only to allegorical settings in paintings and theatre (in particular by Wagner), but also led towards a sense of the essential role that festivals played in orienting both ancient Greek and Italian city-states. This instinct did not articulate the deeper dimensions of "*decorum*"—the natural conditions upon which city life is founded and depends, and Romanticism tended towards inwardness and "a simplicity at one with nature".[7] The rebirth of the tradition of festivals at Hellerau, admittedly within the theatre school of Émile Jaques-Dalcroze, sat within and around a quasi-urban temple-theatre, is evidence of attempts in early modernist design culture to reunify the arts (architecture, stage design, music, dance, opera etc) along with the senses (light, sound, movement).

Hellerau offered an opportunity for the eurhythmic theories of Jaques-Dalcroze, and Appia's own notions

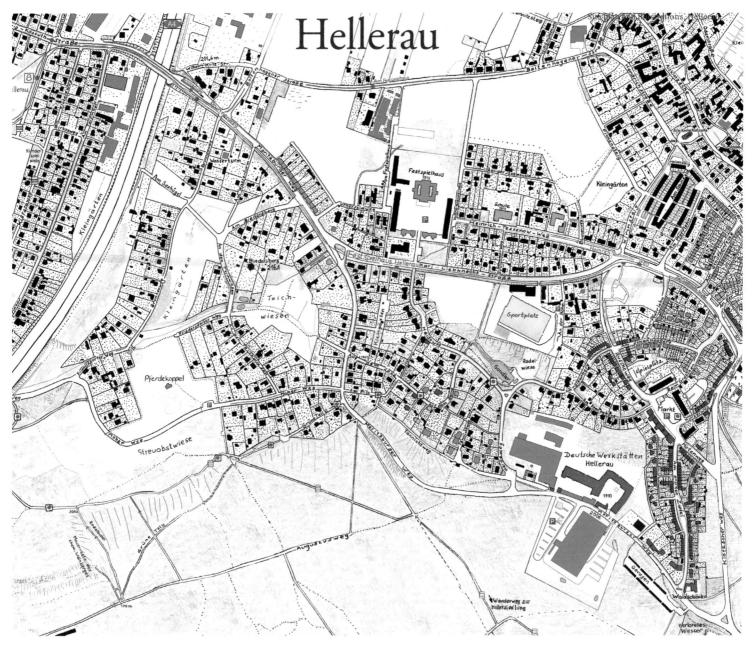

of rhythmic space, to become articulate in a quasi-urban setting—a small town devoted to craft and to art. Appia's set designs and Jaques-Dalcroze's performances were, as it were, the summit of a quite broad cultural pyramid whose layers included the *Werkstätten* of Hellerau and Tessenow's urban design, residential and school buildings, interiors and furniture.

Hellerau is in fact a suburb of Dresden (a city particularly made up of semi-independent suburban satellite towns), one of the most significant urban achievements of both Baroque culture and Enlightenment *Bildung*. The rhythms of the wider city and of the natural world informed the life of Hellerau, which reached a sort of profane apotheosis in eurhythmics.

The enchanted setting of theatre offered a possibility for reconciliation of the mythopoetic themes of the nineteenth century—which had previously only existed in paintings and in music—with a theory of movement and spatiality in general. What is revealed by Appia at Hellerau is the role that rhythm plays in communicative spatiality generally. The communicative power of his stage sets is an aspect of the "synaesthesia" that Vesely identifies as vital to orientation, of which movement is key. Rhythm may in fact be a crucial aspect of urbanity, but we need to step beyond the frame of theatre in order to encounter it, because urbanity is not a spectacle.[8]

8 There are numerous examples in which architects mistake the monumental effects of light and shade, such as one sees in the drawings of Appia and in the paintings of De Chirico, and a vaguely classical architectural language for urbanity per se. Whilst the Italian architects of the 1930s made some useful interventions into cities (see Giovanni Michelucci's post office in Pistoia, and the Santa Maria Novella train station in Florence), attempts to create whole cities or city quarters from monuments are problematic not least because of the problem of domesticity in relation to civic life (see Esposizione Universale Roma). It seems to work best for mortuaries or set design (see Aldo Rossi's San Cataldo Cemetery in Modena, Italy).

Opposite: Site plan of Hellerau, Dresden, 1908–1912.

Right: Adolphe Appia, *Dessin de Rythmique—Prométhée*, 1929.

Heinrich Tessenow, drawings of the workers' housing at Hellerau, 1908.

Festspielhaus, Hellerau by Heinrich Tessenow, 1910.

Henri Lefebvre on Rhythmanalysis and Paris

Whilst it might be commonplace to suggest that cities
exhibit rhythms, it is also perhaps too obvious to
say that all aspects of life are rhythmic. So obvious, in
fact, that we do not notice that rhythm characterises
the world and our being in it in biological, ecological
and social terms. In *Rhythmanalysis: Space, Time and
Everyday Life*, Henri Lefebvre sketches a "portrait" of
"the rhythmanalyst" who is attentive to this continuity
between self and world, one who "calls on all his senses":

> He draws on his breathing. The circulation of his
> blood, the beatings of his heart and the delivery
> of speech as landmarks. Without privileging any
> one of these sensations, raised by him in the
> perception of rhythms, to the detriment of any
> other. He thinks with his body, not in the abstract,
> but in lived temporality.[9]

Acknowledging his debt to Gaston Bachelard's "topo-
analysis" (and his investigations into *The Poetics of
Space* and *The Psychoanalysis of Fire*), Lefebvre adopts
a quasi-phenomenological approach towards what
he calls "The Critique of the Thing", that nonetheless
juxtaposes as "categories" those characteristics which
phenomenological enquiry seeks to reveal as continuous
and reciprocal viz "quantitative and qualitative",
"continuous and discontinuous".[10] He posits the idea of
"secret" as against "public" rhythms; and "fictional" versus
"dominating rhythms";[11] and whilst Lefebvre claims that
"the characteristic traits" of "the real" are that it is "truly
temporal and rhythmic, not visual", his analytic approach
is based upon a series of conspicuously theoretical
metaphors.[12] Lefebvre claims that:

> To release and listen to rhythms demands attention
> and a certain time. In other words, it serves only
> as a *glimpse* for entering into *murmur*, noises,
> cries. The classic term in philosophy, "the object",
> is not appropriate to rhythm. "Objective"? Yes, but
> exceeding the narrow framework of objectivity,
> by bringing to it a multiplicity of (sensorial and
> significant) **meanings**.[13]

However, his critique of "the thing" lapses into a
description of rhythmanalysis as subjectivity, claiming
that it comes close to "the poet".[14] Lefebvre's descriptions
of "children leaving school, some very noisy" etc, are
exuberant and keenly observational, and like Bachelard
he writes well and evocatively, even if the meaning of his
words sometimes slips away within the "wave" of verbal
rhythms. Some sense of the inter-subjective quality of
phenomenological "measurements" is evident in his
description of a "window overlooking the street" that
"is not a mental place":

> The window offers views that are more than
> spectacles; mentally prolonged spaces. In such a
> way that the implication in the spectacle entails the

explication of this spectacle. Familiarity preserves
it; it disappears and is reborn, with the everydayness
of both the inside and the outside worlds. Opacity
and horizons, obstacles and perspectives implicate
one another because they complicate one another,
imbricate one another to the point of allowing
the Unknown, the giant city, to be glimpsed or
guessed at. With its diverse spaces affected by
diverse times: rhythms.[15]

These rhythms he then calls "the music of the city".
Writing at the beginning of the 1980s, in central Paris,
Lefebvre observes changes to the city with a mixture of
delight and horror. He sees evidence of city music in the
ways in which "the squares have refound their ancient
function, for a long time imperilled, of gathering,
of setting the scene and staging spontaneous
popular theatre":

> Here on the square, between Saint-Merri and
> Modernism erupts a Medieval-looking festival:
> fire-eaters, jugglers, snake charmers, but also
> preachers and sit-in discussions. Openness and
> adventure next to dogmatic armour-plating.
> All possible games, material and spiritual.[16]

Lefebvre asks if there is "a hierarchy in this tangled mess,
this scaffolding?" "A relation between" what he calls
the "physical flows of movements and gestures, and the
culture that shows itself (and yells) in the enormous
murmur of the junction?" He is resigned that whilst
the "windows, doors, street and facades are measured in
proportion to human size", the "hands that move about,
the limbs, do not amount to signs, even though they
throw out multiple messages". Despite his sense that
people should "impose a law.... An order of grandeur",
and the fact that "the little bistros on *rue R.*, the boutique,
are on a human scale, like the passer-by"; modern
"constructions wanted to *transcend* this scale". Lefebvre
is scathing not only of the modern architecture of Paris,
but also of capitalist property development generally.
"Money no longer renders itself sensible as such", he
observes, "even on the facade of the bank... not long ago
this capital centre retained something of the provincial,
of the Medieval: historic and crumbling". Just as modern
banks no longer show the presence of money but hide it:

> [The architects of Beaubourg] leave known
> dimensions and also all models past and possible
> behind; leading to the exhibition of metal and
> frozen guts, in the form of solidified piping, and
> the harshest reflections. And it's a meteorite
> fallen from another planet, where technology
> reigns untrammelled.[17]

"Capital", he declares, "kills social riches. It produces
private riches", and he continues:

> just as it pushes the *private* individual to the fore,
> despite it being a public monster. It increases

9   Lefebvre, Henri, *Rhythmanalysis:
    Space, Time and Everyday Life*,
    London: Bloomsbury, 2013, p 31.

10 Lefebvre, *Rhythmanalysis*, p 19.

11 Lefebvre, *Rhythmanalysis*, p 27.

12 Lefebvre, *Rhythmanalysis*, p 41.

13 Lefebvre, *Rhythmanalysis*, p 41.

14 Lefebvre, *Rhythmanalysis*, p 33.

15 Lefebvre, *Rhythmanalysis*, pp 42–43.

16 Lefebvre, *Rhythmanalysis*, p 44.

17 Lefebvre, *Rhythmanalysis*, p 43.

18 Lefebvre, *Rhythmanalysis*, p 40.

19 Lefebvre, *Rhythmanalysis*, p 102.

20 Lefebvre, *Rhythmanalysis*, p 64.

21 Richard Rogers: Inside Out, exhibition at the Royal Academy, 18 July–13 October 2013: Rogers made this claim in a film that was shown in the exhibition. I will refer to this and other interviews in more detail below.

22 Dalibor Vesely remarked on the (limited) success of the public space in front of Beaubourg in our interview for the Venice Biennale of Architecture (Interview with Dalibor Vesely, "Inhabitable Models: Eric Parry Architects, Haworth Tompkins, Lynch Architects", Common Ground, Venice Biennale of Architecture 2012) which I see as deriving from the failure of Rogers' to instigate his plans for the space: "A good analogy is to think of the space in front of Beaubourg in Paris (Centre Pompidou), where the piazza is. I remember, when it was under construction, I was talking to Richard Rogers and looking down from the second floor onto to the huge piazza below, and he described to me his vision of this going to be the future flower market of Paris. That was his intention. Obviously, it didn't happen. But it's probably quite good that it didn't happen, because then it would be a monologue, just flowers.... So now it's open to events, as they come and happen, and whatever happens happens, and it's a sort of city space, which sometimes is more interesting than the exhibitions inside. That's fine."

political struggle to the extent that states and state-apparatuses bow down to it. With regard to social richness, it dates from an earlier time: gardens and (public) parks, squares and avenues, open monumentality, etc. Investment in this domain, which is sometimes reliant on democratic pressure, grows rarer. What sets itself up is the empty cage, which can receive any commodity whatsoever, a place of transit, of passage, where the crowds contemplate themselves (example: the Beaubourg (Pompidou) Centre—the Forum in Paris—the Trade Centre in New York). Architecture and the architect, threatened with disappearance, capitulate before the *property developer*, who spends the money.

Just as Lefebvre juxtaposes a definite distinction between individual and state, he draws absolute distinctions between "everyday" spatial settings and "modernism"—between the city and architecture in fact. This is an extension of what he calls "repressive" "state apparatuses" to encompass capitalist space also. He even describes these as exhibiting different rhythms—even different geometries. What he calls "the cyclical" is "social organisation manifesting itself. The linear is the daily grind, the routine, therefore the perpetual, made up of chance encounters."[18] He elaborates on the distinction between the "everyday time" of city dwellers and "the state" in an essay entitled "An Attempt at the Rhythmanalysis of Mediterranean Cities" (published in the same volume in English), drawing particular attention to the theatricality of Venice:

> Isn't it that because of a privileged form of civility, of liberty, founded in a dialectic of rhythms, gives itself free-rein in this space? This liberty does not consist of being a free citizen within the state—but in being free in the city outside the state. Political power dominates or rather seeks to dominate space; whence the importance of monuments and squares, but if palaces and churches have political meaning and goal, the townsfolk-citizens divert from it: they appropriate the space in a non-political manner. Through a certain use of time the citizen resists the state. A struggle for appropriation is therefore unleashed, in which rhythms play a major role. Through them, civil, therefore social time seeks to and succeeds in withdrawing itself from linear, unrhythmic, measuring/measured state time. Thus public space, the space of representation, becomes "spontaneously" a place for walks and encounters, intrigues, diplomacy, deals and negotiations—it theatricalises itself. Thus the time and rhythms of the people who occupy this spaces are linked back to space.[19]

Lefebvre is clearly unwilling to admit that "the public" and "the secret" "imbricate" each other in both traditional and modern cities—despite his evocation of the masked balls of Venice and his description of the

windows of Paris. Whilst it is clear that modern cities suffer from modern buildings that appear as "empty cages", it is less clear how what he calls "the capitalists" seek to gain from the creation of asocial space. Lefebvre hopes that "perhaps ancient truths will come to pass through a language other than that of the modern, and the position in favour of the social".[20] What these "ancient truths" might be, Lefebvre resists mentioning.

I share his distaste for Beaubourg and I do not accept Richard Rogers' assertion that he and Renzo Piano represented and came from the populist social movements that inspired the events in Paris in 1968.[21] It is named, after all, after the right wing president that commissioned it, Centre Pompidou. It is clear that whilst the creation of a vast and vastly expensive art gallery (and spectacular if ultimately anti-dynamic escalator ride) occurred as a response to civic unrest and replaced spontaneous civic life with spectacle. The Centre Pompidou is purely a visual spectacle. It has nothing in common with the rhythmic experience of a Medieval city that Lefebvre (and the Situationists) saw as a vital contrast to modernism.[22]

The public and private aspects of buildings and spaces in traditional cities are not as antagonistic, or as absolute, as Lefebvre claims. Nor is it impossible today to imagine design that is oriented towards "the social". This social life is a mode of theatricality, as Lefebvre suggests, but he does not describe the transformational power of theatricality that overturns typological categories. Such inversion and metamorphosis was specifically observed in 1930s Naples by Walter Benjamin to reside in the balconies and deep facades of buildings and in the streets. Benjamin was much more of "a poet" than Lefebvre of course, and he saw theatre as a quality of immanence and latency. Benjamin describes theatricality as metamorphosis, and as a form of spatial, temporal and architectural porosity that characterises the city of Naples and its inhabitants:

> As porous as the stone is this architecture. Building and action impenetrable in the courtyards, stairways and arcades. In everything they preserve the scope to become new unforeseen constellations. The stamp of the definitive is avoided. No situation appears intended forever, no figure asserts it's 'thus and not otherwise'. This is how architecture, the most binding part of the communal rhythm, comes into being here: civilised, private, and ordered only in the great hotel and warehouse buildings on the quays; anarchical, embroiled, village like in the centre, into which large networks of streets were hacked only forty years ago.... Porosity results not only from the indolence of the Southern artisan, but also, above all, from the passion for improvisation, which demands that space and opportunity be at any price preserved. Buildings are used as a popular stage. They are all divided into innumerable, simultaneously animated theatres. Balcony, courtyard, window, gateway, staircase, roof are at the same time stage and boxes.... Irresistibly

the festival penetrates each and every working day.
Porosity is the inexhaustible law of the life of this
city, reappearing everywhere. A grain of Sunday is
hidden in each weekday, and how much weekday
in this Sunday! [23]

He describes this capacity for transformation as festival
—as "a grain of Sunday" that inhabits each weekday
and vice versa. Lefebvre's description of everyday
life as something defined and ranged against "the
state" or "the capitalists" misses the essential aspect
of urbanity that makes it theatrical—this capacity
for transformation. The fire-eaters that he observed
at Saint-Merri are not enacting a Medieval rite—they
are not engaged in a festive use of the space, their tricks
are not, in fact, communal activity at all—but evidence
of the lack of it. The reason why the jugglers outside
Beaubourg are not actually in a "Medieval city square"
is not simply because the building is an "empty cage"—
or ugly, or lacking in scale in formal terms. What is
problematic in these spaces is the absolute distinction
between public and private life, and gawping at a street
entertainer is not a satisfying form of encounter because
it is not a mode of participation in city life. A spectacle
is fundamentally not participatory, because there is no
"communicative movement" at play.

Dalibor Vesely on Communicative Movement at
Chartres and Würzburg

Having established the importance of "the situational
structure of the world", and the role that *praxis* plays
in revealing this, Vesely then proceeds to explain how
"communicative space" reveals that the distinctions
between form and content, and between autonomous
self and extensive world, are "fictitious". To do so the
role of "communicative movement" is clarified and
shown to play a central role not only in spatiality but
also in representation, ie in both pre-reflective and
reflective experience, revealing both the spontaneous
aspects of space and the role that architecture plays in
culture generally:

> The place of architecture in the continuum of
> culture is special because its reality coincides with
> the reality of primary situations and their mode
> of embodiment. The history of architecture can
> be seen as the history of attempts to represent the
> latent order of nature and create a plausible spatial
> matrix for the rest of culture. The plausibility
> of the spatial matrix rests on a long process of
> interpretations and modifications that established
> an identifiable tradition. [24]

Vesely calls this "the playing field of architecture", and
suggests that "if we extend the notion of playing field
to architecture, then it may be possible to say that what
the playing field is to the game, architecture is to culture
in its broadest sense." [25] What are the grounds for this

claim? Firstly, he cites Erwin Straus to demonstrate
that architectural space reveals the primary character
of spatiality to lie in movement:

> Sensuality and motility are coordinated in the
> tactile sphere in an especially striking fashion.
> We pass our fingers over the table-top and
> apprehend its smoothness as a quality of the
> object. The tactile impression results from the
> completion of the movement. When the tactile
> movement stops, the tactile impression dies out. [26]

Movement is not only inherent in sensuality, but also
essential to embodiment generally, and this is the
crucial aspect of space that enables architecture
to become articulate. In spatial articulation the arts
play a part in "synaesthetic experience" in the same
way that all the senses are coordinated in everyday life
generally. Architectural space "supports" our movement,
providing stability for culture generally (as a playing
field does for sportsmen):

> We experience the most obvious manifestations
> of the structuring role of architecture almost
> constantly in our everyday lives. There is hardly
> a place or a circumstance that is not organised
> by spatial intentions (or in the case of natural
> surroundings, experienced as organised). The
> encounter with things and their spatial order is
> an encounter with the otherness of our situation,
> accessible through the dialectics of revealing and
> hiding.... However, we need to see these terms
> (embodiment and articulation) in their dialectical
> relationship: it is by resistance that architecture
> supports our intentions and the appropriate
> meaning of a situation. We are aware of this most
> intuitively each time we move up a staircase, travel
> through uncomfortable corridors, enter rooms with
> certain expectations, or recognise the purpose of
> a building from its layout and physiognomy. [27]

Vesely furthermore suggests that there is a play between
the "silence" and "resistance" of space and the role that
architecture has in "supporting" and "articulating" the
"unity" of the arts in traditional buildings, which reveals
the profound contribution that it has in situating and
orienting us in the world. He offers some architectural
examples to explain the role movement plays in our
experience of space and in our comprehension of the
representative aspects of it (whilst noting that "the
process of bringing the latent world to visibility is
most clearly demonstrated in the design of gardens,
where the cosmic conditions are revealed in a visible
order"). [28] In each, "the natural world" provides the
means of and measure of experience. Firstly, the rose
window on the west front at Chartres Cathedral
represents the second coming of Christ (*Parousia*) and
the fulfilment of Christian cosmogony, which began
with the "incarnation of the word". Vesely insists that
"the body of the cathedral provides a background for

23 Benjamin, Walter, "Naples",
    *Reflections: Essays, Aphorisms and
    Autobiographical Writings*, New York:
    Schocken, 1986, pp 165–168.

24 Vesely, Dalibor, *Architecture in the
    Age of Divided Representation: The
    Question of Creativity in the Shadow
    of Production*, Cambridge, MA: MIT,
    2004, pp 103–104.

25 Vesely, *Architecture in the Age of
    Divided Representation*, p 106.

26 Vesely, *Architecture in the Age of
    Divided Representation*, p 82.

27 Vesely, *Architecture in the Age of
    Divided Representation*, p 106.

28 Vesely, *Architecture in the Age
    of Divided Representation*,
    pp 83–84: "The order is always
    a result of dialogue between the
    representative structure of space and
    the spontaneity of natural change,
    manifested in the changing nature
    of the seasons, growth and decay of
    the flora, changing weather."

The rose window at Chartres Cathedral, c 1235.

29   Vesely, *Architecture in the Age of Divided Representation*, p 64.

30   Vesely, *Architecture in the Age of Divided Representation*, pp 66–67.

31   Vesely, *Architecture in the Age of Divided Representation*, pp 77–78.

32   Vesely, *Architecture in the Age of Divided Representation*, p 77.

33   Vesely, *Architecture in the Age of Divided Representation*, p 78.

34   Vesely, *Architecture in the Age of Divided Representation*, p 79.

the articulation of the more explicit meanings visible in the physiognomy and iconography of the sculpture and colored windows".[29] This articulation occurs as interplay between a relatively inarticulate rhythm of columns and arches (of the barely articulated stone architectural space), and the highly articulated rhythm established by the sun's movement (illuminating the stained glass):

> The relationships between these levels of articulation and their equivalent modes of embodiment are brought together in the east to west movement of the sun, the visible source of light, which culminates in the sunset. The correspondence between the Last Judgement in the rose window and the sunset illustrates very beautifully the link between the invisible phenomena of death and resurrection, their visible representation in the window, and their embodiment in the hierarchical structure of the cathedral, animated by the movement and light of the sun. The crucial observation at Chartres is how the body of the cathedral, itself abstract and silent, is capable of revealing and supporting a very subtle and highly articulated meaning of salvation—a meaning that can be brought down to earth tangibly and concretely.[30]

Vesely's other examples of "communicative movement" in architectural space involve both the description of the typical Parisian cafe as a "field of references" and as a "visible text" and a Baroque staircase.[31] The latter reveals that embodiment is movement, not simply materiality (although this plays a supporting role as "resistance" enabling and "supporting" movement). Vesely refers repeatedly to the example of staircases, noting that a stair is "in one sense a pure object,

intended to serve a defined purpose", but also as "a field of relationships—not always visible and obvious, but permanently available".[32] Before dealing in some detail with a particular example he alludes to a theme that unites his term "continuity of references" with "communicative movement" as something that is both spatio-temporal and cognitive. *Decorum* is introduced as a matter of the "institutional nature" of "the French café" example, "rooted in the habits, customs, and rituals of French life... the invisible aspects of culture and way of life are embedded in the cafe's visible fabric, as if they were a language conveyed in a written text".[33] He is insistent that this institutional character is not available via "conventional typologies, relying solely on appearance" because:

> Identity is not a property of things or structures; it is constituted in the continuity of references to the ultimate sameness of the most regular movement in reality as a whole—that is, to the celestial movement, measured by the stability of the earth.[34]

Nonetheless, whilst the ultimate reference for us is gravity and seasonal time, human finitude etc, there is a network of relationships which situate each reference in relation to each other; cognition and comprehension of this occurs instinctively and provides orientation. This is why staircases possess particular and usually typical identities, since they are part of a "field of relationships" that make up typical situations; we might call such a collection of typical situations urbanity, and it is something that exists between things in a building and amongst individual buildings. Staircases connect, bring together and define as distinct, different spatial characters and identities within and also beyond buildings. "These relationships", he declares, "are available in all our

The Bishop's Residence at Würzburg,
Treppenhaus, with fresco by Tiepolo,
Apollo and his Continents, 1752–1753.

preliminary design decisions, including about the staircases' general character and overall spatial arrangement". In fact, staircases facilitate not only physical but also perceptual and communicative or ontological movement; they facilitate spatial recognition and orientation:

> When we speak about the character of the staircase being domestic or public, simple or monumental, we have in mind a precise relationship between the space, the light, the size and material of the staircase, and the movement that occurs on it. There is a striking contrast between the inexhaustible richness of possible interpretations and the limited number of plausible or optimal solutions. This limitation is even more puzzling in more complex designs such as those of residences, libraries, theatres, and concert halls. Most spatial situations show a remarkable level of identity that cannot be derived from spatial characteristics alone; it is something more complex and enigmatic. [35]

In the case of the example of the Baroque staircase at the Bishop's Residence at Würzburg, this enigmatic complexity is a characteristic of an elaborate iconographic scheme in which the architecture of Balthasar Neumann and the frescoes of Tiepolo are unified. Both resistant stone and painted ceiling combine to situate actual and imaginary space in relationship to each other—"one art participates in the reality of the other"—and this unity is achieved through movement. [36] "The unity of space", Vesely reminds us, "depends on the continuity of references, which in our case is the continuity of embodiment understood not as

the materiality of a particular art but as situatedness and participation in movement" (whose ultimate reference is "earth"). This unity "reveals the tension between the anonymity and silence of the architectural body and the iconicity that can be anticipated", and results from the "universality of the imagination" that enables architect and artist to anticipate the culmination of each other's efforts, which in this case occurs on the landing of the staircase at which point it becomes clear that the ceiling represents an image that resolves itself through "communicative movement":

> What we can understand through our experience is the structure of the articulated world in which we can directly participate. This is precisely what we do when we move through the foyer and enter the ceremonial stair hall. The staircase itself is aligned with the movement of the sun, represented by Apollo; this gives orientation not only to the staircase but to the room as a whole. As we ascend to the first landing and turn, the staircase becomes part of the structure of the room; the four walls transform themselves into four continents and eventually disappear into the light of the ceiling. [37]

Both Appia's stair-stage at Hellerau and the Baroque staircase at the Bishop's Residence at Würzburg use rhythmic ascent/descent to embody a change of state. The Hellerau stair is descent to the chthonic realm of Orpheus, whilst the Würzburg stair is ascent to Apollo's luminous realm (the Hellerau stair is "beneath" the Würzburg stair). Both imagine themselves to be stair-rooms (*treppenhaus*) with theatric attributes, the earlier as part of Baroque reception ceremony (in which one

35 Vesely, *Architecture in the Age of Divided Representation*, p 77.

36 Vesely, *Architecture in the Age of Divided Representation*, p 86.

37 Vesely, *Architecture in the Age of Divided Representation*, p 88.

38 Vesely, *Architecture in the Age of Divided Representation*, pp 106–107. Vesely is citing Heidegger, Martin, "The Origin of the Work of Art", *Poetry, Language, Thought*, New York: Harper & Row, 1971.

39 Vesely, *Architecture in the Age of Divided Representation*, p 91.

40 Vesely, *Architecture in the Age of Divided Representation*, pp 71–73.

41 Vesely, *Architecture in the Age of Divided Representation*, p 72.

42 Vesely, *Architecture in the Age of Divided Representation*, p 91. Vesely continues: "Resonance... casts light on the spontaneous formation of identities and differences, similarities and analogies, and more generally on the metaphorical nature of all communication. At the same time it is closely linked with rhythm, proportion, and harmony. It is well known that the primary meaning of proportion is analogical; and while analogy belongs to the metaphoricity of discourse, proportion more explicitly represents its structure, which can be eventually expressed in numbers. We do not need to be reminded that proportion was, until recently, at the center of thinking about architecture and its order. But it is not always understood or acknowledged that proportional thinking was primarily mediation between the ideas of a potential unity of the world and the uniqueness of a particular situation or phenomenon. In the history of Western culture, this process became a mediation between the celestial and the terrestrial order, between divine and human reality, and finally between the universal and particular in the understanding of the world." (pp 91–92)

43 Carl, Peter, "Praxis: Horizons of Involvement", *Common Ground: A Critical Reader*, David Chipperfield, Kieran Long and Shumi Bose eds, 13th International Architecture Exhibition, La Biennale di Venezia: Marsilio, 2012, pp 67–81.

44 Carl, "Praxis: Horizons of Involvement", p 73.

45 Carl, "Praxis: Horizons of Involvement", p 73.

might participate... its effect depends on actually passing through the telamones and arriving at that landing); the later more as spectacle/drama (in which one participates through witnessing) The earlier is for nobles, the later for child actors representing Ancient Greeks; the earlier situates its mythic elements in a lived present, the later is both more historicist—using ancient costumes—and more abstract, atemporal, light, and concerns movement as such. The first carries many more layers of reference—and many more kinds of rhythm—with its ornament and frescoes; the second strives to be more timeless, eternal, a specific insight into "being-human". The first is vastly expensive, required Europe's best artists, stuccoists, architects and is structurally sophisticated (the thin vault survived the Second World War bombing); the second is temporary, inexpensive, more image than substance, more stage set than architecture as such.

However, embodiment is body-in-movement and since "situation is communication" our bodily situations provide a clue to the nature of *decorum*. I will discuss *decorum* as an aspect of ornament, and ornament as the orientation provided by art experience in some detail below. Vesely alludes to this as the role that "decor" plays in architecture, and it is significant that in the architectural examples he offers of "communicative space", artworks play a vital role in revealing the "reciprocity between the articulated world and its embodiment". He suggests that this reveals "Heidegger's effort to grasp" the significance of "earth" and the role that "the work of art" plays in situating world and Being in relation to each other:

> The setting up a world, does not cause the material to disappear, but rather causes it to come forth for the very first time and to come open of the work's world. The rock comes to bear and rest and so first becomes rock; metals come to glitter and shimmer, colors to glow, tones to sing, the word to speak. All this comes forth as the works sets itself back into massiveness and heaviness of stone, into the firmness and pliancy of wood, into the luster of metal, into the lighting and darkening of color, into the clang of tone, and into the naming of the word.[38]

Vesely also situates geometry and "resonance" as aspects of spatiality that place architecture as central to the formation of communicative culture generally. Both aspects of communicative space are closely related to rhythm and to proportion, he suggests.[39] He contends that "what logic and grammar are to verbal language, geometry is to the visual world", asserting the central role that it played in pre-Enlightenment culture "on the boundary of visible realities".[40] Vesely suggests that "geometry is subtly linked to language by movement and gesture" and that "even at its most abstract level, geometry depends on certain basic movements and gestures, such as measuring and drawing, visual analysis, and making models".[41] Once again architecture is seen to exhibit aspects of "communicative movement" not only as spatial experience in a finished building, but in the corporeal and imaginative act of design, which is a form of orientation itself. Like craft or sport, design is a mode of "communicative movement". Resonance and rhythm are aspects also of relationships that imply orientation as *decorum*, and as such are part of a hierarchy of relationships implied by analogies and "the communicative nature of movement, imagination, and language".[42] I will discuss in more detail below the particular relationships between geometry and analogy that made it central to Greek thinking about poetry and architecture, and the vital role that rhythm plays in this.

Peter Carl on *Praxis* as Horizons of Involvement

Vesely's description of the primary importance of communicative space in Western culture and his claim that this enables architecture to "create a plausible spatial matrix for the rest of culture" implies, as he suggests, the central place that *praxis* plays in our lives. The creation of a "spatial matrix" reveals the important place that institutions play in both spatial and ethical orientation, and the role that urbanity has in stabilising and acting as a mode of *praxis*. *Praxis* is typified by institutions and cities, since they provide the "horizons of involvement" that situate ethical action and reflection, Peter Carl contends:[43]

> The phenomena summarised as a city's culture... prevail as institutions, always already there. Institutions of this kind are more or less visible as such, but are activated as soon as one becomes involved, as is evident in greetings—at a formal dinner or a garage, to a junior or a senior, to an animal, or according to someone's customs. Institutions are typicalities (conceptually) with attached constituencies (concretely). These constituencies are mostly anonymous (and mostly deceased, recollected), but are manifest in the particular person whom one seeks to greet properly, or in the character/direction of the context into which one seeks to intervene architecturally. Gadamer's term for horizon, "tradition", reflects this depth of anonymous, ancient constituency as the conditions for freedom (which we are as free to get wrong, or misunderstand, as we are to profoundly understand). Here lies the source and authority for architecture's capacity for memory.[44]

In contrast to formalist readings of institutions as physical types or concepts, Carl proposes that we should think of them as "latent background/context, awakened and made compelling in the situation/involvement".[45]

He continues to describe the "horizons of involvement" in a series of diagrams that reveal the relationships between the "basic situation of the claim of a topic"; "the stratification of embodiments"; and "fundamental reciprocity of conditions and possibilities", that "give the structure of any poetics, the basis for references, allusions, metaphors". [46] The grounds for this are both concrete and ontological, and Carl describes the city in terms of "architecture and urban topography" that "provide particular structures of embodiment, situated in a particular place and for a duration in history, of the more universal phenomenon".

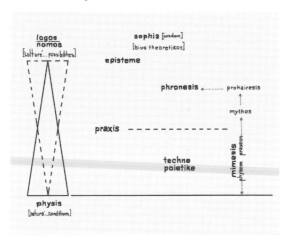

Architectural mimesis/interpretation set within the stratification of Aristotle's *Nicomachean Ethics*, book vi by Peter Carl as illustrated in Carl's essay "Praxis: Horizons of Involvement".

Recognising the primary role that *topos* and "topic" play in urbanity situates architectural imagination in regards to both "actual natural conditions" ("a garden, wilderness, materials, light") and the "ontological natural conditions" that they are "concrete manifestations of" ("called *physis* in the Greek philosophical tradition").[47] He continues, "*praxis* is civic life", stating that this has "two dimensions… action and reflection". Both confront the natural conditions or "earth/*physis*" and whilst action "revolves around choice rooted in judgement, and is always a matter of concrete/particular instances of choice"; reflection ("called by Aristotle *theoria*") "is essentially ethical speculation on the nature of our understanding of the good, the divine, the common to all".[48] There is an inevitable theatricality to the enactment of judgement, and Carl points out that "all the principal institutions of Aristotle's polis were characterised by *agon*/conflict and its resolution—judging and making laws, tragic drama, religious sacrifice, games, symposia". These events were situated somewhere but "architecture is not the drama", Carl insists. Rather, "architecture is a discipline of peripheral vision, of setting the conditions and horizons of *praxis*".[49]

Carl situates the theatricality of "architectural *mimesis*/interpretation set within the stratification of Aristotle's *Nicomachean Ethics*, Book VI" in order not only to explain that *praxis* is both an imitation ("play between *mimesis praxeos* and *mimesis physeos*") but also a form of practical wisdom that now involves *phronesis* directly with *techne*:

Architectural design now requires being able to reconcile primordial spatial and material

phenomena with a range of discourses, techniques and people that move between technical specialists, bureaucrats, users or constituents, politicians, journalists, scholars, and so on. It is not easy to preserve the integrity of the topic/question where the building codes are the most explicit representation of common-to-all. Something like practical wisdom is needed if we are to recover technological making for ethical reflection. Because it incorporates the embodying conditions of participation/understanding and can communicate with the most abstract discourses, the closest we have to a practical philosophy is phenomenological hermeneutics.[50]

This mode of enquiry comes closest to Platonic dialogue, which is not simply a matter of discussion between different individuals' points of view (nor of systematic visions of city in terms of this or that social class and the ultimate triumph of either). Socratic dialogue, Carl reminds us, is a matter of "ascent and descent through levels of participation/understanding" that "has its roots in the collaborative *agon*, a trusting of the disagreement to help to find the truth of a topic". Carl is clear that "we cannot avoid these conditions" and that *praxis* "is a matter of interpreting them well or badly".

Elsewhere he describes the vertical hierarchy between topics and ideas, the primary dialectic, in Heideggerian terms as between "*da*", ie earth, and "*sein*", ie being/comprehension.[51] This finds curious resonance, Carl remarks, with Le Corbusier's comment about the chapel at Ronchamp, that architecture is "word addressed to earth".

The conditions of mediation between the ontological and actual "earth" correspond with architectural settings that "establish the conditions for participation and for witnessing", he believes, and it is this that orients the polis with *praxis*. In other words, it is the ornamental character of architecture, and its role in mediation that means that it is associated with beauty by Gadamer. Carl contends that the "time out of time" aspects of festival resonate with the theatricality of architectural settings.[52] Both are typified by rhythm—be it poetic, seasonal, rhetorical, mathematical, structural, light-shade, geometrical and analogical—and by mediation. In order to see how the affiliation of beauty with mediation enables Carl to assert that dialogue is the basis of civic life itself ("*Convivimus Ergo Sumus*"), we need to now see how "communicative movement" situates art experience as an aspect of urbanity, and the role that architecture plays in this in concert with the other arts.

In particular, Carl's emphasis upon Heidegger's observation that "the city gives a definite direction to nature" reveals the particular role that architecture and sculpture play in the specific spatial and cultural mediation that is known as "civic *decorum*".[53] The role that rhythm plays in "communicative movement" is a key aspect of spatiality, suggesting its importance in the potential recovery—alongside the reappearance of urban topography—of the civic depth of urban architecture.

46 Carl, "Praxis: Horizons of Involvement", pp 74–75.

47 Carl, "Praxis: Horizons of Involvement", p 74.

48 Carl, "Praxis: Horizons of Involvement", p 74.

49 Carl, "Praxis: Horizons of Involvement", p 76.

50 Carl, "Praxis: Horizons of Involvement", p 78.

51 Unpublished seminar notes on "Being and Time" by Peter Carl.

52 Carl, "Praxis: Horizons of Involvement", p 78 and see also Carl, "Convivimus Ergo Sumus".

53 Carl, "Praxis: Horizons of Involvement", p 67. The Heidegger citation is from Heidegger, Martin, *Being and Time*, Oxford: Basil Blackwell, 1962, p 71 (this is erroneously credited in *Common Ground* as SCM Press, London.)

possibilities,
emancipation,
articulation,
world-*sein*

symbol/concept

speech/language

significant gesture

intentional arc,
symbolic structure
of situation

habit (hexis)

corporeal scheme (body)

domain/field

conditions,
participation
embodiment
earth-*da*

physis

INDIVIDUAL   COLLECTIVE

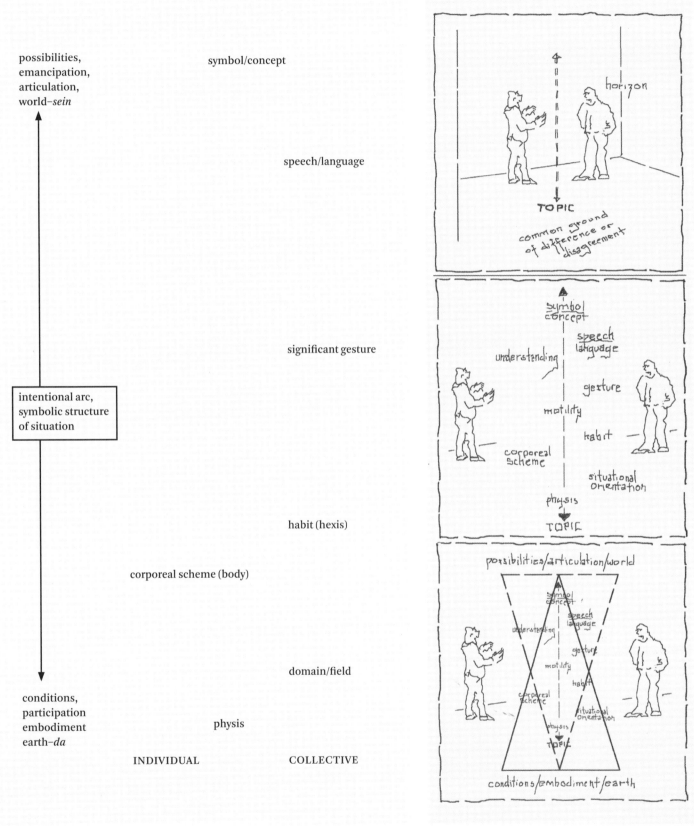

Peter Carl, diagram articulating the stratified structure of embodiment/
articulation of worldhood of world; the layers on the right correspond to
"institutional horizons".

Peter Carl, horizons of involvement, as illustrated in Carl's essay "Praxis:
Horizons of Involvement".

The City Gives a Definite Direction to Nature:
Decorum, Temporality and Urbanity

Hans-Georg Gadamer on Art and Architecture as Ornament, *Decorum* and Play

> The city gives a definite direction to nature.
> —Martin Heidegger, *Being and Time*

The analogous role that nature plays in ornament needs to be made explicit if we are to understand the profound contribution that rhythm makes to the *decorum* of civic culture, and to the revelation of the civic dimension of urban ground.

Dalibor Vesely described the role that *decorum* and ornament play in structuring urbanity in an interview that I conducted for our contribution to Common Ground, the Venice Biennale 2012:

> What we have been saying about the appropriate, right, corresponding—call it whatever—location, situatedness of particular things in the structure of the city—is a question of being proper (*prepon*). And proper, of course, eventually is *decorum*, and *decorum* means fits the purpose, something which fits the purpose. *Decorum* is when you're dressing for a particular event: you can be overdressed or underdressed, because you're missing the *decorum* of the event... and the *decorum* is subordinated to the overall notion of order... what is "proper" etc, is order as a whole, it fits into the overall order of things. And from then on you can also begin to understand or derive the meaning of terms like what is "common good"? And what is "good"? Because the good is part of what fits the purpose of the whole, and responds to it. And *decorum* is of course subordinated to the notion of order, and order—in the original term for it—is "*kosmos*". And it's interesting that *kosmos* can be translated into Latin as 'ornament'. Ornate; ornament; order; *cosmesis*: because *kosmos* is ordering. And it's still preserved in the current term "cosmetics". You order yourself for a particular purpose; you paint your face. You re-order yourself, and so on. So, eventually, underneath that term, is ornament. Ornament is ordering. Ornament is a language, which is mediating between the different levels of reality, and eventually brings things into coherence and harmony and to existence. But it's an ordering principle, bringing things into overall order. That's why you ornate, because you are referring to something beyond its own presence. That's what people don't appreciate anymore in modern terms of ornament, that ornament is not there just to embellish, to make it more interesting. If we say it makes it more interesting, we have to finish the sentence with "interesting for what?" For a purpose: In order to make it part of a larger whole, to situate it, and therefore make it part of the overall order of things, because it's only from the overall order of things that you can understand, or derive, the order of the particular thing.[1]

Vesely's emphasis on *decorum* echoes Hans-Georg Gadamer's emphasis upon ornament as orientation and mediation, and ultimately, his ambition in *Truth and Method* is to "free" the concept of play "of the subjective meaning that it has in Kant and Schiller and that dominates the whole of modern aesthetics and philosophy of man".[2] Gadamer makes it clear that:

> When we speak of play in reference to the experience of art, this means neither orientation nor even the state of mind of the creator or of those enjoying the work of art, nor the freedom or subjectivity engaged in play, but the mode of being of the work of art itself.

One of the most potent aspects of art is that it is "an experience that changes the person who experiences it", and "contains its own, even sacred seriousness".[3] Gadamer's insistence that art is primarily a mode of play does not diminish the importance of art in culture, but, rather, emphasises the ubiquity and centrality of art (play) to society generally. This central importance lies in its symbolic character, and the essential role that symbols play in culture.

Fra Carnevale, *La Città Ideale*, c fifteenth century.

The key aspect of play that makes artistic play a mode of the symbolic is that it too is primarily physical. "Play", Gadamer insists, "is the occurrence of movement as such", and "it renews itself in constant repetition".[4] Whilst it might be tempting now to settle for the fact that "movement" or "repetition" are closely related with rhythm, and of course play is all of these things at once, what is more significant in Gadamer's chapter "Play as the Clue to Ontological Explanation" is that play is also imitation of the creative processes at work in nature. Gadamer cites Friedrich Schlegel:

> All the sacred games of art are only remote imitations of the infinite play of the world, the eternally self-creating work of art.

In other words, play is a mode of *mimesis*. Art, as play, possesses some of the rhythmic character of the natural world; it is temporal, situational, territorial, "requires a playing field" whilst being paradoxically a "sphere of play" closed off from the world.[5] As important as the physical aspect of play is the fact that "the cognitive import of imitation lies in recognition".[6] This is why a play-world is credible no matter how apparently absurd—it can be a world, eg *Alice in Wonderland*.

1 Interview with Dalibor Vesely, "Inhabitable Models: Eric Parry architects, Haworth Tompkins architects, Lynch Architects", Common Ground, Venice Biennale of Architecture 2012. See Carl, Peter, "Ornament and Time", AA Files 23, 1992, pp 49–64: "Plato 'played upon the modalities of that term (*kosmos*) which include the world or universe, order as arrangement (and therefore, as *kosmiotes*, propriety or *decorum*) and ornament and embellishment" (and the footnote 112 to this in which he acknowledges that "Vesely put me onto this problem many years ago by observing the presence of ornament in *kosmos*". Vesely makes the same point somewhat differently in the chapter "Communicative Space" in *Architecture in the Age of Divided Representation: The Question of Creativity in the Shadow of Production*, Cambridge, MA: MIT Press, 2004, p 94.

2 Gadamer, Hans-Georg, *Truth and Method*, London: Sheed and Ward, 1993 (1960), p 101.

3 Gadamer, *Truth and Method*, pp 102–103.

4 Gadamer, *Truth and Method*, p 103.

5 Gadamer, *Truth and Method*, p 107. Gadamer acknowledges at this point that "Huizinga rightly points out" that the field of play "sets off the sphere of play as a closed world". He is referring to Huizinga, Johan, *Homo Ludens: A Study of the Play-Element in Culture*, Boston: Beacon Press, 1955, p 17.

6 Gadamer, *Truth and Method*, p 113.

7 "No one will be able to suppose that for religious truth the performance of the ritual is inessential", Gadamer, *Truth and Method*, p 116.

8 Gadamer, *Truth and Method*, p 116.

9 Gadamer, Hans-Georg, *The Relevance of the Beautiful and Other Essays*, Cambridge: Cambridge University Press, 1986.

10 Gadamer, *The Relevance of the Beautiful*, p 123.

11 For an example of the relevance of this to architecture see Lynch, Patrick, *The Theatricality of the Baroque City: The Zwinger and Dresden*, Saarbrücken: Verlag Dr Muller, 2011.

12 Gadamer, *Truth and Method*, p 152.

13 Gadamer, *Truth and Method*, p 154.

14 Gadamer, *Truth and Method*, p 156.

15 In other words, the facade is the site of representation and participation in architecture. These terms are usually reduced to "transparency" today, and confused with "political transparency", eg Foster's GLA Building is glass but impossible to enter without an invitation. OMA's Prada store in Los Angeles has no door during the day, but does have security guards.

16 See Harries, Karsten, *The Ethical Function of Architecture*, Cambridge, MA: MIT Press, 1998, p 81. Harries is citing Heckscher, August, *The Public Happiness*, New York: Antheneum, 1962, p 50, whom Denise Scott Brown refers to in her preface to the revised edition of *Learning from Las Vegas: The Forgotten Symbolism of Architectural Form*, Cambridge, MA: MIT Press, 1977, p xvii.

17 See Koolhaas, Rem and Bruce Mau, *S,M,L,XL*, New York: Monacelli Press, 2002. In his essay "What ever happened to Urbanism?" Koolhaas proposes "the architecture of Bigness", claiming that "small" equals private or domestic architecture (as if a small church was somehow not public, or a merchant's house in Spitalfields also not a place of work and trade); and he generally misuses the term "scale" when he actually means size. Similarly, Colin Rowe elided size with scale, claiming that New York is similar to Rome *because it has large buildings too*: "to move from Rome to London, to New Haven, and finally, to Manhattan, is still to receive a version of the same message. For, in Manhattan, the earlier skyscrapers (almost everything built before 1950) are still obedient to the principles observed in Rome. No doubt New York City is a vertical excess, but, until very recently, almost every skyscraper behaved approximately like Sant'Agnese in Piazza Navona. The Woolworth, the Chrysler, the Empire State buildings all behave this way. Below a certain level they are reticent and no more than street furniture; and at this level while they accommodate the street, they make no insistence. At street level they are quiet. They are not big and bold and grand. Instead, they only display what they intend to become above a highly calculated elevation. Below this, they are tranquil; and above this, they are disposed to be exuberant. The set-piece, the celebration of object, the *fioritura*, belong on top". Rowe, Colin, "The Present Urban Predicament", *As I was Saying,* iii: Urbanistics, pp 201–202. Rowe's use of the phrase "*fioritura*", literally "flowery" in Italian, is borrowed from opera criticism. What Rowe says about the lack of insistence of office buildings at ground floor is fine in terms of *decorum*, but the extrapolation of this to include Sant'Agnese inflates the point to the extent that it takes off like a hot-air balloon of rhetorical hubris; so that all the attention is suddenly upon the balloon-like dome of a church in Italy, and the reality of a street in Manhattan gets forgotten. We now have whole city quarters made up of office buildings without the Piazza Navona, and office blocks that strain to take off like rockets.

18 What Heidegger calls art, *aletheia,* means "disclosure" in ancient Greek, and "truth", he claims.

In the same way that children have a need to be recognised as playing a part—as being disguised—the character of "art-as-play" reveals the theatrical character of *decorum* and civic life. Gadamer is able to make this claim because he demonstrates that all aspects of play reflect aspects of city life. Play becomes "transformed into structure" as it assumes ever more theatrical roles in culture, sport, the law, religion, education and art itself; all are modes of play that reveal the essential character of public life to be representation.[7] "Thus imitation", Gadamer is able to declare, "as representation, has a special cognitive function", and therefore, he continues, not only is it pointless to discuss art in terms of objects (formalism), but also:

> The being of art cannot be defined as an object of aesthetic consciousness, because, on the contrary, the aesthetic attitude is more than it knows of itself. It is part of *the event of being that occurs in presentation*, and belongs essentially to play as play.[8]

"Play as play" is heuristic and pedagogic, and is a means by which children learn of course. It is not "a mere subjective variety of conceptions", because what emerges is "possibilities". Gadamer likens this to any experience noting that not all artworks reveal their secrets at the same rate, and our response to them changes over time.[9]

Gadamer goes on to claim that temporality is essential to one's cognition of art, as "it has its being only in becoming and return". He elaborates on this theme in his later writing about festivals.[10] (I have written elsewhere about the essentially theatrical nature of certain cities, particularly Baroque cities, for which festival was inspirational and central to public life, to the design of buildings and public spaces.)[11] In *Truth and Method*, Gadamer proposes that "the spectator is an essential element in the kind of play we call aesthetic", freeing play from the subjectivist bias that relegated art to something private on the one hand, or petrified into objects for scrutiny on the other. He is able to recover the public and civil character of art experience by showing that not only is art temporal, but that it is also symbolic:

> There is an obvious distinction between a symbol and a sign, for the symbolic is more like a picture. The representational function of a symbol is not merely to point to something that is not present. Instead, a symbol manifests the presence of something that is really present.[12]

The power of a symbol to "take the place of something" lies in the fact that it "makes something immediately present".[13] In the next chapter, "The Aesthetic and Hermeneutic Consequences", Gadamer suggests that "architectural monuments" do not owe their meaning to "the public act of consecration or unveiling" but to the thing which they commemorate. In order to

achieve their function of commemoration they must be participated with through use. Just as in the case of a festival, in which the spectator is a key participant in the event, the user of an architectural edifice—albeit a building or a monument—determines its significance and success. This is what is meant by "immediately present", and Gadamer is adamant that it is true not only for monuments but for buildings in general:

> A building is never only a work of art. Its purpose, through which it belongs in the context of life, cannot be separated from it without it losing some of its reality. If it has become merely an object of aesthetic consciousness, then it has merely a shadowy reality and lives a distorted life only in the degenerate form of a tourist attraction or a subject for photography. The "work of art in itself" proves itself to be a pure abstraction.[14]

In the context of my argument, a building or monument should be seen within the rhythm of life and as a setting for typical recurring situations. The "becoming and return" that characterises cognition are described as aspects of play in terms of "movement" and "repetition", recalling Dalibor Vesely's phrase "communicative movement". "Communicative movement" arises in participation, with knowledge, and in particular this arises in the heuristic experiences of work and artwork. Art is a form of work, Heidegger claimed, just as work is a mode of play (as we will see below). Gadamer continues this theme, in proposing that play is a form of knowledge that specifically brings us closer to life. This is the basis for all of the cultural games that comprise civilised society and which are housed in buildings, Gadamer suggests. What we should focus on when looking at and thinking about a city, to paraphrase both of them, is not primarily the form of the buildings that make up a city, but the situations housed within buildings and the equipment and spatial settings that support them. It is the rhythm of these spatial settings and the typical situations that they accommodate that determine the character of city life.

The *decorum* of individual buildings seems to derive from the ways in which facades of individual buildings relate to their neighbours, and in doing so both reveal and enclose spatial settings, and can even act as spatial settings themselves, both as niches for performances, and as thresholds for demonstrations. Traditionally, sculptures activated the analogous role of buildings as settings for commemorative and significant public events.[15] Certainly a city is not simply "crowds of anonymous individuals without explicit connection with each other" as Denise Scott Brown suggests.[16] It is not enough simply to make certain buildings large and to claim that this makes them civic: nor to suggest that all large buildings are civic.[17] In traditional cities, buildings disclose the spatial settings housed within.[18] The measure of a building's success—as something alive and part of "reality", "manifests the presence of something *that is really present*". The relationships between buildings that are "really present", yet withheld and the network of specific situations, relies upon the wit and imagination of architects working together at different times, collaborating together to play a game whose aim could be said to be the representation of something already present there, but sometimes not "really present". In other words, the task of an architect involves re-presenting the city anew, and renewing the relationships of the typical situations that make up city life with the conditions of life in general.

The "special importance of architecture" for Gadamer lies in the "element of mediation without which a work of art has no real '*presence*'".[19] He continues:

> [Architecture] gives shape to space. Space is what surrounds everything that exists in space. That is why architecture embraces all the other art forms of representation: all works of plastic art, all ornament. Moreover, it gives a place to the representational arts of poetry, music, acting, and dancing. That perspective is decoration. Architecture safeguards it even against those forms of art whose works are not decorative but are gathered within themselves through the closure of the circle of meaning.[20]

The "special importance of architecture" for the other arts is that it situates them ("ornament or decoration is determined by its relations to what it decorates, to what carries it. It has no aesthetic importance of its own that is thereafter limited by its relations to what it is decorating").[21] In doing so it transforms the play of rhythm as movement into the communicative (or ontological) movement of cognition, as imitation becomes representation.

The closeness of a building to "the context of life", to which Gadamer claims it properly belongs, occurs at the same moment as the recognition that the architectural imagination, as a mode of play, is "imitation and representation". This brings Gadamer to a discussion of the purpose of architecture as ornament, and the ultimate purpose of this is said to be *decorum*. He begins his exegesis by restating his position regarding the artistic content of a building:

> A building should certainly be the solution to an artistic problem, and thus attract the viewer's wonder and admiration. At the same time it should fit into a way of life and not be an end in itself. It tries to fit into this way of life by providing ornament, a background of mood, or a framework. The same is true for each individual work that the architect carries out, including ornament, which should not draw attention to itself but function as a decorative accompaniment. But even in the extreme case of ornament it still has something of the duality of decorative mediation about it.... It is not intended that the forms of nature used in an ornament

should be "recognised". If a repetitive pattern is seen as what actually is, then its recognition becomes unbearably monotonous.[22]

The representational character of ornament distinguishes pattern from decoration. The role of "architectural ornament" as "mediation" distinguishes it from patterns of natural phenomena in a reproduced mechanical fashion, (as various architects from Owen Jones to Foreign Office have attempted to do as a way to "connect architecture to culture").[23] Architecture would not need to be connected to culture, or connected to a city, if it were conceived of situationally (reaffirming the topographic continuity-in-difference). The problem of non-site-specific sculpture that Serra raged against (Henry Moore's sculptures randomly dropped into strange settings), finds its echo in the recent attempt to retrofit formalist (technical) design methodologies into "culture".

Gadamer claims that sculpture should not be thought of free from situation:

> Even the freestanding sculpture on a pedestal is not really removed from the decorative context, but serves to heighten representationally a context of life with which it is decoratively consonant.[24]

Gadamer sees the potency and relevance of sculpture to reside not only in its site-specificity, but also in its *consonance* with a site. He extends this argument to spatial settings to demonstrate that all of the arts are contingent upon witness.

> Poetry and music, which have the freest mobility and can be read or performed anywhere, are not suited to any space whatever but one that is appropriate: a theatre, concert hall, or church. Here too it is not a question of subsequently finding an external setting for a work that is complete in itself but of obeying the space-creating personality of the work itself, which has to adapt to what is given as well as to create its own conditions (think only of the problem of acoustics, which is not only technical but architectural).[25]

In other words, *decorum* reflects the contingent character of art itself. Gadamer re-establishes ornament as "something that belongs to the self-presentation of the wearer", enabling one to understand its public character. This enables him then to redefine the role of architecture as *decorum*, since it establishes what Gadamer calls "a universal ontological structural element of the aesthetic, an event of being". This structure sets up the potential for spontaneity, because it keeps in motion, or sets into play again, the recurring and repetitive rhythm of becoming. In doing so, the ontological significance of culture is revealed to lie not so much in pattern, or "gestalt" or form, but in rhythmic spatiality—manifest in ornament and in the way that architecture acts as what Vesely calls a "playing

19 Gadamer, *Truth and Method*, p 157.

20 Gadamer, *Truth and Method*, p 157.

21 Gadamer, *Truth and Method*, p 159.

22 Gadamer, *Truth and Method*, p 158.

23 See Kubo, Michael and Farshid Moussavi, *The Function of Ornament*, New York: Actar and Harvard GSD, 2008. Ornament, they claim, is a "mechanism to connect architecture to culture" (p 1). In contrast to this mechanistic and Hegelian reading of culture and of ornament (as pattern), see Brett, David, *Rethinking Decoration: Pleasure and Ideology in the Visual Arts*, Cambridge: Cambridge University Press, 2005, which provides a hermeneutic account of Gadamer's work on ornament and its relevance to contemporary *praxis*.

24 Gadamer, *Truth and Method*, p 157.

25 Gadamer, *Truth and Method*, p 157.

26 Vesely, *Architecture in the Age of Divided Representation*, p 106.

27 Gadamer, *Truth and Method*, p 159.

28 Baron, Hans, *In Search of Florentine Civic Humanism: Essays on the Transition from Medieval to Modern Thought*, vol I, Princeton: Princeton University Press, 1980, pp 236-237. Baron is commenting upon and citing Alberti's texts *Vita Civile* and *Della Famiglia*.

29 "Do you not seek great praise, glory, and immortality in this magnanimity of yours? Not only with pomp: not with ostentation, nor with crowds of flatterers will you earn real whole-hearted praise, for this can only be won by virtue." Alberti, cited in Borsi, Franco, *Leon Battista Alberti: The Complete Works*, London: Harper & Row, 1977, p 20.

30 Białostocki, Jan, "The Renaissance Concept of Nature and Antiquity", *Studies in Western Art*, ii: *Renaissance and Mannerism: Acts of the Twentieth International Congress of the History of Art*, vol 2, Princeton: Princeton University Press, pp 19–30.

field".[26] This mediation is the "old, transcendental meaning of the beautiful", Gadamer declares, concluding that:

> The truth is that the concept of decoration needs to be freed from this antithetical relationship to the concept of art based on (personal) experience (*Erlebnis*); rather, it needs to be grounded in the ontological structure of representation, which we have shown to be the mode of being of the work of art. We have only to remember that the ornamental and decorative originally meant the beautiful as such. It is necessary to recover this ancient insight. Ornament or decoration is determined by its relation to what it decorates, to what carries it. It has no aesthetic import of its own that is thereafter limited by its relation to what it is decorating. Even Kant, who endorsed this opinion, admits in his famous judgment on tattooing that ornament is ornament only when it suits the wearer. It is part of taste not only to judge something to be beautiful per se but also to know where it belongs and where not. Ornament is not primarily something by itself that is then applied to something else but belongs to the self-presentation of its wearer. Ornament too belongs to presentation. But presentation is an event of being; it is representation. An ornament, a decoration, a piece of sculpture set up in a chosen place are representative in the same sense that, say, the church where they are found is itself representative.... What we mean by "representation" is, at any rate, universal significance of play, we saw that the ontological significance of representation lies in the fact that "reproduction" is the original mode of being of the original artwork itself. Now we have confirmed that painting and the plastic arts generally have, ontologically speaking, the same mode of being. The specific mode of the work of art's presence is the coming-to-presentation of being.[27]

The re-presentation of being involves also the formulation of public roles. The creation of public *personae,* and the ritualistic and performative aspects of society mirror the representational and transformational character of art (*mimesis*). Both contribute together to the creation of culture, and what we refer to as "civic" values. Civic is the transformation not only of play into structure (laws, rituals etc); but also the transformation of natural conditions in ornament, ie, *decorum*. This is why we can talk of the *decorum* of people, costumes, buildings and situations etc. *Decorum* in architecture concerns, therefore, not only the facade but also the disposition of spatial situations and the relationships between these parts and the whole, the immediate context, natural conditions etc.

This was seen in the Medieval period to have limits set by the laws of blasphemy, but architecture played a central role in re-establishing the power and beauty of city life in the Renaissance. Ultimately, imitation, *decorum* and playful imagination reoriented the introverted scholastic mind outwards towards the world. Emphasis upon the textual character of holiness was reoriented towards the Hellenic ethos of the city as the site—and the purpose and the means— for love and wisdom.

"Civic" is a term traditionally associated with Renaissance Florence, and in particular with its use by Hans Baron. Baron uses the term "Civic Humanism" to define and distinguish between the Medieval emphasis upon poverty as grace in Franciscan and Dominican theology, and the proto-modern (Neo-Aristotelian and Neo-Platonic) world of Marsilio Ficino, Giordano Bruno, Petrarch and Alberti. Of course we recognise that Petrarch was once a poet, philosopher and gardener, and that Alberti was a priest, philosopher and architect. These factors define the essence of "Renaissance Man". Civic Humanism was the expression of this "tradition"—it was possible at this point in history to lead a contemplative and an active life, Alberti argued, to be at once engaged in city life in a generous and imaginative way, without being a slave to committees or to greed. What we now call "modern" is also defined by this tradition—a tradition of belief that "Virtue needs material possessions in order to appear dignified and beautiful."[28]

This belief leads directly to acknowledging that creating beautiful buildings and civic amenities is virtuous—and that mercantile trade is virtuous if it supports these works with finance. In fact, without orientation beyond profit towards virtuous expression in architecture, trade was considered dangerous—as wealth leads to the fear of losing it, and to sins that follow on from this fear. Civic Humanism is the rebirth of antique values that promoted the individual and the city they inhabited through the virtue of transforming wealth into beauty. Machiavelli and Erasmus called this the "exercise of virtue" and "organ of virtue". Alberti saw architecture as the professing of virtue, and one role of the architect was the teaching of virtue to patrons. Architecture manifests virtue he believed, representing it as something civic.[29]

One other aspect of *decorum* is revealed in Jan Białostocki's attention to the Renaissance concern with "*Natura Naturans*". "*Natura Naturata*" is defined as "the imitation of created nature", a tradition which the Humanists inherited from the Greeks along with Ovid's emphasis upon "Metamorphosis". This was a tradition in which artists and farmers engaged together with what Petrarch called "cultivation". Cultivation of the natural world was seen in the Renaissance as an example of divine will ("*Natura sive Deus*"). "For the Stoics", Białostocki contends, "Nature was identical with life-giving power", something that was also revealed in imitation.[30] *Mimesis* (as an act of cultivation) revealed man's cultivation, his participation with cosmic order. "*Natura Naturans*" is "a second concept, that of the imitation of creating nature". Alberti "employs this second concept when he calls nature 'marvellous artificer of things' and says, 'nature itself seems to delight in painting'". Białostocki points out that this "concept enables him to consider architecture as an art of imitation", and that "Alberti then tries to establish which laws are being followed by nature as she strives towards perfection". Alberti places nature foremost as a model for representation and nature's laws as a guide for what is practical and ideal, calling this a "general law" of congruity (*concinnitas*).

Alberti translates Aristotle's idea of *mimesis* into his proposition not only of nature as a guide to representation (*decorum*), but extends this to claim that nature is transformed by imagination and thus renews itself in the artist or architect's "perfection of nature". Białostocki distinguishes this from the scholastic tradition, since "Medieval writers always considered nature as a divine creation superior to human art", stating that "Human art could never, until the Renaissance, have been considered as surpassing nature." Alberti "formulated a new idea of great importance", Białostocki claims, "Nature is perfect as a harmonious whole, but her elements are not", enabling Humanists to see their task as the completion, and perfection, and participation with nature. From the scholastic idea that man cannot surpass nature, that "art is infallible as nature" (Grosseteste), arose the idea that the "world is a living, animated, and intellectual being" (Ficino). Whilst for Alberti art begins with the imitation of nature, Białostocki claims that for "Leonardo it is replaced by creation based on knowledge of necessity and inherent laws of nature". Białostocki's argument is that whilst Alberti views nature as transformational, as a natural mode of *mimesis*, the innovations of Leonardo da Vinci and Mantegna ignore nature as transformation, seeing it instead as "perfect form". Białostocki defines this as the beginning of Mannerism in art, whereby the history of artworks became the model for artistic inspiration, "an order discovered by the searching mind and an analytical eye": in other words, Academicism, or Historicist Formalism. In contrast, the intense relationships between ornament and *decorum*—and between urbanity and the natural world—form the basis of the continuity between architecture, sculpture and site; and this reciprocity underlies the communicative dimension of the role that rhythmic spatiality plays in civic ground.

Clare Lapraik Guest on Figural Cities and Florence

Clare Lapraik Guest describes the eloquent character of "Figural Cities", in terms of rhetoric and "the 'body' of civic virtue".[31] Guest sees in the funeral oratory of Florentine Renaissance noblemen a movement from "allegory to scenography" that relates the rhythm of speech to ornament, since this means "reflecting, or participating in universal order".[32] "Such reflections", she notes, "drew their meaning from their relation to metaphysics; where this ontological background is neglected the invocation of ornament will remain superficial and things which are not objects of artifice, such as city states, be treated as though they were art objects." Guest demonstrates that *decorum* represents "civic harmony":

The civic virtues of Florence—its prudence, justice, magnificence—correspond to Aristotle's *Ethics*, but these virtues have become embodiments of the measure and harmony of virtue, as well as exhibiting the splendour and excellence of the city.

For the fifteenth-century Florentine chancellor Leonardo Bruni *decorum* is at once a matter of Ciceronian rhetorical harmony (*convenientia*) and the Albertian conception of mathematical harmony (*concinnitas*).[33] Guest declares that for Bruni and Alberti:

The city is asserted as a totality, but it is a totality asserted (almost imposed) by rhetoric, which insists on the architectural fabric as *ornamentum* in relation to its virtues.... Bruni's work shows quite clearly the rhetorical background to Alberti's efforts to articulate the union of harmonious body of a building or the city, and the harmonious body of *decorum*; in each writer rhetorical ornament *concinnitas* plays an important role. Fundamental to the union of physical fabric and "body" of *decorum* is the understanding of justice as measure... as we should see Aristotle's discussion (*Ethics*) as essential to Alberti's view of proportion as ethical and mathematical.... As *decorum* requires that virtue has an outer form of corresponding splendour, so the visual aspect of the city places its virtues before the eyes, as in the funeral oration for Nano Strozzi, which celebrates the city through epideictic eloquence and "the magnificent display of things". The splendour of the city is not therefore a mere outer dress for the virtue of its inhabitants, but an excellence which penetrates through every part of the fabric of the city.[34]

Bruni conceived of "the city as ornament", since ornament is a mode of virtuous contemplation. In making a connection between ethics and civic virtue, Guest reveals that ornament is an expression of "*praxis*, the essence and praise of civic life".[35] Bruni boasts that "In our City there is no street or district which is not filled with the most eminent and ornate buildings", and "links rhetorical arguments for unity of form and content with the analogy of the building as body so important in Humanist architectural writings".[36] In contrast to Florence, Bruni claims:

The "*ornamenta* of other cities are instantly visible to a traveller, as an outer covering or shell... but anyone who goes... to the core or marrow (of Florence)" will find harmony between the buildings of a city, its parts, furnishings, paintings, streets: "the outer walls have not more ornament and magnificence than those within it, nor is one street or another handsome or beautifully kept and refined, but the parts of the whole city are thus".

Bruni also relates the "magnificence of ceremony" to the excellence of its festivals and this to its civic virtue

31 Guest, Clare Lapraik, *Rhetoric, Theatre and the Arts of Design: Essays presented to Roy Eriksen*, Novus Press: Oslo, 2008, p 157. See also, Guest, Clare Lapraik, *The Understanding of Ornament in the Italian Renaissance*, Leiden: Brill, 2015.

32 Guest, *Rhetoric, Theatre and the Arts of Design*, p 178. Guest cites Cicero's "discussion on rhythm" in *De Oratore*, III.xlv.

33 Guest, *Rhetoric, Theatre and the Arts of Design*, p 158.

34 Guest, *Rhetoric, Theatre and the Arts of Design*, pp 159–160.

35 Guest, *Rhetoric, Theatre and the Arts of Design*, p 166.

36 Guest, *Rhetoric, Theatre and the Arts of Design*, p 160.

Andrea Mantegna, *Portrait of Carlos de Medici*, 1459–1466 (although often said to be a portrait of Alberti).

Left: Facade of Alberti's Santa Maria
Novella, Florence, 1470.

Right: Facade of Alberti's Sant'Andrea,
Mantua, 1790.

Left: The west gate of Alberti's
Sant'Andrea, Mantua, on Good Friday,
2002, during the evening procession of
the relic of the Saint.

Right: The west gate of Alberti's
Sant'Andrea, Mantua, on Good Friday, 2002.

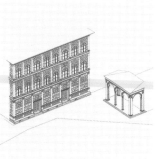

(ornament is thus revealed as a mode of *ethos*). Guest illustrates Bruni's conception of civic ornament with the examples of rhetorical figures of speech in paintings of dancers depicted as celestial bodies; and the "harmony between the external and internal parts of each building and between the districts which comprise parts of a city".[37] Bruni also brings the relationship between the city of Florence and the neighbouring countryside into his rhetorical "*topoi*", Guest claims, and she notes "a topographical continuum of garden and city which has its first architectural expression in *Quattrocento* villa architecture, for example in Michelozzo's Villa Medici in Fiesole".[38] Bruni laminates the rhetorical figure (of noble lives) as "stars" shedding light on the world (the "lights and colours" of noble speech), with his assertion that Florentine villas have "fallen from heaven rather than been built by human hand". He thus unites ornament and *decorum* in a continuum between the natural and man-made aspects of the world. The city gives a definite direction to nature, "which allows for a whole which is both graduated and harmonious", Guest suggests. Ornament is essentially orientation. This is what enables Gadamer to insist upon the relevance of the beautiful.

As we saw in the examples of Borromini's work in seventeenth-century Rome, *decorum* is not simply the imitation of other buildings, nor merely the re-presentation of tradition. Its relation to natural conditions reveals a vital aspect of *decorum* as ornament.

In order to illustrate the veracity and relevance of this vital aspect of architecture, I propose to discuss Eduardo Chillida's sculptures at San Sebastián and Rafael Moneo's Kursaal there; Sigurd Lewerentz's Church of St Peter, Klippan—even though this is usually considered

to be aniconic and purely materialistic; and Álvaro Siza's church of Santa Maria near Porto, which situates an acute sense of architectural history with the specific tectonic characters of local geography, one mediated by ornaments and artwork that amplify and intensify one's sense of reality. I aim to show that, even in the late twentieth century, collaborations between architects, clients and artists can reveal the latent urbanity of a situation, even one that appears on the surface to be otherwise dominated by technology. The revelation of the profound potential of civic ground is my aim in the following chapters, concluding with its reappearance on Victoria Street in the City of Westminster.

This latent urbanity is characterised by, and could be defined as, spatial settings that offer *a definite direction to nature*. In order to avoid the trap of facile and shallow "operative criticism", and to understand the continuity of sculpture and architecture in a modern setting, we now need to explore the reciprocity of philosophical, geometric and spatial aspects of an analogical and ornamental understanding of "nature". This needs to be clarified if we are to fully understand the contribution that modern philosophy has made to modern art and architecture. This contribution is important to enabling us to see how the representational presence of the natural world in modern architecture and art need not imply traditional or kitsch copies of classical models. What matters is the content of ornamental representation, as this is what allows it to persist through so many cultural transformations and across so many cultures. Ultimately, Guest suggests this content resides in trying to make sense of how history can be reconciled with cosmic conditions.[39]

Left: Palazzo Rucellai (left) with Stoa (right), Florence by Alberti, 1451.

Top: Ground plan of Alberti's Palazzo Rucellai and Stoa, Florence, 1451.

Above: Axonometric drawing of Alberti's Palazzo Rucellai and Stoa, Florence, 1451.

37 Guest, *Rhetoric, Theatre and the Arts of Design*, p 161.

38 Guest, *Rhetoric, Theatre and the Arts of Design*, p 165.

39 Guest, in conversation with Peter Carl, 13 April 2016.

Giusto Utens, Palazzo Pitti, the Boboli
Gardens and Fort Belvedere, 1599–1602.

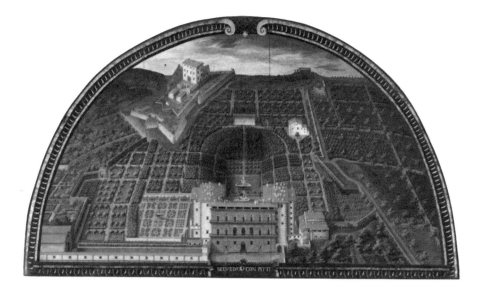

Giusto Utens, Villa Medici di Poggio a
Caiano, 1599–1602.

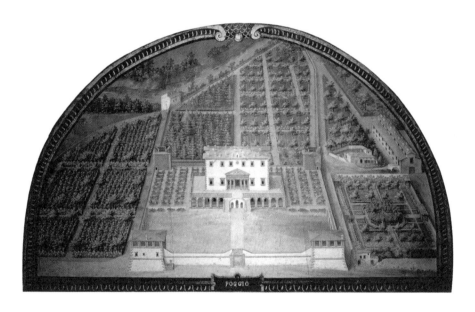

Giusto Utens, Villa Medici di Poggio a
Caiano, 1599–1602.

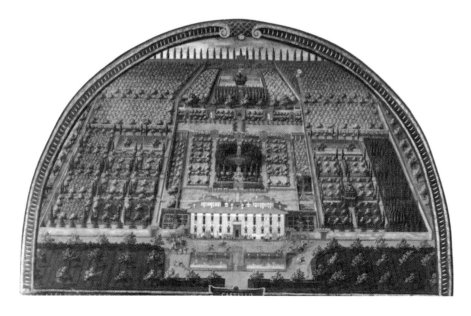

Geometric and Rhythmic Spatiality in the Heidegger-Chillida Collaboration

Art and Space

Here concern means something like
apprehensiveness... This term (Sorge—care or
concern) has been chosen not because Dasein
happens to be proximally and to a large extent
"practical" and economic, but because the Being of
Dasein itself is to be made visible as care... because
Being-in-the-World belongs essentially to Dasein,
its Being towards the world is essentially concern.
—Martin Heidegger

Whilst the twentieth-century German philosopher Martin
Heidegger's interest in architecture is well documented,
his intense interest in modern art, and in sculpture in
particular, has only recently come to the attention of
scholars, although he was active and quite well known
in his lifetime as a protagonist in what we now call "the
art world". In "Art and Space", produced in collaboration
with the Basque sculptor Eduardo Chillida, Heidegger
elaborated on his belief that "the physically-technologically
projected space" of "modern man" leads us to assume that
the world is a thing available for "utter control".[1]

Martin Heidegger, Max Bill, et al, 1964, from *Heidegger Amongst the
Sculptors* by Andrew J Mitchell.

In contrast to a materialist conception of the world—one
that "is only as old as modern technological natural
science"—Heidegger saw in certain works of sculpture the
characteristics that have the potential to disclose Being.
Sculpture defines the world "by demarcation" and by
"setting up an inclosing and excluding border". Heidegger
quotes Aristotle (*Physics*, Book IV) in his preface:

It appears, however, to be something overwhelming
and hard to grasp, *the topos*—that is, place-space.

One way of grasping this overwhelming condition is
provided by Chillida's sculpture, Heidegger infers,
not only because "sculpted structures are bodies" but
because these demarcate borders and territories.
Are these "articulated spaces, artistic space, the
space of everyday practice and commerce", he asks,
"only subjectively conditioned pre-figurations and
modifications of one objective cosmic space?" And if
this is so, how is this possible if we now only believe
in "objectivity of the objective world-space"?

In his essay "Weak Architecture", the Catalan
architect Ignasi de Solà-Morales discusses Heidegger
and Chillida's collaboration, and he concludes with
the suggestion that in an age that cannot build bell
towers or traditional monuments, there is poetic
resonance still in the "tremulous clangour of a bell that
reverberates after it has ceased to ring".[2] We are in the
age after monuments, he suggests, perhaps in unwitting
accordance with Hegel's belief that we live in a period
after art. Ignasi de Solà-Morales' essay is evocative and
cautious, but does not fully reveal the depth of the power
of the collaboration between Heidegger and Chillida,
nor the consequences of their work on space for architects.

Paul Crowther was the first contemporary scholar
to emphasise the ontological significance of sculpture
in his essay "Space, Place and Sculpture: Working
with Heidegger". Crowther's work inspired a recent
book *Heidegger Among the Sculptors* by Andrew J
Mitchell, to which I will also refer below. According
to Crowther/Mitchell, Chillida's sculptures reveal the
"unconcealment of Being": this is, the conditions of
worldhood, ie the situated character of Being-in-the-
World. Crowther's essay draws our attention to some of
the specific aspects of Heidegger's "thinking through
sculpture". These can be summarised as: the truth of
space is revealed in art that then illuminates the relations
between things to be part of the nature of places; spatiality
belongs to places; place is revealed by art, and this is
a preparation for dwelling; place is the home of Being;
Being is unconcealed in places through actions and
activities that reveal its embodied character (dwelling).[3]

I suggest that this shows that there is less an explicit
"turn" or "*kehre*" in Heidegger's thinking—from Being
towards space (as Vattimo and others suggest)—and
instead continuity based upon the examples of work
and play that Heidegger sees to reside in sculpture.[4] In
particular, Crowther insists that whilst some studies
insist that "space" is the dominant theme in Heidegger's
late work, his "main thematic in the essay is not the
problem of space itself but the way in which it is *overcome*
in the sculptural work".[5] What he means by this, I think,
is that sculpture is exemplary of spatiality, rather
than abstract space; and it is this ambiguity between
space/place in *topos* to which Heidegger is drawing
our attention. What is continuous, Crowther suggests,
are Heidegger's insights that "making room admits
something", and that "clearing away is the release of
places towards which the fate of dwelling turns".

Heidegger insists that we acknowledge that "once it
is granted that art is the bringing-into-the-work or truth,
and truth is the unconcealment of Being, then must
not genuine space, namely what uncovers its authentic
character, begin to hold sway in the work of graphic art?"
Crowther suggests that:

[Space] is that which can be linked to the
unconcealment of Being. This "genuine space"
is the primordial basis of *all* spaces, and hence
the artistic space of sculpture must involve some
distinctive articulation of it.[6]

1   Heidegger, Martin, "Art and Space",
Charles H Seibert trans, *The
Heidegger Reader*, Günter Figal ed,
Bloomington: Indiana University
Press, 2007 (Heidegger, Martin,
*"Die Kunst und der Raum", Aus der
Erfahrung des Denkens*, St Gallen: SG
Erker Verlag, 1969).

2   Solà-Morales, Ignasi de, "Weak
Architecture", *Architecture Theory
Since 1968*, ed KM Hayes ed, p 623.

3   Crowther, Paul, "Space, Place and
Sculpture: Working with Heidegger",
Continental Philosophy Review, vol 40,
no 2, June 2007, p 152.

4   Vattimo, Gianni, *The Adventure of
Difference: Philosophy after Nietzsche
and Heidegger*, Baltimore: Johns
Hopkins University Press, 1993;
and Richardson, William, *Martin
Heidegger: Through Phenomenology
to Thought*, New York: Fordham
University Press, 1993.

5   Crowther, "Space, Place and
Sculpture", p 152.

6   Crowther, "Space, Place and
Sculpture", p 156. Crowther reads
"Art and Space" in concert with
"Building Dwelling Thinking" as
he sees the articulation of genuine
space to be the fact that, "It lets
openness hold sway which, among
other things, grants the appearance
of things present to which human
dwelling sees itself consigned....
Place always opens a region in
which it gathers the things in their
belonging together." Crowther
understands the significance of this
to be a question of practical wisdom,
and ultimately one of dwelling. He
calls Heidegger's notion of "making
room" for example, "place in its
relational sense", and suggests that
whilst "modern technologically and
scientifically determined thought
sometimes reverses this order of
priority", in "Art and Space" and
in "Building Dwelling Thinking",
"Heidegger emphatically restores it."
Whilst it might appear that relational
place is "rather anthropocentric",
Crowther believes that "there are
considerations that mitigate against
such an interpretation... humans find
places through adapting to locations
already laid though the interaction
of processes. Human dwelling
can transform these; through
technological and environmental
abuse it can erase them, but they will
always remain a part of its character,
and may even retain something of
their individuality within this." He
illustrates this point by referring to
Heidegger's example of a bridge in
"Building Dwelling Thinking" "where
the edifice does not come simply
to some empty location, but rather
defines a location through being
constructed there". For Heidegger
therefore, "spaces receive their
being from locations and not from
abstract "space".

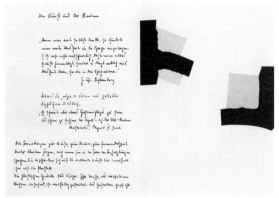

Above: Cover of Heidegger, Martin, *Die Kunst und Der Raum*, with Eduardo Chillida, photograph by Alberto Cobo.

Right: Pages from Heidegger, Martin, *Die Kunst und Der Raum*, with Eduardo Chillida's artwork, photograph by Alberto Cobo.

Below: Martin Heidegger and Eduardo Chillida examining a copy of *Die Kunst and Der Raum*, 1969.

Indeed, Heidegger does allude in "Art and Space" to the "something" which is revealed in art as that which allows "the release of places toward… the preserve of home", and Heidegger continues comparing this to the "brokenness of homelessness" or "complete indifference to the two". This cosmic dimension of space conditions all involvements—what is called in "The Origin of the Work of Art" the "strife of earth and world"—is participatory (like work), and is a mode of "involvement" and "interest" in "places as a region". The specific reason why Heidegger "turns" towards art and towards the problem of space, I suggest, is that what is revealed there is the embodied nature of territories. Heidegger is not only writing about some specific sculptures by Chillida in "Art and Space", but also declaring what he thinks sculptures in general should be like, and how they should be another mode of work revelatory of both Being and dwelling:

Sculpture would be the embodiment of places. Places, in preserving and opening a region, hold something free gathered around them which grants the tarrying of things under consideration and a dwelling for man in the midst of things.

Heidegger's phrase "in the midst of things" describes the situation in which we find ourselves called to work. The first thing to recognise when starting work, something which we also recognise in works of art, Heidegger suggests, is that "Emptiness is not nothing. It is also no deficiency." He continues, "In sculptural embodiment, emptiness plays in the manner of a seeking-projecting instituting of places." This suggests that art refers us to things outside of and defined by the object-like presence of a material thing—not to the "failure" of the space it occupies. Crowther calls this "relational place", insisting that it is not anthropocentric.

Heidegger cites an analogous situation described by Georg Christoph Lichtenberg in regards to language:

If one thinks much, one finds much wisdom inscribed in language. Indeed, it is not probable that one brings everything into it by ones self; rather, much wisdom actually lies therein, as in proverbs.[7]

This colloquial and idiomatic sense of language—what Heidegger calls "idle chatter" in *Being and Time*—is something like tradition, not in an academic sense, but as one aspect of global knowledge—of the world in which we are situated by language and things. Sculpture might appear to be an unusual means by which to discuss the character of Being as territorial, and abstract modern sculpture might seem an unusual way to discuss the way in which we are situated in the world by language.

What Heidegger seems to have been thinking about, I would like to suggest, is the ancient sense of "rhythm" as geometry, measure and as representation. In particular, he seems to have been thinking of Plato's *Philebus*, when Socrates refers to the ways in which thought is situated in the world. Socrates explains to Protarchus that "the letters of the alphabet" are "sound", "which passes through the lips whether of an individual or of all men is one and yet infinite". We are able to speak without realising that language is "infinite", and yet "grammarians" possess "knowledge of the number and nature of sound" and musicians possess the same knowledge understood as "harmonies". Both speech and music are comprised of "intervals and their limits or proportions", which, Socrates claimed, have "affections corresponding to them in the movements of the human body" that when measured "by numbers ought... to be called rhythms and measures".[8]

There is a further connection between thought and movement, which the Greeks understood as "rhythm". One clue to this lies in the etymology which "to draw" shares with "to pull" or to "draw out", and which relates "shape or pattern" to the character of a man, which has also been "formed".[9] These influences and forces that work upon the world shape thought and "the rhythm of a building or a statue", yet rhythm is not only movement, but also the positions that a dancer was made to assume "in the course of a dance":

Rhythm is that which imposes bonds on movement and confines the flux of things... the original conception that lies beneath the Greek discovery of rhythm in music and dancing is not *flow* but *pause*, the steady limitation of movement.[10]

Rhythm in dance was made up of steps that "were naturally repeated, thus marking the intervals in the dance". Whilst dance is movement, it is also "pattern and schemata". Dance set the rhythm of music in Greek theatre, and "this explains why the basic component of music and poetry was called a "foot" (Plato) or a "step" (Aristotle). Thus the dynamic art of dance related directly to a static art like sculpture, because it was

seen to represent "rests" or "points at which fleeting movements came to a temporary halt, thus enabling the viewer to fasten his vision on a particular position that characterized the movement as a whole."[11] In this way, ancient Greek musical theory and poetics generally, and the static arts of sculpture and architecture, were united by the notion of "rest" or "pause"; the beats between notes and movements, dividing the whole into rhythmic sections. In other words, "time-out-of-time", just as festivals and rites punctuate the year.

As we have seen, Vitruvius distinguishes *symmetria* and *eurhythmia*". The latter requires adjustments to proportions: "optical illusion and distortion must be taken into account by an architect" who must use his "*ingenium*" in order to "achieve proper affect." And Vitruvius continues to give the example of the need to adjust the proportions of a door to suit the "décor" of a temple so that the "appearance of *eurhythmia*" results, thus linking questions of appropriateness and *decorum* to the rhythmic relationships established between situations which are mediated by spatial thresholds—spaces in-between.[12]

It is clear that in antique culture measure was established by rhythm, and that this is a special form of silence or pause, something that relates things together in a way that their interdependence comes to visibility and makes them whole. It is also clear that all of the senses were combined in appreciation of rhythm, and that rhythm can change from a musical beat to a poetic metre, to the lines of a statue, to the gesture of a doorway placed into a wall. This is a form of measured relations that describes things not as single forms, but as parts of a greater whole, fitted to and revealing of an unseen but imagined and sensed order, like pauses in a musical piece, or movements in a game. Geometry describes relationships that move from analogues to proportions, from ratio to harmony, and it reveals the nature of continuity-in-difference that establishes communication between things; and so geometric order is a way to demonstrate similarities and differences. This was the means by which, for Plato, one's soul might participate in World-Soul.

What comes to life in music and in poetry, and in sculpture and in architecture, is the relational character of things, their dependence upon and proportional relation to each other. Like moves in a game, the relation between pause and step is both spontaneous and part of an overall order, and we are able to go from dance step to declamation, from line to plane, and from part to whole.[13]

What is revealed in the silence of a sculpture is a world of rhythm that is otherwise invisible to us. Rhythm structures traditional sculptural settings, enabling the eye to move from different scenes and between parts and the whole. We saw in Dalibor Vesely's example of the rose window in the west facade at Chartres Cathedral how the background of the church acted as a setting for sculpture and coloured light, all of which was animated by the movement of the sun—bringing the death of each day into poetic resonance with the Christian concept of the Resurrection. At the Bishop's Residence at Würzburg

7   Heidegger, "Art and Space", 1969.

8   Plato, *Philebus,* 17a—17b: "But when you have learned what sounds are high and what low, and the number and nature of the intervals and their limits or proportions, and the systems compounded out of them, which our fathers discovered, and have handed down to us who are their descendants under the name of harmonies; and the affections corresponding to them in the movements of the human body, which when measured by numbers ought, as they say, to be called rhythms and measures; and they tell us that the same principle should be applied to every one and many;—when, I say, you have learned all this, then, my dear friend, you are perfect; and you may be said to understand any other subject, when you have a similar grasp of it. But the infinity of kinds and the infinity of individuals which there is in each of them, when not classified, creates in every one of us a state of infinite ignorance; and he who never looks for number in anything, will not himself be looked for in the number of famous men".

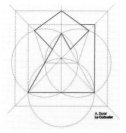

Le Corbusier, geometric construction after Albrecht Dürer, *Le poème de l'angle droit* and the *Section d'Or* in which he discovered the Bull.

Tilman Riemenschneider, *The Holy Blood Altarpiece* at St Jakob in Rothenburg ob der Tauber with detail of the Last Supper (bottom left).

9   Pollitt, JJ, *The Ancient View of Greek Art*, New Haven: Yale University Press, 1974, p 138.

10 Jaeger, Werner, *Paideia*, Gilbert Highet trans, 3 vols, 1939–1944, p 126, cited in Pollitt, *The Ancient View of Greek Art*.

11 Pollitt, *The Ancient View of Greek Art*, p 139; Pollitt is citing Plato, *Republic*, 400A ("foot"); and Aristotle, *Metaphysics*, 1087b37 ("step").

12 Vitruvius, *Ten Books on Architecture*, 6.2.5, cited by Pollitt, *The Ancient View of Greek Art*, pp 147–148.

13 See Ghyka, Matila C, *Esthetique des proportions dans la nature et dans les arts*, Paris: Gallimard, 1938; and Ghyka, Matila C, *Le Nombre d'Or— Rites et Rythmes Pythagoriciens dans le Développement de la Civilisation Occidentale*, Paris: Gallimard, 1959. Joseph Rykwert reports having seen two copies of the latter in the Le Corbusier archive; one had un-cut pages, the other was heavily annotated (telephone conversation 5 April 2014). These studies border on the occult and mystic numerology, which Corbusier's own interests also veered towards.

14 Summerson, John, "Heavenly Mansions: An Interpretation of Gothic", *Heavenly Mansions and Other Essays on Architecture*, New York: WW Norton, 1963, pp 1–28.

the ambiguity between actual and painted spaces is unified by "communicative movement". In both cases, individual spaces are unified through the synaesthetic qualities of artworks and architecture. These combine to situate particular places in relationship to other implied territories. In this way, ontological movement—or "communicative movement"—reveals a latent order of reality made up of perception, anticipation, imagination and memory, and this synaesthetic aspect of spatiality is key to orientation generally.

Whilst the Holy Blood Altarpiece by Tilman Riemenschneider at St Jakob in Rothenburg ob der Tauber, Germany, is a very different affair from modern artworks such as Chillida's metalwork posted in the rocks at the San Sebastián shoreline, in both cases rhythmic spatiality is the key to the phenomenon of space-place revealed by sculpture.

It is very clear how this is built up in the Holy Blood Altar (from folds in cloth and skin to the curlicues of hair and beards and trees and clouds; the rhythm of gestures/postures of the protagonists at the Last Supper for example leads the eye outwards towards the aedicule that frames the setting; and again the repetition of this type (a flattening of the curved arches made by trees, and the arched space implied above the figures seated at the table by their gestures) enables the series of microcosmic scenes to become part of the architecture setting also.

The rhythmic repetition of the aediculae situates the sculpture within and as part of a building, ultimately Heavenly Jerusalem.[14] Its placement at the back of

the altar and role in the rites is established by the repetition of the rhythm of use—the temporal rhythm of the space. From this temporal stability the viewer of the iconographic content is able to oscillate between sites, from Jerusalem to the Mount of Olives to a dining room in a house situated in a forest beneath the Christian universe. The altar was built to situate worshipful attention and prayer upon the blood of Christ, which is believed to be housed there, making the church the focus of pilgrimage, and so the sculpture makes explicit the theatrical re-enactment of the Eucharist and the analogical structure of supper-wine, and sacrifice-blood. The aedicule situates the Eucharistic Rite in continuity with the Last Supper and the church as part of the universal "Church". It is a "model" of re-enactment, time-out-of-time, symbolic.

At the same time the sculpture is one of many aedicular moments in the church, which is itself a threshold on the route to St James Church in Santiago de Compostela, Spain (Jakob/James/Iago). Interaction and participation with the sculpture, both imaginatively (in contemplative prayer) and in ritual, complete the rhythmic motion set into play by the sculptor. The topics contained within the sculpture describe mental and actual topographies that are united by the rhythmic articulation of the lines and pauses orchestrated by the artist, but which makes sense fully only in use. The rhythm is counterpoised between human events, mythical events and the natural world beyond the church, and geographic (actual) and imaginary (real or otherwise) realms are united.

Museo Chillida-Leku and *The Wind Comb* by Eduardo Chillida at San Sebastián

Chillida poses rhythmic spatiality as a question: the metal lines are opposite in form to—and mediate between—both rocks and sea, but otherwise are both assertive and vulnerable, leaving us suspended between shoreline and the instinct/insight of the sculptor. In this case however the crash of the waves against the sea wall describe the space between the metal tines, and along with the wind they make the sculptured spatiality sing, like a tuning fork. In both cases, temporal rhythm, and in particular the rhythm of the seasons (Christmas and Easter at St Jakob—summer and winter storms at San Sebastián) situate the sculptures in particular locations. The sculptures make the places specific in both instances, opening this specificity to orientation and to universality, and ultimately to Being.

As well as the huge metal tuning forks, Chillida and the architect Luis Peña Ganchegui burrowed under the sea wall creating points at which the seawater bursts out of the boardwalk like liquid fire works. The energy and violence of the sea is trained and tempered and revealed as sculptural spatiality. The structure of this rhythmic order incorporates:

A   The Beach—Sea/Shore
B   Tides and Seasons—Storm/Calm
C   Marking the Place
     i   locations
          (a play with horizons, shore, peninsula,
          island, stones etc)
     ii   burrowing and terracing
     iii metal figures
     iv wind chimes

Chillida's sculptures "spatialise" the place, by which I mean, they make explicit the spatial relationships the town has with the sea. The space itself is the subject of the sculptures, just as it is in the drawings in "Art and Space".

In particular, in both the lithographs by Chillida and in his sculptures at the town, space is not nothingness or a lack, and the island in the bay does not appear as an isolated object, but part of a network of rhythmic relationships. In the case of San Sebastián the space

between things is aqueous—almost solid—and this is transformed in the artworks into air and light and sound. This theme of spatial inversion, whereby space becomes visible as light, is continued in Rafael Moneo's Kursaal.

In fact, Chillida describes spatiality as volumetric:

> A dialectic exists between the empty and full space and it is almost impossible for this dialogue to exist if the positive and material space is not filled, because I have the feeling that the relation between the full and empty space is produced by the communication between these two spaces. You can't simulate volume.[15]

Volume is given strong spatial orientation in his work either by the relationships that are established with existing conditions, or through the intense directionality of topography. Chillida's sculptures are in some cases more like rooms or gardens, in which one discovers a sculptural object.

I would like to suggest that the drawings and prints that Chillida made for "Art and Space" are attempts to describe the volumetric "dialect" of his sculptures. Territories are described and rooms appear within the thickness of walls. Traditional figure-ground relationships are distorted and one cannot speak of object or void.

What is apparent is the equal weight given to the space of the page that has not been inscribed: this equivalence is echoed on Chillida's sculptures, perhaps most notably in the *Crucifix* in the church of Santa Maria at San Sebastián. Chillida's sculptures are attempts to answer a question that he phrased in poetic terms in a series of meditative dialogues published posthumously in Spanish in 2005 by Museo Chillida-Leku:

> Rhythm—time—silence
> Is matter not also space, a slower space?[16]

Chillida's "museum" is in fact a sculpture park in a village called Leku (meaning "place" and "space" in Basque) 10 km west of San Sebastián. It consists of a garden; a small new building housing his archive (by Ganchegui, a close friend and collaborator, also the designer of the landscape surrounding the *The Wind Comb*); and a renovated Medieval barn, which has the

15 Wagner, Sandra, "An Interview with Eduardo Chillida", *Sculpture Magazine* (online), nd.

16 Chillida, Eduardo, *Escritos*, Gavin Henneberry and Patrick Lynch trans, Gipuzkoa, Spain: Museo Chillida-Leku, 2005, p 28. See also, Chillida, Eduardo, *Eduardo Chillida: Writings*, Dusseldorf: Richter Verlag, 2009.

Left: The Basque Liberties Plaza, Vitoria-Gasteiz by Eduardo Chillida, 1980.

Right: Monumento a los Fueros in The Basque Liberties Plaza, Vitoria-Gasteiz by Eduardo Chillida, 1980.

Patrick Lynch, plan of San Sebastián
showing the locations of The Wind Comb
(on the left of the image, to the west of La
Concha Bay) and the Kursaal (at the head
of the River Urmea, to the east).

Eduardo Chillida, *The Wind Comb*,
San Sebastián, 1977.

The Museo Chillida-Leku.

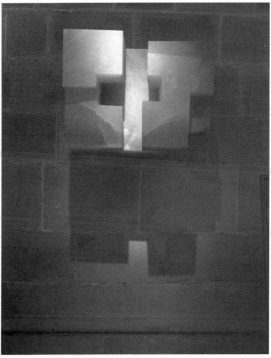

Left: The Barn at Museo Chillida-Leku by
Eduardo Chillida.

Right: Eduardo Chillida, *Crucifix*, Santa
Maria, San Sebastián, 1975.

Opposite top left: Eduardo Chillida,
Eulogy to the Horizon, Gigon, 1990.

Opposite top right: Photograph from the
southern edge of *The Wind Comb* site
showing the relationships between the
breakwater in the bay, Isla Santa Clara,
and the town.

17 Luis Chillida, in conversation with the author, 8 April 2014, at Leku. He noted also that his father was visited by Frank Gehry when he was designing the Guggenheim at Bilbao, who asked for a Chillida sculpture to sit in front of the entrance: "the reason my father refused was because he didn't want his sculpture to compete with Gehry's".

18 See Chillida's many book projects included an edition of the poem "Parmenides", published in Paris, 1990. Gaston Bachelard wrote the catalogue essay for Chillida's first solo exhibition (Maeght Gallery, Paris, 1956) and Octavio Paz wrote the catalogue essay for Chillida's retrospective at the Guggenheim (New York, 1980); see also de Beistegui, Miguel, "The Work and the Idea", *Parrhesia*, no 11, 2011, pp 1–34 and de Beistegui, Miguel, *Aesthetics After Metaphysics: From Mimesis to Metaphor*, London: Routledge, 2012. Beistegui sees sculpture for Heidegger as the "presentation of truth that takes the form of a strife between world and earth... the original strife between clearing and concealment." Heidegger saw the "danger" of "wanting to reduce earth to world", and sees in sculptures a hyper-sensibility that transcends "the *mondialisation* of earth". Heidegger's influence is clear also in the work of Richard Deacon, I suggest: "Deacon draws an analogy between the work in the world and language in society... by emphasising the fabricated aspect of his sculptures, points to their own syntactical quality and their kinship with language... an affinity can be seen between the artist's and the philosopher's shared understanding of the role of language. 'All reflective thinking is poetic, and all poetry in turn is a kind of thinking'. Deacon is concerned with how language exceeds itself, and how it cannot be reduced to the status of a tool when used for poetic or reflective thought." Lynch, Patrick, "Language and the Poetic", *RD: Richard Deacon*, Penelope Curtis and Clarrie Wallis eds, London: Tate Publishing, 2014, pp 27–28.

19 Luis Chillida, in conversation with the author: "at his death, when all else had deserted him, my father spoke on the words of St Juan de la Cruz", Chillida, *Escritos*. Luis confirmed the profound influence of Michelangelo upon his father's thinking.

20 Chillida designed a monument for the poet Jorge Guillén.

21 Bull, George ed, *Michelangelo, Life, Letters and Poetry*, Peter Porter trans, Oxford: Oxford University Press, 1987, pp 142 and 153.

22 Exhibition text in the barn, Eduardo Chillida, Museo Chillida-Leku.

23 Wagner, "An interview with Eduardo Chillida".

status of an artwork (since it failed to comply with any building regulations).

Chillida sat many of his sculptures into the grounds in order that they patinate before being moved to their intended locations elsewhere. In some cases, sculptures made for commission were, in fact, never installed and so the "museum" consists of pieces that he either couldn't bear to part with, or which the original patron did not want.[17] These are arranged in the park as a sequence of rhythmic spatial and material encounters with sculptures that are complementary both to each other, the site, and architecture.

Many of Chillida's sculptures were made in series, and their titles reveal that not only was his work site-specific, but also that his sculptures were inspired by recurring and particular preoccupations. Sometimes the work is made in response to a certain material, and *The Depth of Air XVII*, for example, is one of a series of works that investigate the spatial possibilities within a number of blocks of red Indian granite that Chillida discovered in the scrapheap of one of his local stone merchants. The stone works can be seen in the tradition stemming from Michelangelo's poetic search for the spatial and figurative possibilities of a material, as his son, Luis Chillida, suggests. Chillida was particularly attracted to the work of poets, philosophers,[18] Christian mystics,[19] and poet-artists.[20]

His stone work, I suggest, was influenced by Michelangelo's invocation of the inherent presence of space of life in matter: "No block of marble but it does not hide/the concept living in the artist's mind—/pursuing it inside that form, he'll guide/his hand to shape what reason has defined" (Sonnet 151).

In contrast, Chillida's metal works are primarily but not solely geometric studies, recalling Michelangelo's contention that, "Only fire forges iron/to match the beauty shaped within the mind" (Sonnet 62).[21] In *Homage to Luca Pacioli* the importance of Chillida's study of geometry in the architecture school at Madrid (ETSAM) in the 1940s is evident.

The text that he wrote accompanying the artworks displayed in the barn at Leku makes it explicit that the work should be seen in terms of groups of works relating to various possibilities found in each material; wood, stone, metal, concrete, ceramic, felt, paper etc.

In particular, the importance of alabaster to Chillida is made explicit as "a direct source of inspiration from architecture" that in the creation of "a space... establishes a direct link to the universe".[22]

A general equivalence between solid and void is also particularly evident in *The Wind Comb* and in *Eulogy to the Horizon*.

Chillida's motivations for making a work that explicitly deals with the horizon is acknowledgement not only of his relationship with Heidegger, he explains, but also because of the public nature of sculpture itself:

> Public works are open to the horizon and are in a public scale, the scale of man. Horizon is very important to me, it always has been. All men are equal and at the horizon we are all brothers, the horizon is a common homeland.[23]

Whilst this statement could be said to oscillate between political naivety and New Age generalities, Chillida's sculpture hints at something essential, the shared nature of a common horizon. The oscillation between matter, volume, distance and involvement introduces also a stylised mode of "deserved spatiality". It is the rhythm within the pieces, and the rhythm of the participant's involvement with them that is called into play, which enables a mode of what Heidegger called "deserved spatiality".

The special importance of *The Wind Comb* in Chillida's oeuvre is clear from only a cursory glance at the tourist stalls in San Sebastián—it is a symbol of the city and can be found on t-shirts and key rings, fridge magnets etc.

The Wind Comb sits at the extreme western edge of the bay of La Concha, beyond the breakwater that connects this to the island of Santa Clara over which the Atlantic waves dissolve. This protected "shell" cove was the first modern tourist resort in Spain, its safe and beautiful bay becoming fashionable in the mid-nineteenth century as a bathing resort. This led to the creation of a boardwalk in the 1860s, illuminated originally by gas lamps, that houses fresh water and changing facilities and staircases, and which supports cafes and bars. The main boulevard that was built beside this accommodates not only cycle paths and

Eduardo Chillida, *The Depth of Air XVII*,
Museo Chillida-Leku, 1997.

Eduardo Chillida, *Homage to Alabaster*,
Museo Chillida-Leku, 1965.

Eduardo Chillida, *Homage to Luca Pacioli*,
Museo Chillida-Leku, 1977.

The Wind Comb viewed from the top of
the stone landscape set up to capture its
relationship to the horizon.

24 See Chillida, *Eduardo Chillida:
Writings*, p 70: "There is a series of
laws in my works—I am referring
to my entire body of work—that are
fundamental and that are at the
root of the freedom with which I
work. They are before and ahead of
forms. The dialogue between forms,
whichever they may be, is much more
important than the forms themselves."

25 Chillida, *Eduardo Chillida: Writings*,
pp 50–53.

a promenade, but also is home to dozens of hotels,
including Hotel Niza, which was founded by Chillida's
grandmother's family and is still owned by them.

The Wind Comb completes this nineteenth-century
project, creating a space to encounter the natural
world just beyond the safe edge of the bay. Chillida's
sculpture can be seen as the evolution of the
hollow boardwalk from civic facility into a highly
mediated encounter with nature—one which is also
an encounter with one's self, and yet also public, a
thrilling, pleasurable entertainment.

It is saved from the solipsism of Romanticism,
I suggest, because it is deliberately scaled as a public
space and this has enabled it to become appropriated
by wedding parties, by school parties, by courting couples,
gangs and individuals.

Its popular and artistic success derives, I suggest,
from the fact that it is a collaboration between the
architect Ganchegui and Chillida. The potency of this
reveals the rhythmic and communicative potential
of site, architecture and sculpture. It is in no way
populist or patronising, and is in fact quite dangerous
and austere. I believe that the artist and architect were
intensely conscious of the spatial resonance that the
landscape and sculptures would have with the island,
the geometry of La Concha Bay, and the materials and
colours of the site.

Its rocks leach iron ore onto the granite landscape,
which *The Wind Comb* only seems to exaggerate and
to intensify. The wind is almost overpoweringly loud,
and quite painful, yet one is aware of being carefully
situated in close proximity to the ocean, the island, the
bay and the hotels, and the stone steps accommodate
and invite seated bodies quite comfortably.

I suggest that *The Wind Comb* is a form of speculation
in space of the relationships between the natural world,
human and geological time, and the inter-relatedness or
"dialogue" between the visible and invisible aspects or
reality.[24] Chillida asks us to consider that:

There must be a relationship between the rhythms
of—for example—the bark of a fir tree and the
directions in space in which its branches sprout.
Between the infinitely similar and varied forms
made by a breaking wave and the forms, in this
case spatial, made by erosion. On the rocks of the
coastline the relationship of form is clear, but the
laws that in such distinct processes come to produce
such similar results are worthy of being searched
for and consulted.... It is very simple: absolutely
everything can be reduced to learning and asking....
On the edge of shrillness, silence. To cross space
silently. To find mute vibration.... Beyond and
behind knowledge there is a language....[25]

Patrick Lynch, sketch of La Concha Bay
at San Sebastián with *The Wind Comb* on
the left and the town hall and old town on
the right connected by the boardwalk and
the boulevard.

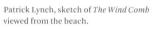

Patrick Lynch, sketch of *The Wind Comb*
viewed from the beach.

Patrick Lynch, sketch of *The Wind Comb* viewed from the southern edge of the stone landscape.

Patrick Lynch, sketch of *The Wind Comb* looking out to sea.

Patrick Lynch, sketch of *The Wind Comb* viewed from the northern edge of the stone landscape.

Patrick Lynch, sketch of *The Wind Comb* showing the relationships between the plateau of the stone landscape and Isla Santa Clara.

Patrick Lynch, sketch *The Wind Comb*
showing the plateau of the stone landscape.

Patrick Lynch, sketch of *The Wind Comb*
site showing the relationships between
the plateau of the stone landscape, Isla
Santa Clara and the town.

Patrick Lynch, sketch of *The Wind Comb*
and the Kursaal shown in the context of
the ocean and the town of San Sebastián.

The Kursaal by Rafael Moneo at San Sebastián

The volumetric and rhythmic characteristics that Chillida refers to in his descriptions of his sculptures seem to have been noticed also by the architect Rafael Moneo.[26] Moneo confirmed to me in April 2014 that "the Kursaal is a project concerned with geography" and identified "two types of space in Chillida's sculptures: space defined by lines, usually lines of metal; and carved space, especially space carved from alabaster that is matter and also light. The Kursaal is informed in part by the latter."[27]

The Kursaal sits between the edge of the ocean and the town of San Sebastián—between natural time and the life of the town, in-between the rhythm of music festivals and popular culture, and the institutional and regional character that typifies public life generally.

Two translucent glass boxes house timber-lined auditoria, sat upon a plinth made up of an aggregate of stones arranged to form a highly synthesised version of a rusticated battered base, or sea wall. The intensely mixed quality of this ground is exposed towards the water and appears as a compressed and artificial mounding up of stones and driftwood—a sort of waterborne archaeology of densely compacted groins

that at night are playfully revealed to be part of a group of translucent layers.

In contrast to the very porous threshold to the city, and the seemingly solid sea wall to the north, the concert halls within are slickly polished hulls marked by thousands of thin oak boards. The scale of the timber is echoed in the thin glass panels that form the facades. Concave and stippled glass planks create another layer of rhythm of light and shadow, distort the watery light into a semi-solid background state akin to mist or spray, enabling salt particles to collect and frost the surface of the building. The aqueous nature of the rhythmic glass and its contrast with the wooden hull of the concert halls exhibits a dialectics of remoteness and proximity. Moneo exaggerates this further through the device of platforms and landings, contrasting the intimate spaces of the concert halls to the distant sea, with the landings sat half-way between them—literally and figuratively in between them, making the contrast remarkable.

Within this intense background, the concert hall is revealed as a series of thresholds that echo with the rhythm of the crowds of concert goers flooding the interiors, and whose mass temporarily fills the voids between the strand and the city. It goes without saying

26 Rafael Moneo, in conversation with
    the author at the Biennale Finnissage
    dinner in Venice, 24 November 2012.

27 Rafael Moneo, in conversation with
    the author at his office in Madrid,
    28 April 2014.

Patrick Lynch, comparisons between
the topography of San Sebastián as two
"shells" of water and the Kursaal as two
"shells" of light.

Patrick Lynch, sketch of San Sebastián,
The Wind Comb and the Kursaal.

The Kursaal, San Sebastián by Rafael
Moneo, 1999, seen from the sea wall
and boardwalk.

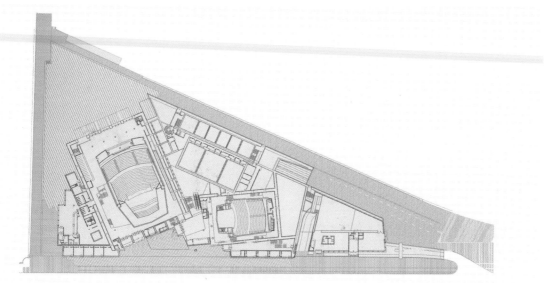

Ground floor plan of the Kursaal, San
Sebastián by Rafael Moneo, 1999.

that the music plays an important part in this dramatic rhythmic spatiality, and it is to Moneo's credit that the architecture enables one to participate in the drama of its situation—and, like the Chillida sculptures, it makes the place itself the main protagonist.

The spatial threshold between the town and the ocean, to which Chillida draws our attention in the natural rhythms of salt spray and wind and water, is deepened by the *decorum* of the Kursaal. Moneo could be said to have inserted a series of mediating territories into the deep threshold set up by Chillida's sculptures.

Moneo's building responds not only to the conditions of the natural world, but also to rhythms of concert-going, making the experience of visiting the building at dusk a dramatic and satisfying one. A transformational and tense equilibrium is established between everyday situations, seasonal time, and the festive time embodied by music. The commingled character of these is exaggerated, creating a witty mode of experiential *decorum*. One becomes aware of the extremely contingent character of a concert hall, at once part of the *oikos* of the town, the Basque region, national politics etc. What is also apparent is the strange character of modern musical performances that are powerfully immersive and distant from

everyday life. Yet this experience is immediately followed by a sort of shock, when one is plunged back into the world. The site-specific character of Chillida's sculptures is accompanied by Moneo's carefully calibrated spatial territories. In both cases, architecture and sculptures act as thresholds between the diverse psychic, organic and imaginative realms that situate music in the life of San Sebastián, as if orientation itself is at stake.[28]

I believe that just as Chillida completed a nineteenth-century project by making an edge and limit to the town and the natural world, Moneo's Kursaal owes a profound debt to the spatial communication established by the sculptures, urban design and infrastructure of San Sebastián. There are obvious and perhaps significant similarities between Chillida's sculptures and the Kursaal in terms of material and composition of course.

However, beyond formal or material similarities, there is also a deeper correspondence between the work of Chillida and Moneo at San Sebastián, and this lies in the communicative aspects of spatiality and site. Both projects sit on the edge of the city, and occupy and make inhabitable a liminal situation between pure rhythm and human situations.

28 Moneo has written about the "problems" of the concert halls in "Reflecting on Two Concert Halls: Gehry versus Venturi" (Walter Gropius lecture, Graduate School of Design, Harvard University, 25 April 1990) published in *Rafael Moneo: Imperative Anthology 1967–2004*, Madrid: El Croquis, 2005. In particular he notes the "very specific circumstances" of Gehry's concert hall: "Los Angeles is movement, change. Things do not endure there. Everything lives together. There is tolerance and looseness. Gehry's architecture does not care about context; being contextual in Los Angeles means to ignore context." Moneo has a different reading of the "pretentious" attitude Gehry takes towards his work, believing that: "Gehry is employing a subtle strategy to survive. Art—painting, sculpture, and even more, contemporary architecture has always been fragile. And yet we preserve art, and treat it with the utmost care because of its value. Gehry understands that the only way to guarantee architecture's durability today is to upgrade it to the status of "work of art" (p 627). This might be true of the situation of a concert hall in Los Angeles, but at San Sebastián Moneo does not need to play this trick, as the city is the work of art that completes the beauty of the natural setting. Chillida knew this too I suggest, and *The Wind Comb*, like the Kursaal, recognises and draws our attention to the stability and vulnerability of human situations.

The Kursaal, San Sebastián by Rafael
Moneo, 1999, view of the ocean and
town in the early evening 7 April 2014
during the interval of a performance.

Left: The Kursaal, San Sebastián by
Rafael Moneo, 1999, view of the grand
stairs connecting the auditoria to the foyer.

Right: The Kursaal, San Sebastián by
Rafael Moneo, 1999, view of the grand
stairs connecting the auditoria to the foyer.

Left: The Kursaal, San Sebastián by Rafael Moneo, 1999, view from the bridge.

Right: The Kursaal, San Sebastián by Rafael Moneo, 1999, view from the bridge at night.

Left: The Kursaal, San Sebastián by Rafael Moneo, the threshold to the town.

Right: The Kursaal, San Sebastián by Rafael Moneo, the threshold to the town at dusk.

29 See "Glass", *Wikipedia*: "Glass is an amorphous (non-crystalline) solid material that exhibits a glass transition, which is the reversible transition in amorphous materials (or in amorphous regions within semicrystalline materials) from a hard and relatively brittle state into a molten or rubber-like state."

30 Gadamer, Hans-Georg, *The Relevance of the Beautiful and Other Essays*, Cambridge: Cambridge University Press, 1986, p 40.

31 See also Carl, Peter, "Ornament and Time", *AA Files* 23, 1992, pp 49–64.

Opposite: The Kursaal, San Sebastián by Rafael Moneo, 1999, view from the beach at night.

Just as the spatial forms of La Concha bay are represented in microcosm by the arcs of the *The Wind Comb,* Moneo's Kursaal represents the topography of two "shells" of water as two shells of light. Physicists famously define the aqueous character of glass as "a very slowly moving liquid"—and Moneo's Kursaal recalls Chillida's question cited above ("Rhythm—time—silence/Is matter not also space, a slower space?").[29]

The Kursaal situates the playful activity of concert going at the threshold between the worlds of work and pleasure, at the edge of man-made shoreline and natural conditions. In his profoundly mimetic exaggeration and amplification of the geometry and morphology of the town he audaciously accommodates poetic sound—music—within a practically poetic structure—architecture. The difficulty of acoustically isolating and lighting two structures is achieved with a wonderfully inventive and witty device: the outer skin is a grand luminaire, in imitation of the crystalline lanterns that deepen and enchant the night and the boats at anchor there. Moneo and Chillida's imaginations seem to have synchronised in a profound manner, transforming the somewhat banal spectacle of promenading along the coast into a powerful encounter with the forces of nature and human ingenuity. Town and ocean, and work and play meet each other in a series of spatial and material settings that are primarily typified by rhythm. In this encounter a series of rhythms of association are revealed and can be enjoyed, which situate one in a pleasurable domain of wit and physical exuberance, silence and repetition, noise and stillness. An equilibrium is established at certain times of the day and year—the calm inversion of states that typifies art

experience—what Gadamer calls "festive still" ("time out of time").[30]

Chillida made a crucifix for the cathedral and for the church of Santa Maria. In the cathedral the cross projects out of a stone background, and a kilometre away this finds its echo and answer in the spatial recesses of Santa Maria. Inversion is clearly a theme at play in Chillida's sculptures at San Sebastián. Moneo seems to have intuitively understood and responded to this, and to the lamination of everyday and festival at play at the city edge; and his Kursaal is a profound example of the appropriateness of extreme architectural exertion made to appear ludic and graceful.

Rhythmic play characterises the world of the workroom and reveals it as a "*Spielraum*". Play is work transformed into contemplation; and when work becomes action, a mode of ontological movement is established that extends rhythm into understanding. In his study *Heidegger Among the Sculptors*, Andrew J Mitchell touches upon the ludic quality of sculpture, referring to the fact that Chillida almost became a professional footballer (he played in goal for San Sebastián), citing what he wrote about the similarities:

There are a lot of connections between football and sculpture. The conditions you need to be a good goalkeeper are exactly the same as the conditions you need to be a good sculptor. You must have a very good connection, in both professions, with time and space....[31]

Mitchell claims that the "sculpture shapes the space of collaboration" and that everything from Heidegger's

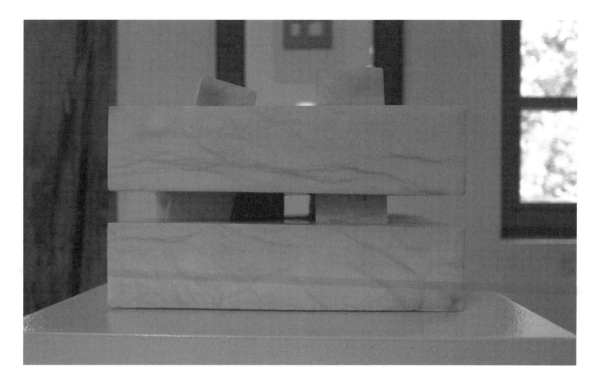

Eduardo Chillida, *Homage to Marble*,
Museo Chillida-Leku, 1969.

text "written in gothic characters from his bare hand", at Chillida's request, upon the Bavarian Solnhofen stone that Chillida engraved his lithographs, should be seen as a form of "teamwork".[32] This slightly crass metaphor is redeemed by the insight that art experience of space "is preparatory for dwelling, for if there is to be dwelling for humans at all, it must be amid and between the things and others of the world... we are able to dwell because we are already permeated by these places and things".[33] He concludes that "the truth of sculpture is the truth of being: mediation."

Heidegger declares in "Art and Space" that art should not be "a domination of space" or "a technical conquest of space", but the revelation of place. His famous example of a Greek temple in "The Origin of the Work of Art", which as well as "raising up" the hill on which it sits towards the sky (the gods) also "saves the stone" that it is made of so that it is not "passed over".[34] Instead of abstract space and objectified matter, what is revealed by the temple is "a place". Heidegger emphasises the "work" character of "the work of art" and also its status as a "thing". He calls art that has been taken out of its context examples of "world-withdrawal and world-decay", and laments the tendency of "art historical study (that) makes the works the objects of science".[35] In contrast, works of art are part of the "living world" and the places that are revealed by art reveal an ultimate reference in "the earth". The earth is revealed as that from which "man bases his dwelling", and Heidegger's famous and evocative passage on the temple—albeit discussed in isolation from its "world" and relation to any actual *polis*—evokes a proto-ecological sense of "earth":

The temple's firm towering makes visible the invisible space of air. The steadfastness of the work contrasts with the surge of the surf, and its own repose brings out the raging of the sea. Tree, grass, eagle and bull, snake and cricket first enter into their distinctive shapes and thus come to appear as what they are. The Greeks called this emerging and rising into itself *phusis*. It clears and illuminates, also, that on which and in which man bases his dwelling. We call this ground the earth. What this word says is not to be associated with the idea of a mass of matter deposited somewhere, or with a merely astronomical idea of a planet. Earth is that whence the arising brings back and shelters everything that arises without violation. In the things that arise, earth is present as the sheltering agent.[36]

Earth is the primary reference for Being, Heidegger insists (what Peter Carl calls "the common limit of human finitude"). The situational character of art enables it to provide orientation in relation to this. Art is primarily situational, Heidegger contends, and "situation always prevails", he insists: "we hear the door shut in the house and never hear acoustical sensations or even mere sounds.[37] In order to hear a bare sound we have to listen away from things, divert our ear from them, ie listen abstractly".[38] I suggest, therefore, that Heidegger's emphasis upon the "work" character of art (in "The Origin of the Work of Art"), should be seen in concert with his emphasis upon work-places in *Being and Time*: because what unites these two discussions is the "situational" character of everyday things and artworks. Both reveal that the directional and orientation character of spatiality lies in our situational involvement with *things in space*, ie at a particular place.

32 Mitchell, AJ, *Heidegger Among the Sculptors: Body, Space, and the Art of Dwelling*, Palo Alto: Stanford University Press, 2010, pp 83–84. A similar point is made by Vesely in his book, *Architecture in the Age of Divided Representation: The Question of Creativity in the Shadow of Production*, Cambridge, MA: MIT Press, 2004, pp 80–81: "the topography of the ground, the rules, previous experience constitute a preunderstanding of the game... each [layer] is able to translate the kinesthetic reality into its visual equivalents, and conversely, respond kinesthetically to a situation that can be assessed only visually. Even more surprising is the contrast between the constant changes in the game and the stability of the field to which each player refers at all times. This contrast reveals the role of our corporeal scheme, sometimes less appropriately referred to as a 'body image'." This insight is confirmed by the dance critic Edwin Denby who writes of the reciprocity of the urbane character of a town, and the rhythmic nature of human situations and movement: "In ancient Italian towns the narrow main street at dusk becomes a kind of theatre. The community strolls affably and looks itself over. The girls and the young men, from fifteen to twenty two, display their charm to one another with a lively sociability. The more grace they show, the better the community likes them. In Florence all in Naples, in the ancient city slums the young people are virtuoso performers, and they do a bit of promenading any time they are not busy.... Their stroll is as responsive as if it were a physical conversation.... Their liveliness makes these courteous formalities—which recall ballet—a mutual game of skill... ballet was originally an Italian dance... [with] the lively sociability of its spirit and of its forms." Cornfield, Robert ed, "Forms in Motion and in Thought", *Edwin Denby: Dance Writings and Poetry*, New Haven: Yale University Press, 1998, p 301. For a further discussion on the reciprocity between play and urbanity see *Man, Play and Games*, Roger Caillois, University of Illinois Press, 2001.

33 Mitchell, *Heidegger Among the Sculptors*, pp 86–87.

34 See Sallis, John, *Stone (Studies in Continental Thought)*, Bloomington: Indiana University Press, 1994.

35 Heidegger, Martin, "The Origin of the Work of Art", *Poetry, Language, Thought*, New York: Harper & Row, 1971, p 40.

36 Heidegger, "The Origin of the Work of Art", p 42.

37 Heidegger, "The Origin of the Work of Art", p 25.

38 Heidegger, "The Origin of the Work of Art", p 26.

39 Heidegger, "The Origin of the Work of Art", pp 26–27: "That which gives things their constancy and pith but is also at the same time the source of their particular mode of sensuous pressure—colored, resonant, hard, massive—is the matter of things. In this analysis of the thing as matter (*hule*), form (*morphe*) is already composited. What is constant in a thing, its consistency, lies in the fact that matter stands together with a form."

40 Heidegger, "The Origin of the Work of Art", p 19.

41 Heidegger, "The Origin of the Work of Art", p 23.

42 Heidegger, "The Origin of the Work of Art", p 29.

43 Heidegger, "The Origin of the Work of Art", p 25.

44 See Kant, Immanuel, *Critique of Pure Reason*, London: Penguin, 2007. By emphasising the heuristic aspects of art as "work" Heidegger recovers aesthetic judgment from Kantian pure sensibility, irrationality and solipsistic subjectivity. Gadamer extends Heidegger's work on art and space to include specific aspects of this, such as festivals, and he grounds Heidegger's claims that "man dwells poetically" in the urban situations that involve ornament and *decorum* with the playful aspects of civic life generally. Merleau-Ponty's critique of Kant is based on his observation that "Kant's conclusion was that I am a consciousness which embraces and constitutes the world, and this reflective action caused him to overlook the phenomenon of the body and that of the thing.", Merleau-Ponty, Maurice, *The Phenomenology of Perception*, Routledge, 2013, p 303.

45 Heidegger, "The Origin of the Work of Art", p 75.

46 Heidegger, "The Origin of the Work of Art", p 74.

47 Heidegger, "The Origin of the Work of Art", p 75.

48 Heidegger, "The Origin of the Work of Art", p 41.

49 Heidegger, "The Origin of the Work of Art", p 71: "Truth, as the clearing and concealing of what is, happens in being composed, as a poet composes a poem. All art, as the letting happen of the advent of truth of what is, is, as such, essentially poetry. The nature of art, on which both the artwork and the artists depend, is the setting-itself-into-work of truth. It is due to art's poetic nature that, in the midst of what is, art breaks open an open place, in whose openness everything is other than usual."

50 Heidegger, "Art and Space", p 8.

51 Mitchell, *Heidegger Among the Sculptors*, p 91.

Whilst Heidegger is happy to suggest that "the thing is formed matter" and that in a "synthesis of matter and form a thing-concept has finally been found which applies equally to things of nature and use objects"; he contends that "form and content are hackneyed expressions under which anything and everything may be subsumed".[39] Instead of these categories, Heidegger insists furthermore upon the directionality of things. Remarking that: "the interfusion of form and matter prevailing here is served by jug, ax, shoes. Such usefulness is never assigned or added on afterwards to a being of the type of a jug, ax, or pair of shoes. But neither is it something that floats somewhere above it as an end." Art is somewhat different to a pair of shoes of course, and Heidegger is careful to distinguish natural, equipmental and artistic things, whilst insisting nonetheless that:

> Works of art are familiar to everyone. Architectural and sculptural works can be installed in public places, in churches, and in dwellings.... If we consider the works in their untouched actuality and do not deceive ourselves, the result is that the works are naturally present as things. The picture hangs on the wall like a rifle or a hat.[40]

However much artworks are things, the "presence" that they embody is "the basic Greek experience of the Being of beings"; and this was revealed in the belief that "the core of the thing was lying at the ground of a thing, something always already there".[41] It is the basic reticence of things and their resistance to appropriation and consumption that typifies artworks also:

> A piece of equipment, a pair of shoes for instance, when finished, is also self-contained like the mere things, but it does not have the character of having taken shape by itself like the granite boulder. On the other hand, equipment displays an affinity with the artwork insofar as it is something produced by the human hand. However, by its self-sufficient presence the work of art is similar to the mere thing which has taken shape by itself and is self-contained. Nevertheless, we do not count such works among mere things. As a rule it is the use-objects around us that are the nearest and authentic things. Thus the piece of equipment is half thing, because characterized by thingliness, and yet it is something more: at the same time it is half artwork and yet something less, because lacking the self-sufficiency of the artwork. Equipment has a peculiar position intermediate between thing and work, assuming that such a calculated ordering of them is permissible.[42]

In emphasising the situational character of things, and of artwork's "thingliness", Heidegger attempts to overcome the clichés of "useless art" and of "form and content" in which "form is correlated with the rational and matter with the irrational".[43] Ultimately, he refutes

Kant's idea that art is irrational, proposing instead that "what we call feeling or mood, here and elsewhere, is more reasonable—that is, more intelligently perceptive—because more open to Being than all that reason which, having meanwhile become *ratio*, was misinterpreted as being rational. The hankering after the irrational, as abortive offspring of the unthought rational, therewith performed a curious service."[44] Heidegger declares that the "reason" that we find in art is a function of language itself, and that "the nature of art is poetry",[45] since "language is poetry in its essential sense".[46] Poetry is "the founding of truth" because "the poetic projection of truth that sets itself into work... [is] never carried out in the direction of an intermediate void." Poetry—as work—is projected towards "the opening up or disclosure of that into which human being as historical is already cast. This is the earth, and for an historical people, its earth, the self-closing ground on which it rests together with everything that already is, though hidden from itself."[47] Poetry is an aspect of "openness" and in fact "the Open" is an ontological state that "poetry lets happen". It recalls the openings or clearings that we find in the world, and also "time-out-of-time" or "festive" moments in which we encounter "the earth" as the "ground of Being".

This is why a sculpture is important for Heidegger—not as a thing, or even simply the abstract space between things—rather, its importance lies in the relationships that it opens between things, since "the work belongs, as work, uniquely within the realm that is opened up by itself. For the work-being of the work is present in, and only in, such opening up."[48] For Heidegger "opening up" enables "the unconcealedness of Being" (he refers also to the "unconcealment of Being" in "Art and Space"), and this, because it is "the setting into work of truth", he insists, "is not necessarily dependent on embodiment".[49] Heidegger continues and concludes "Art and Space" by citing Goethe:

> It is not always necessary that what is true embody itself; it is already enough if spiritually it hovers about and evokes harmony, if it floats through the air like the solemn and friendly sound of a bell.[50]

Mitchell declares that "space is the truth, the space through which, as Goethe says, what is true resounds, not as raw noise but like a bell, that is, as something rippling through a medium."[51] This seems to me to rely still upon a structured movement between embodiment and articulation, which the metaphor a "friendly sound of a bell" *overcomes*.

The Brunnenstern and *Hütte* at Todtnauberg

Heidegger would have been conscious also of the analogical character of geometry, not only because of Edmund Husserl's *The Origins of Geometry*, but also through his study of Plato and Aristotle. Geometry is traditionally understood as the logical description of relationships.[52] For this reason, Husserl was able to demonstrate Aristotle's proposition that geometric relationships are metaphoric, ie a verbal expression is a geometric construction implying a relation; A is to B as B is to C, for example, describes a continuous proportion as well as a syllogism.[53] It is this observation that enables Heidegger, in his poem "The Thinker as Poet", to make the claim for poetry as a form of philosophy, since it is an expression of *logos* and reveals the "topology of Being":

> When the cowbells tinkling from
> the slopes of the valley
> where the herds wander slowly...

> The poetic character of thinking is
> still veiled over.

> Where it shows itself, it is for a
> long time like the utopism of
> a half-poetic intellect.

> But poetry that thinks is in truth
> the topology of Being.

> This topology tells Being the
> whereabouts of its actual
> presence.[54]

Heidegger is referring to a tradition of thinking that is now almost entirely concealed beneath a flood of rationalist misinterpretations of presence and Being, and of the role that geometry plays in traditional dialectics. It is worth quoting at length from an essay by Peter Carl entitled "Geometry as Discourse", as he explains the differences between Aristotle's and Plato's understanding of geometry and rhetoric, and the status poetics holds for both in terms of revelation of truth:

> Plato's Divided Line and Aristotle's comparison between geometric proportion and the syllogism... have in common the desire to understand the mediation of difference through analogy, expressed in terms of geometry. This is rooted in *logos* itself, which is not only discourse but also account, accounting, counting. Thus Plato and Aristotle are both moving within agonic *logos* between concrete dialogue and dialectic, with the common aim of rescuing the weakness of the *logoi*, their capacity for error or untruth. If, however, both agree on the importance and nature of concrete dialogue, they differ on the nature of dialectic. For Plato, dialectic is the highest stratum of *noesis*, whereby, through *analogia,* the individual soul has the potential to participate (*methexis*) in the structure of the world-soul (*Republic, Timaeos*).

According to the ascending and descending movement, the individual is reconciled with the truth of the order; and the many of the *polis* is oriented to the ethical

coherence (the one) that is always-already-there, common-to-all, divine. Although Aristotle preserves the stratification (in the movement from the knowledge of *praxis* to *episteme* to *sophia* in the *Nicomachean Ethics*) and speaks of particular (individual, historical) and universal (the order of the whole, eternal) in the *Metaphysics*, in his texts which concern the nature of *logos* in the *polis*, he brings dialectic into the work of discourse. These texts comprise the *Topics*, concerning the common-places which are typical of *polis*-discourse (common agonic situations), the *Rhetoric*, which addresses the nature of the common framework of discourse for all political and celebratory affairs of the *polis* (the framework which claims all participants, like the *polis* itself), and what has become known as the *Organon,* the collection of texts on logic, of which the syllogism (A:B:B:C) is the basis for all logical expressions. Logical discourse or thought is distinguished from rhetorical discourse, and in this sense recalls Plato's sense of a separation of dialectic from everyday *logos*. However, particularly in the *Topics* (judged to be the earliest of this series of texts), one can see Aristotle working with the notion that dialectic might be more involved with clarifying statements in political and legal *praxis*. Similarly, whilst Plato decants mimetic discourse to the milieu of *doxa*—all the while building it into the presentation of his dialogues, which move from everyday jokes through carefully structured argument to myth—Aristotle separates mimetic discourse from the work of politics and logic in his *Poetics*. At the same time, he makes the central thesis of his treatment (of, mostly, tragic drama) the proposition that poetics is a *mimesis* of *praxis*; and the basis of this *mimesis* is what he terms *mythos* (usually translated as "plot"). Accordingly, one can see that Plato and Aristotle are responding to the life in *logos* in different ways, but that the life in *logos* itself harbours a commonality that claims all speakers. One always finds oneself in an agonic movement between particular and universal, between concrete many and symbolic one, between dialogue and dialectic. As the very nature of "finding oneself", being-there-being, this *agon* would be reframed by Heidegger as one between earth (conditions) and world (possibilities), which points to the universal nature of "situation" (all situations involve interpretation). His formulation captures the deeper similarity between Plato and Aristotle, and suggests why one always finds them in reciprocity in the subsequent history of philosophy. Put simply, Aristotle articulates how the amplitude of the practical life is embodied in the spectrum of discourses which one finds woven together in Plato's evocation of being in the *logos* of finite beings.[55]

Despite the absence of involvement with the geometric tradition in his writings (certainly by comparison to Gadamer), there is some evidence that Heidegger took a concrete interest in geometry, and that in acting as a geometer he saw himself fulfilling his aim to situate thinking in the world, even that he saw thinking as situated geometry. We are grateful to Adam Sharr for revealing to us the origins of Heidegger's *Hütte* (hut) at Todtnauberg in Bavaria, but until recently the

52 See "Origin of Geometry", Appendix to Husserl, Edmund, *The Crisis of European Sciences and Transcendental Phenomenology: An Introduction to Phenomenological Philosophy*, Evanston, IL: Northwestern University Press, 1970; Derrida, Jacques, *Edmund Husserl's "Origin of Geometry": An Introduction*, Lincoln, NE: Bison Books (1962), 1989; and Carl, Peter, "Geometry and Discourse", unpublished essay, 2010.

53 Aristotle, *Topics*, 159a1, 161a35.

54 Heidegger, Martin, "The Thinker as Poet", p 12.

55 Carl, "Geometry and Discourse".

Left: View of the Brunnenstern looking towards Heidegger's *Hütte* (the green shutters are closed in front of his study window).

Top right: Digne Meller Marcovicz, photograph of the Brunnenstern and Heidegger fetching water *Hütte*, 23 September 1966.

Bottom right: View of the *Hütte* poste with a crude reconstruction of the star carved as Z planes—the original Brunnenstern is now in the Martin-Heidegger-Museum at Schloss Messkirch.

56 Sharr, Adam, *Heidegger's Hut*, Cambridge, MA: MIT Press, 2007, p 42. The "well" is drawn but not annotated on the plan on p 25, nor included on the model photographs which appear on pages 27 and 28. The historical and intellectual context of the hut is discussed but not its actual physical context, and Sharr can be accused of committing a Heideggerian error; he concentrates on the hut as an object, missing the relationships set up between Heidegger's study and the landscape, the view of which is mediated by the analogical device of the Brunnenstern.

57 Heidegger, Martin, *The Question of Being*, Lanham: Rowman & Littlefield, 1958.

ornamental geometric figure that was constructed atop of the drinking fountain was not considered significant. Sharr simply notes that "a split hollowed log is fed with water from a spout in another, upright log connected to a natural spring. A star carved in relief from a timber cube sits on this upright", and the "well" is not included on the model that he makes of the *Hütte*.[56]

Ross Anderson delivered a paper at the Kyoto conference on phenomenology in 2011 entitled "Brunnenstern: The talismanic presence of the architecture and ornament of philosopher Martin Heidegger's *Hütte* at Todtnauberg, Germany, 1922", in which he proposed that:

In a photograph from 1968, Heidegger is captured walking back to the *Hütte* having filled a bucket with water from the *Brunnen*. The unusual cubic-stellar ornament atop the continually filling trough demands attention. It sits incongruously in the rustic setting otherwise thoroughly purged of excess, carefully attuned to a paradigmatic mountain existence. Given there is little ornament elsewhere in the *Hütte*, there is cause to suspect this assertive element was of personal significance to Heidegger.

In fact, Heidegger's son Hermann confirms that his father "used to sit here at the desk and look out at the water trough, which had a special significance for him".

Anderson admirably investigates the meaning of the symbolism in archaic Teutonic culture, and suggests that the *significance* that the fountain held for Martin Heidegger is partly historical symbolism, and also as a demonstration of his philosophical stance.

[It] prompts thought of Heidegger's *Totenbaum* (tree of the dead) in "Building Dwelling Thinking", known more generally as a *Baumsarg* (tree-coffin); a casket finished from a single oak tree trunk. When relating how the fourfold ordered the black forest, Heidegger writes that "it made room in its chamber for the hallowed places of childbed and the *Totenbaum* (tree of the dead)... and in this way it designed for the different generations under one roof, the character of their journey through time."

Totenbaum is a term local to Baden-Württemberg, for what in German is more generally known as a *Baumsarg* (tree-coffin), referring to a casket finished from a single tree-trunk split lengthways and hollowed out for a corpse. Heidegger would thus have been reminded of the essential characteristic of Dasein as "being towards death" as he wrote in his study each morning, facing the rising sun, and contemplating the well/fountain.

Sein itself was marked in *The Question of Being* as crossed through, indicating the limit of being, like a *memento mori*.[57] Anderson also suggests that

Left: Illustration of a stella octangula by
Leonardo da Vinci in Luca Pacioli's *De
Divina Proportione*, 1509.

Right: Sequence of images tracing the
process of fabricating the Brunnen
ornament out of a cube of timber, with
the stella octangula as a polyhedron of
two tetrahedra. Computer renderings,
model and photographs by Ross Anderson.

there is rhetorical significance in the form of the
Brunnenstern itself:

> Geometrically it can be classified either as a
> polyhedron compound of two tetrahedra, or as a
> stellation of an octahedron. The composition is of
> particular interest because both the tetrahedron
> and octahedron are Platonic solids, as articulated
> in Plato's *Timæus;* a cosmogony paired with the
> Republic, whose divided line presents an ontology
> of understanding demonstrating how the individual
> soul participates in the world soul. In the *Timæus*
> each solid was accorded the qualities of an "element"
> (earth, air, water and fire). Earth was associated
> with the cube, air with the octahedron, water with
> the icosahedron, and fire with the tetrahedron.
> Geometry, *analogia*, is implicated in the origins
> of the thinking-being that Heidegger derives from
> Parmenides, and there exists a highly provocative
> possibility that he might have sought to bring his
> own idiosyncratic fourfold of "earth, sky, divinities,
> mortals" into dialogue with the more classical
> "fourfold" of earth, air, water and fire.[58]

Anderson continues to propose a symbolic reading
of the sculpture, suggesting that "the significance of
the *Brunnen* to Heidegger may in part be as a heavily
sublimated self-effacing reminder to himself" of the
task of thinking as mediation, "the philosopher
between fool and interpreter of truth". He discusses
the analogical significance of the star as a form of
memory aid,[59] and demonstrates that whilst appearing
complex it is in fact "unexpectedly simple to carve".[60]
It is tempting to see in this its value to Heidegger as an
embodiment of de-severance—the prone coffin-tree
receives water from the erect tree-fountain with its
stellate "capital" positioned like a font along the path
to the hut and alternately part of the land at a distance
and ready-to-hand offering water. It demonstrates the
embodied character of knowledge, as ideas become
visible under what Michelangelo called the "thinking
hand of the sculptor".[61]

These allusions to the history of representation are
quite typical in the ornamentation of villas, which are in
essence thresholds between the natural world and the
life of contemplation, and the negotiations of political
life.[62] It maybe "incorrect" in formal architectural terms,
or in terms of style, to think of the *Hütte* as a villa, but
villas are not so much typological models as examples
of a particular mode of dwelling.[63] Heidegger's modest
building is adorned with a perceptible grandeur through
the position and constellation of the Brunnenstern, as is
the act of thinking—which is revealed in this arrangement
not only to be the act of moving water, of carrying it, its
weight, wetness etc, but also as orientation (it is to
the east of the house). What is clear is that a) it is not
plumbing (like his critique of the dam, nature as standing
reserve) and b) as a figure, as something like sculpture, it
is not taken for granted, simply used, but exerts a claim
upon reflection—which includes distance, eastward
orientation for thinking, dying-reviving, tree/human, tree/
geometry, body/head etc. That is, the thinker is situated
through activating the horizons of reference.

In other words, the situation is made up of a number
of activities of things at hand and ready at hand which
precede thought and which situate contemplation as an
act occurring specifically somewhere, overlooking the
valley, facing the morning sun. Just as the house is said
to have its sunny side, it has a view onto a region of life
in which the desk, the chair, the pen and the hillside
are all part of a workroom situated and oriented in part
by the fountain. It ornaments the natural conditions
otherwise implicit in the view from the study, bringing
to the surface a rhythm of sound and moving light.
Heidegger was emphatically in place there, the fountain
and the Brunnenstern situating and representing the
themes of life/death implied by the movement of the
water from "tree/body" to geometric "capital/head".

58 Peter Carl claims that "this is an
    error—it comes from Plato's *Gorgias*."

59 Anderson, Ross, "Brunnenstern:
    The talismanic presence of the
    architecture and ornament of
    philosopher Martin Heidegger's
    Hütte at Todtnauberg, Germany,
    1922", *From the Things Themselves:
    Architecture and Phenomenology*,
    Benoît Jacquet and Vincent Giraud
    eds, Kyoto: Kyoto University Press,
    p 6: "The second possible reference
    comes from Meno, which contains
    a demonstration of anamnesis; the
    notion that certain knowledge is
    innate and 'recollected' from the past
    lives of the immortal soul. Socrates
    induces one of Meno's slaves to
    'remember' how to find half the
    area of a square. He draws a square
    in the sand, and through a series
    of questions and accompanying
    drawings passes through a series
    of false conclusions based on partial
    logic in order to eventually arrive at
    the correct solution."

60 Anderson, "Brunnenstern", p 7.

61 Michelangelo, "Only Fire Forges
    Iron", *Michelangelo, Life, Letters
    and Poetry*, George Bull trans, pp
    142 and 153, cited in Lynch, Patrick,
    "Only Iron Forges Fire", *Drawing:
    The Process*, Leo Duff ed, Chicago:
    University of Chicago Press, 2005.

62 See Lynch, Patrick, "Sanctified
    Leisure: The Villa is not a Temple
    or a Barn: The Villa as Archetype
    and Paradigm", *The Lives of Spaces:
    The Irish Pavilion at the Venice
    Architecture Biennale*, Dublin, 2008;
    and Lynch, Patrick, "All imagination
    has to be re-imagined: the villa and
    the architectural imagination",
    Architectural Research Quarterly,
    vol 9, no 2, Cambridge: Cambridge
    University Press, 2005.

63 See Ackerman, James, *The Villa:
    Form & Ideology of Country Houses*,
    Princeton: Princeton University Press,
    1992, in which it is made clear that
    "the villa typology" is not pure (they
    can equally be courtyards or barns
    with temple fronts). Despite the title,
    Ackerman is more insightful on the
    activities of villa life than the terms
    "form" and "ideology" would suggest.

64 Anderson, "Brunnenstern", p 10: "We
can place an episode from Heidegger's
'Letter on Humanism' in the context of
the dignity of everyday ritual relating
to heating from a stove. He reports an
incident recorded by Aristotle, where
a group of curious strangers come to
visit Heraclitus and are perplexed by
their first glimpse of his abode. They
had expected to catch sight of him
at that very moment when, sunk in
profound meditation, he is thinking.
The visitors want this 'experience'
not in order to be overwhelmed by
thinking but simply so they can
say they saw and heard someone
everybody says is a thinker. Instead,
they find him warming himself at a
stove. "In this altogether everyday
place he betrays the entire poverty
of his life. The vision of a shivering
thinker offers little of interest.... The
visitors are on the verge of going away
again. Heraclitus reads the frustrated
curiosity on their faces.... He invites
them explicitly to come in with the
words.... 'Here too the gods come
to presence'." Heidegger seeks to
replicate this condition in general with
his *Hütte*, and possibly more explicitly
via one of the staged photos in a folio
by Digne Meller Marcovicz, in which
he sits idly by the stove".

65 Anderson, "Brunnenstern", p 10.

In other words, it imitates and represents his belief that thinking grows from the everyday world of nature and work, which is in this case typified by the play of water and the rhythmic qualities of the natural world present in the fountain as part of the background to the workroom.

The fountain also acts as a figurative middle ground between the hills beyond the hut, and the desk on which Heidegger's hand sat. Anderson suggests that the photographs that Heidegger staged with Meller Marcovicz allude to the stories about the lives of various philosophers; Heraclitus sat by a stove etc.[64] He also suggests that it fulfils the purpose of linking the practical and symbolic aspects of everyday life to Heidegger's notion of the fourfold:

The Brunnenstern is approximately aligned with the major wall halving the interior of the cabin in the east-west direction, and therefore is aligned approximately with the stove. This may symbolise a relationship between water and fire; the movement from the spring in nature to the ritualistic everyday human need to heat water for cooking, washing and so forth.[65]

I would like to suggest an equally presumptuous reading of the situation, but one grounded in Heidegger's experience of the Brunnenstern, and drawn from the evidence of staged photographs. In the photographs of Meller Marcovicz, Heidegger sets the scene for us— he looks as if he is having fun, he appears playful, he even smiles in one image. Anderson observes that the fountain is strongly figurative:

The vertical trunk looks like it would fit into the recess of the trough, further enhancing its anthropomorphic character. In this context it is to be observed that the photograph of Heidegger returning to the *Hütte*, having filled a bucket of water at the Brunnen displays the same motif

Patrick Lynch, drawing of the spatial
relationship between the workroom
and the well at Heidegger's *Hütte* at
Todtnauberg.

repeated twice: once as vertical and horizontal
tree and once as Heidegger and his bucket. It may or
may not be an accident. The fact that he is carrying
the bucket in his left hand whilst walking back
towards the *Hütte*, thus exactly duplicating the
configuration speaks for deliberateness. Therefore,
the Brunnenstern is also the "capital" of the column,
just as a person rests on earth and whose head
symbolises *nomos* (thought).[66]

Anderson suggests that Heidegger has staged a photograph
of himself beside a sculptural artefact that he surely
must have designed. It is in fact impossible to prove who
designed the Brunnenstern; perhaps in order to tell us
something? Anderson's insistence on "the vernacular"
character of the hut (he compares and contrasts it to Le
Corbusier's *Cabanon*) somewhat misses the grandeur
that the sculptural fountain adds to the hut. My assertion
that the hut is in fact a type of villa is based in part on the
importance of contemplative work in the writings of his
student and lover, Hannah Arendt,[67] who makes a case
for contemplation as something vital and committed to
reality.[68] In particular, she emphasises the contribution
contemplative thought makes to politics, which can be
rephrased as the contribution the *vita contemplativa*
makes to the *vita activa*; as the contribution the villa
makes to the city; the contribution play makes to work
and vice versa: it is a form of reconciliation of opposites,
of agonic sublimation, poetic commingling, analogical-
geometric thinking.

The hut is placed exactly at the point at which
the cultivated landscape gives way to forest, at the
threshold between the world of men and the mountains.
Heidegger's workroom is situated overlooking a valley,
on the edge of rising ground, above which the tree line
begins. It is not in the wilderness like a hunter's lodge
or cabin, but at the extreme edge of urbanity—just
as villas traditionally occupy and construe a threshold
between cities and the natural world.[69]

Villas typically house galleries from which to
contemplate this distinction, and these rooms
are traditionally decorated to reflect the themes of
transformation and of the commingling of mythic
themes and natural conditions, in which thought
and physical labour unite the various meanings of
cultivation. Heidegger's study exhibits exactly these
spatial characteristics, and his view of the natural world is
mediated not only by contemplative action (philosophy),
but by the Brunnenstern, which represents the unity
of visible and invisible worlds—the work of a geometer-
philosopher, as Heidegger saw it.

I do not wish to base an argument upon one image—
my observation is based on the series of images that
were made that day and upon what they enable us to
reconstruct in our minds, ie how they mediate reality
and communicate to us the relationships between the
hut, and the inhabitants, and the natural world in
which everything sits. From his work chair, Heidegger
could observe the fountain and the water constantly
falling and splashing into the trough—eternal, self-
replenishing potential. His study has two windows
facing east. These are the only windows on this face of
the building and they appear like eyes, looking directly
at the log and mast of the fountain. Meller Marcovicz's

66 Anderson, "Brunnenstern", p 10.

67 Safranski, Rüdiger, *Martin Heidegger:
    Between Good and Evil,* Cambridge,
    MA: Harvard University Press, 1998.

68 Arendt, Hannah, *The Human
    Condition*, Chicago: University of
    Chicago Press, 1958.

69 See Lynch, "All imagination has to
    be re-imagined".

70   Heidegger, addendum to "The Origin
     of the Work of Art", pp 82–83.

71   Heidegger, *Being and Time*, p 369:
     "With regard to that space which it has
     ecstatically taken in, the 'here' of its
     current factical situation (Lage bzw.
     Situation) never signifies a position
     in space, but signifies rather the
     leeway (*Spielraum*) of the range of that
     equipmental totality with which it is
     most closely concerned—a leeway
     which has been opened up for it in
     directionality and deserverance."

72   Heidegger, *Being and Time*, p 369.

73   Heidegger, Martin, "Building
     Dwelling Thinking", *Poetry, Language,
     Thought*, New York: Harper Perennial,
     1975. If we compare this to Peter
     Eisenman's statements about
     individualism versus "total order" in
     his PhD, it is clear that his "formal"
     reading begins with an erroneous
     understanding of the nature of
     creativity, and that his arguments
     rely upon an idealist juxtaposition
     of subjects (subjectivity) versus
     objects/forms (objectivity); hence
     his need for "total order" to counter
     "individualism", and for "form" rather
     than situation, since the latter is
     "relative". Dalibor Vesely has shown
     that "typical situations" mediate
     the unique and universal dichotomy
     that Eisenman is trapped within.
     See Vesely, *Architecture in the Age of
     Divided Representation*.

photographs of Heidegger in his workroom show him sat in his chair looking out, one of which is taken low down from the position of someone sat in a chair in conversation with him.

In this image, and in the other photographs made in the study, you notice that Heidegger has hung a small circular wreath onto the wall, to the left of his desk. It appears in the photographs to float above his head, almost a halo; a small sun. The wreath is probably a votive offering from the harvest festival, a reminder of the commingling of solar symbolism in Christian eschatology with the seasons of the year, with images of rebirth and sacrifice in Teutonic culture, and in the intellectual context that Heidegger occupied from Parmenides onwards. I would like to suggest that this contextual reading is an example of the task of the thinker that Heidegger set himself, and that only analogical thinking enables one to move between the universal and the particular. The universal aspect of this task is suggested to us by the resolution that the circle offers the quartered star, sat above the endless rhythm of the spring. Heidegger's star sits in the world of work, contemplated by the philosopher-geometer, and set in place by thought. The role of contemplation is important in the disclosure of Being of course, and poetry—like art in general—establishes the grounds for dwelling. In this instance, Heidegger's thought and action came together in a particular mode of rhythmic spatiality at his *Hütte*, situated between the earth, the forest, seasons, customs, traditions, habits, domestic life and rituals of life and death. Death and renewal are symbolised by the Brunnenstern, marking the ground as a bridge across a stream; and practical and poetic life (the well is a drinking fountain and a semi-sacred "font"-tree) combine together to set in motion the conditions of poetic dwelling.

Heidegger insists in "The Origin of the Work of Art" that whilst "art is the setting into place of truth" to "'fix in place' can never have the sense of rigid, motionless, and secure", because "boundary in the Greek sense does not block off.... Boundary sets free into the unconcealed... the work's being is '*energia*'".[70] This energy is always directed, "never carried out in the direction of an indeterminate void", just as a statue is directed at a "historical group of men", "letting a statue be set up... means laying down an oblation". Heidegger sees the directed nature of art to exhibit the characteristics of work, and he explicitly refutes both Kant and Hegel in the Addendum of "The Origin of the Work of Art", just as he set out to destroy Descartes' errors in the introduction to *Being and Time*.

Heidegger suggests that a workroom is a type of "*Spielraum*" in *Being and Time*,[71] presumably since skill entails a form of playful engagement with reality, and because "Being-busy which is 'absorbed in the thing one is handling'... in such bringing close, the essential structure of care—falling—makes itself known".[72] I suggest that this is why he then addresses what the modern world considers to be "mere play" in order to show that art is a form of work ("the setting into work

of truth"). Along the way he draws back the mystical veil thrown over art by the subjectivity of Kant from "the German Romantics onwards", and he also moves art out from under the shadow of "German Idealism", "rationalism" and "technological-scientific thinking". This is the obverse of what he achieves in *Being and Time*, whereby thought is saved from individualism and method. He does this in "Building Dwelling Thinking" by showing how dwelling is a mode of poetry, and that poetry is related to life; and he emphatically links dwelling to art and both to being:

> All creation, because it is such a drawing-up, is a drawing, as of water from a spring. Modern subjectivism, to be sure, immediately misinterprets creation, taking it as the self-sovereign subject's performance of genius.[73]

In contrast, creativity is a "leap" that "throws us into the world", away from subjectivism, overcoming distanced relationships in space, into the rhythms of life.

Heidegger's renewal of the task of "grounded" thinking as a mode of situated geometrics shows us also the mediating power of sculpture in revealing the "communicative movement" between the natural world and human habitat. In this case dwelling in a small summer house is revealed as a mode of serious play and ludic work—as poetic.

Chillida and Moneo responded to the geography and spatiality of the settings for their public works in a similarly mediated and synthetic manner—their projects reveal the full experiential potential of an encounter with culture at the edge of the man-made and natural worlds. The civic dimension of two small churches and community centres in suburban situations otherwise dominated by banal technology— a Lutheran church in Sweden and a Roman Catholic one in Portugal—is the theme of the next two chapters.

Rhythmic Spatiality and the Communicative Movement between Site, Architecture and Sculpture at St Peter's Klippan by Sigurd Lewerentz

Thus the concern about the doctrine of form became bound to a classically-aesthetic conception of form. This canon was a doctrine of empty dimensions into which one poured the stuff of the world—forming meant the minting of dumb material. This teaching based itself on sculptural form and at least it was able to provide classicist buildings. The architecture of antiquity is not false. Aside from the fact that it was once historical, it represents an eternal possibility in building, its symmetry and static quality, can be changed. Therefore a canon that is derived from it is not false and yet it is narrow. It is limited to the validity of this "sculptural form", and like it, this canon is a matter of feeling and taste.... A doctrine which insists on form without imparting the glimmering spark is empty and leaves its listeners cold.
—Rudolf Schwarz, 1923

We are now equipped with an understanding of the importance of the terms "urban topography", "rhythmic spatiality" and "communicative movement" to civic design, and we have seen how they are essential aspects of the urbane art of architecture in its continuity with sculpture and analogical modes of "nature". St Peter's at Klippan demonstrates the serious *decorum* of the play ethos that Hans-Georg Gadamer identifies as the primary characteristic of the artistic imagination. As we have seen, the communicative nature of artistic experience reveals itself in participation, and the potentially public character of play reveals also the orientation that ornament has towards urbanity. It is these aspects of the playful imagination of the architect and his client that make you feel so emphatically in place at Klippan after visiting its church—and suggests a way to recover the civic depth of situations otherwise bereft of any "communicative movement" between site, architecture and sculpture. To understand how this is achieved and the profound contribution that it makes to continuity of the civic ethos in modern architecture is the aim of this chapter.

Sigurd Lewerentz and his client, Lars Ridderstedt, identify and fulfil Gadamer's ambition—discussed previously—which is described in *Truth and Method* as the desire to "free" the concept of play "of the subjective meaning that it has in Kant and Schiller and that dominates the whole of modern aesthetics and philosophy"[2]—in freeing play from subjectivity, the full civic dimension of art and architecture is recovered. St Peter's is an example of the transformed role that ornament plays in modern architecture, in concert with the other arts, in the recreation of a communicative civic realm.

Sigurd Lewerentz's later church buildings, most obviously St Peter's at Klippan, are generally seen to lack traditional iconographic content and to represent pure materialism in architecture. However, Lewerentz continues the tradition of "communicative movement" that characterises the Gothic and Baroque buildings that we have discussed previously. St Peter's also

articulates rhythmic spatial relationships between site, architecture and sculpture, and in particular the hinterland of semi-rural agricultural industry, and semi-urban and suburban settlement are revealed as aspects of the civic depth of Klippan. In solving problems at an urban scale, and also at a bodily or equipmental scale, Lewerentz created an exemplary complex of civic buildings that are as useful to their occupants as they are to the town generally.

Sigurd Lewerentz, drawing of The Way of the Cross for Stockholm Cemetery competition, 1915.

The architecture of St Peter's offers a counter to the contemporary division that clients and critics of architecture usually make between useful but pointless buildings, and aesthetic but useless ones. Its combination of architectural and sculptural artefacts create a richly meaningful urban quarter, redeeming the road engineering of the New Town and situating its inhabitants in continuity with the natural world and the history of Swedish and European urban culture.

The purpose of studying this project in detail is to reveal an exemplary mode of *praxis*. I aim to reveal that St Peter's at Klippan is both a poetic landscape and part of a modern town—an attempt to turn a suburb into a recognisable place. St Peter's is a liturgical theatre that reconciles the town with its natural topography, and which situates Christian mythology into a modern landscape, ie in space. The theatre of the Swedish Lutheran *Mässe* reveals the dramatic presence of events situated in the Holy Land, fusing the ontology of Klippan within the motif of a catholic or universal church (from Greek *katholikos* "universal").[2] In doing so, the ancient notion of a *topic* is recovered in both the history and practice of modern architecture, and with this the full depth of the poetic task of articulation is revealed again. *Topos* inspires in the imagination communication and participation—making and

1   Gadamer, *Truth and Method*, p 101.

2   For a definition of "catholic" as "whole" ("the most important definitions of the word in the early Church stress that calling the Church "catholic" is a matter of grasping that it teaches the whole truth in a way that involves the whole person and is addressed to the whole of humanity"); see the Foreword by Rowan Williams to *The Heart in Pilgrimage: A Prayerbook for Catholic Christians*, Eamon Duffy ed, London: Bloomsbury, p vii. By this definition "catholic" means any Christian who rejects the Calvinistic doctrine of predestination.

3   Mattsson, Helena and Sven-Olov
     Wallenstein eds, *Swedish Modernism:
     Architecture, Consumption and
     the Welfare State*, London: Black
     Dog Publishing, 2010. The
     following citations are from their
     "Introduction", pp 8–33.

recognising places as distinct. This is a practical task oriented towards wisdom. It is practical and interpretative, bodily and macrocosmic, at once useful (*usus*) and representational (*actio*). Less obviously hermeneutic in character, but nonetheless articulate of phenomenal and territorial relationships is the Kursaal at San Sebastián by Rafael Moneo. In both examples, the fundamental relationships between architecture, nature and urbanity—that we saw embodied in both Medieval and Renaissance situations—has remained more or less articulate in spatial terms. Whilst the obviously semiotic content of the architecture is different of course, they remain capable of communicating iconographic and symbolic spatial content. This achievement, I suggest, is derived from and through the revelation of the spatial and temporal dimension of buildings' relationships with sculptures, landscape and social structures. This expanded field might be a way of discussing and defining architecture in both traditional and contemporary contexts, as rhythmic spatiality; and the relationships between site, architecture and sculpture reveal the role that "communicative movement" plays in spatiality and in urban culture generally. These projects embody and articulate continuity in architecture, and demonstrate the possibility of its contribution to civic *decorum* today.

For over 45 years the Swedish Social Democratic Party formed a uniquely stable participatory democratic parliamentary government (1932–1976), enabling the formation of a modern welfare state and establishing a prosperous, well-educated and increasingly urbane nation.[3] In this period, the SDP ruled in concert with "The Farmers' Party". Design played a large part in the industrialisation of Sweden, and quite early in its development the welfare state sought from 1930 onwards to integrate technology into a traditional if increasingly secular public realm. The cemeteries of Stockholm and Malmö that Gunnar Asplund and Lewerentz undertook from the 1920s onwards illustrate very well the integration of large-scale machinery into a pastoral or semi-pastoral setting, and in part these projects also disguise and embed modern transport systems in a pseudo-traditional landscape.

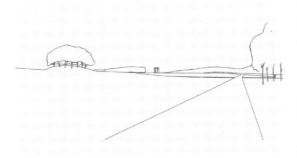

Sigurd Lewerentz, drawing of The Way of the Cross for Stockholm Cemetery competition, 1915.

The great earth mound in the Woodland Cemetery in the suburbs of Stockholm was built not only to resemble a tumulus and to direct the eye to a sacred route towards the Chapel of Resurrection, but also because it blocks one's view of the train station where one has just alighted. This station is, of course, the reason why the new suburbs could exist and why the local population needed a cemetery. Almost from the beginning of his career, Lewerentz seems to have been not only attracted to places where technology and tradition meet, but also to have exhibited an ambivalent attitude towards each. Or rather, it is as if he refused to be drawn in favour of either, accepting that the modern task of design would involve both traditional forms of use with vernacular and semi-classical architectural expression, and in doing so he did not reject the challenges and opportunities created by modern technology.

Eastern Cemetery, Malmö by Sigurd Lewerentz, 1916–1969.

Lewerentz's ambivalence could be seen as a form of creative pragmatism, refusal to discount the possibility for symbolism within ultra-mundane settings. I believe that he saw within the absolutely worldly situations of religious structures in new towns and suburbs and in very precise technical and programmatic problems, the potential for common ground. This common ground is characterised in his work as quite violent juxtapositions between ancient and brute new things, and in between their juxtaposition a continuity of sorts is established and revealed. Sweden's welfare state enabled this ludic attitude towards tradition to prosper. As the nation industrialised, the "Swedish model" of governance by compromise, consultation and representation of difference, led to, and even encouraged, the co-existence of contradictory modes of thought.

Recent histories of Swedish Modernism emphasise the unusual situation of its arrival in the country via the Stockholm Exhibition of 1930. The "first manifesto of Swedish Modernism was published in 1931", Helena Mattsson and Sven-Olov Wallenstein claim in *Swedish Modernism: Architecture, Consumption and the Welfare State*. Published as *acceptera*, the manifesto was "co-

Chapel of Resurrection, Stockholm
Cemetery by Sigurd Lewerentz, 1925.

Stockholm Cemetery by Sigurd
Lewerentz and Gunnar Asplund,
1917–1940.

4   "acceptera (Stockholm, 1931)",
    *Modern Swedish Design: Three
    Founding Texts*, New York: Museum
    of Modern Art, 2008. See also
    Mattsson and Wallenstein, *Swedish
    Modernism*, p 19.

5   Berggren, Henrik and Lars
    Trägårdh, "Pippi Longstocking: The
    Autonomous Child and the Moral
    Logic of the Swedish Welfare State",
    Swedish Modernism, Mattsson and
    Wallenstein eds, pp 50–65.

6   See "List of countries by GDP (PPP)
    per capita", *Wikipedia*.

7   Berggren and Trägårdh refer
    the reader to Borland, Harold,
    *Nietzsche's Influence on Swedish
    Literature*, Göteborg: Kungl, 1955;
    and to *Persöhnlichkeitsidealismus
    und Willenskult: Aspekte der
    Nietzsche-Rezeption in Schweden*,
    Heidelberg, 1945. They also note that
    "The French editors of Pippi found
    her superpowers disconcerting and
    did their best to tone down her self-
    sufficiency and autonomy in relation
    to the adult world", p 63, footnotes
    no 2 and no 7.

written by six of the most prestigious architects and intellectuals of the time: Asplund, Wolter Gahn, Sven Markelius, Gregor Paulsson, Eskil Sundahl and Uno Åhrén".[4] Mattsson claims that it was published at a point at which world economic crisis led to the failure of the avant-garde modernist project elsewhere (*pace* Tafuri). Mattsson and Wallenstein believe that "in its Swedish version, modernism was not portrayed to the same extent as a break with tradition, as was the case with the European avant-garde, but rather, at least if we follow the arguments of *acceptera*, as a programme to reconnect traditional values to contemporary development". This mirrors almost exactly the political situation at the birth of Social Democratic governance, which presented itself as the Swedish model or "the Swedish way", which they define as "a set of ideological motifs centred on 'Swedishness', the spirit of collaboration between labour and capital, and a certain aloofness from the disarray of post-war Europe". Ultimately these motifs are an "ideological illusion", they fear. However, in the "manifesto" of *acceptera*, they see the "primary task of functionalism" to be an attempt to "make the individual identify with the project of modernisation by creating an amalgam of old and new, and a kind of 'patchwork history' became the crucial way to achieve this". This patchwork included what they call "Vernacular Modernism" on the one hand, and also tacit acceptance of Le Corbusier's vision at the end of *Vers Une Architecture*, 1923, that "revolution can be avoided"; and that this "architecture should be capable once more of unifying society and making everyone identify with a given totality".

All Saints' Day at Woodland Chapel, Stockholm Cemetery, by Sigurd Lewerentz, 1935–1940.

This led to a series of tensions within a society in which tension and conflict had been agreed upon as being unproductive, and in which compromise and negotiation were supposedly able to mediate tradition and modernity. In architectural terms these tensions are manifest in the state project of "the million programme", whereby one million apartments were built between 1965 and 1974; the manufacturing of the romantic notion of "*folkhemmet*" ("the people's home"); and the "creation of non-descript suburban milieus".

Mattsson and Wallenstein see the latter as an example of "hatred against urbanity (itself strangely enough understood mainly in terms of the nineteenth-century cityscape that preceded the arrival of modernism), and as an effective way of depriving architecture of whatever artistic and imaginative potentials it might have". Mattsson and Wallenstein adopt a post-Marxist technique whereby Tafuri's analysis of the failure of the avant-garde project is elided with a neo-liberal attitude towards recent history. Extrapolating from their own explanation, "consumption" is inserted betwcen "architecture" and "the welfare state" to explain the passivity resulting from "the Swedish way" of doing politics—reflected in a uniform way of life—and "the Swedish version" of modernism articulated in a suburban architectural landscape.

Against this conformity is contrasted another mode of anti-urban national myth-making found in the children's stories of Astrid Lindgren. *Pippi Longstocking*, 1944, "both offers an extreme version of child autonomy and a resounding confirmation of the social order that surrounds her".[5] Individualism is the key aspect of Swedish life that leads Henrik Berggren and Lars Trägårdh to the conclusion that "though not literally orphaned", the contemporary equivalents of Pippi Longstocking "have been abandoned by working mothers, and yet they are not surrounded by the "gentle paternalists" Pippi knew. They insist that "Sweden, it must be emphasized, is not the middle way between Italy and the United States. Basically, Sweden is a variation of the American situation... [sharing] the dubious distinction of topping international statistics in terms of divorce... the breakdown of traditional support structures through the acceptance of globalization and a competitive market economy. Drugs, sexual promiscuity and strong youth sub-cultures are part of everyday life. Both countries can supply good arguments for a general critique of modern, western civilization." Indeed, both the US and Scandinavia top the tables for GDP per capita, education, research etc.[6]

Berggren and Trägårdh concede that whilst *Pippi Longstocking* is "a fanciful fantasy about the sovereign child", it must be noted that "her world displays most of the characteristics—non-productivcness, idleness, excessive and meaningless consumption, criminality and disorder—that according to the French philosopher Georges Bataille are the characteristics of the "sovereign man" who rejects the normal existence as a "servile man" subordinate to the social contract (*The Accursed Share: An Essay on General Economy*)".

One part of Berggren and Trägårdh's essay has the heading "An Übermensch Disguised as a Child", and they note that, "Nietzsche had a great impact on intellectual life in Sweden at the closing of the nineteenth century".[7] They also suggest that the anti-social aspects of the modern Swedish national heroine Pippi Longstocking are symptomatic of the malign aspects of the Swedish model, which is

Left: Klippan town centre with nineteenth century country house amongst twentieth century buildings.

Right: Town Park notice board with crest of Klippan that is based upon the local topographic features.

Left: Klippan with the blanket factory outlet on the right.

Right: View of St Peter's community centre parish hall from the car park beside the fast food kiosk (the park sign and the park are on the right).

quasi-Nietzschean in character, suggesting that "the temptation on the part of the adult world to view children as a means to an end is great.... We can destroy them by giving them too much or too little freedom." The Welfare State, they claim, legitimised children's rights over their ability to exercise them—making them citizens before they stopped being their parents' responsibility. Such a dramatic account of extreme individual and group pathology contradicts the supposedly benign character of the Swedish Welfare State, and continues the thematic of the "hatred" of the city suggested by Mattsson and Wallenstein. Recent Swedish popular culture has begun to deal with the tensions between a domineeringly benign Welfare State, extreme youth culture, and a conservative and secure business elite (see the removal of Lisbeth Salander's sovereignty by the Swedish state in Stieg Larsson's *Millennium* trilogy).[8] The wartime "neutrality" of Sweden has also been recently suggested to be at best a form of moral equivalence or ethical ambivalence, as well as the cover for a sizeable National Socialist movement—the other example of course of an elision of tradition and modern politics in 1930s Europe. Perhaps traditional culture was reconciled with modernism in the SDP-led Swedish model; but "tradition" and modernity, or at least stylistic or rhetorical interpretations of these terms, were also manipulated by Left and Right for political aims, and by architects to aesthetic and personal intentions.

So, it is perhaps not surprising that despite the tolerance of traditional cultural values within this nascent modern state, when the regional government of Skåne decided upon the establishment of the new town at Klippan in 1945, they did not immediately seek to create it as a new parish, nor to erect a church there. Before its civic foundation, Klippan was remarkable only as a topographic feature, and as a collection of houses known as Alby (which was not a parish). Locals identified a "klippan" or "the cliff" in the river, which must have appeared prominent in the flat Skåne landscape when seen from the road between the large towns of Helsingborg and Hasselholm. The creation of a town at this spot arose in response to the industrial role the river would play, and because the cross-country train lines were built so as to stop at a factory there. Thus Klippan's foundation was essentially economic and bureaucratically profane, and was effectively the recognition of a series of almost haphazard acts of covering the ground with buildings and mills. "Klippan" blankets are the most notable local export—evidence of the role the river plays in manufacturing.

By the late 1950s, the small group of local Lutheran parishioners were keen to elaborate upon their meetings at the local school hall.[9] Slowly this ambition grew into the aim to create a properly designed church setting, and over a number of years they gained confidence and expertise sufficient to gain the attention of the church commission and the local council members. Initially, the plan was for the creation of a modest chapel and a community centre, to be funded partly by the church and local council. The latter group saw that the creation of a

8 Larsson, Stieg, *The Millennium Trilogy: The Girl with the Dragon Tattoo, The Girl Who Played with Fire & The Girl Who Kicked the Hornets' Nest*, London: Vintage, 2010.

9 Ridderstedt, Lars, *Adversus Populum: Peter Celsings och Sigurd Lewerentz sakralarkitektur 1945–1975*, Stockholm: Hallgren & Fallgren, 1998.

10 Ridderstedt published his PhD, *Adversus Populum*, in 1998, and whilst it contains a summary in English, as far as I am aware I was the first person to commission a translation of the chapter on St Peter's by Nina Lundvall in 2011.

11 Ahlin, Janne, *Sigurd Lewerentz Architect: 1885–1975*, Stockholm: Byggförlaget, 1987, pp 11–13.

12 Smithson, Alison, "The Silent Architects", *Sigurd Lewerentz 1885–1975: The Dilemma of Classicism*, London: Architectural Association, 1988.

13 Wang, Wilfried, *Sigurd Lewerentz: St. Petri*, Tübingen: Ernst Wasmuth Verlag, 2009.

14 See Brett, David, *The Plain Style: The Reformation, Culture and the Crisis in Protestant Identity*, London: Black Square Books, 1999. Brett explains in detail the effects of "reformed education" upon domestic spaces and upon design generally; and also the effects of the destruction of traditional image-based memory learning systems upon language

The park reflected in the windows of the community centre parish hall.

acquisition and spatiality in
protestant societies in the US and in
the north of Ireland (he compares
this to the Medieval model that
Frances Yates famously called "the
art of memory" in Yates, Frances, *The
Art of Memory*, London: Routledge;
London: Kegan Paul, 1966). See
also Dryness, William A, *Reformed
Theology and Visual Culture: The
Protestant Imagination from Calvin
to Edwards*, Cambridge: Cambridge
University Press, 2004; and Walsham,
Alexandra, *The Reformation of the
Landscape: Religion, Identity and
Memory in Early Modern Britain and
Ireland*, Oxford: Oxford University
Press, 2011.

15 See the website of the Church
of Sweden for details of the four
"public" sacraments: "Baptism,
Confirmation, Marriage and Funeral:
The occasional services are where
the Church of Sweden comes into
direct contact with the majority oft
the Swedish people, and when the
description 'national church' most
truly applies". The other sacrament
is ordination. They do not recognise
Reconciliation (confession), nor First
Holy Communion (Confirmation
stands in for this in Anglican life too),
nor Coronation.

church might be a necessary compromise, if it led to a community setting with public rooms for the elderly, a youth club and kindergarten. It seems that the local priest's initial thoughts were along similar lines to the politicians—the chapel was to have a straightforward and simple structure, almost an addendum to the community centre.

I hope to show that in building the church of St Peter, the town was retrospectively named and recognised by its inhabitants as a setting for the theatrical rites of passage that mark human time as something essentially public. It also recovered, in part, the ancient relationship between architecture and the natural world and its role as a limit to this— its essentially urban character.

St Peter's came into existence partly due to two pieces of good luck. Sigurd Lewerentz had an exemplary client representative to discuss his work with, the Reverend Lars Ridderstedt. Ridderstedt was an educated and sensitive man who had become a sort of expert-client for the Church of Sweden in the 1950s and 1960s, a "liturgical advisor". He was able to support and encourage and even to participate in the creation of St Peter's, smoothing Lewerentz's way with the local priest, and directing the architect and his ideas. The second piece of good fortune for us today is that Ridderstedt submitted a PhD on the religious architecture of Peter Celsing and Sigurd Lewerentz at the University of Uppsala in 1998.[10] I will draw lightly upon this text, but I aim to move back and forth between a description of the process of work and an interpretation of the project as built.

St Peter's has not been written about a good deal in histories of twentieth-century architecture. It is usually seen as an anomaly, the fruit of Lewerentz's extremely individualist approach to architecture. Certainly, Lewerentz did not write much, nor teach at all. However, it would be a mistake to think that his architecture does not communicate, and I suggest that it is foolish to ascribe a psychological reading of his aloof persona to his buildings, as Janne Ahlin does.[11] Modern critics of literature and the visual arts tend towards this journalese almost as a default setting. Lewerentz did not write, but that does not mean that he was "unaware", as Alison Smithson suggested in her description of him as one of "*The Silent Architects*".[12] The other tendency, which Wilfried Wang uncharacteristically falls into in his recent otherwise excellent record of the design process of St Peter's, is to ascribe to the architecture the somewhat vague Anglo-Saxon cliché that St Peter's represents a "Nordic Protestant ethic".[13] This cliché recurs partly because its architect didn't speak much, and mostly because "Protestant" equals "Calvinistic" for most commentators in the Anglo-Saxon world—even though Luther was an Augustinian monk and his catechism is Catholic if not Papist.[14] The Swedish Church retains five sacraments, and its cathedrals maintain a strong musical tradition.[15]

The other erroneous tendency is the assumption that because St Peter's looks unusual, Lewerentz rejects "the tradition of western sacred architecture". In "Sigurd Lewerentz and a Material Basis for Form" Adam Caruso claims that:

In attending to the raw, existential nature of his materials, Lewerentz privileges a subjective and shifting experience of the world. In this, he is making a decisive break with the tradition of western sacred architecture, which relies strongly on convention to embody a particular ontology. Even Ronchamp makes explicit reference to Neolithic ceremonial structures in order to assert its continuity with a sacred tradition. At Klippan, Lewerentz rejects iconography as a basis for form. In the same way that he makes us look at bricks as if they were a new material, each of us must confront the spaces of St Peter's anew, and on our own. The severely reduced palette of materials has the same effect as a silent space, and we gain an enhanced awareness of the physical presence of the church, a presence onto which we can project meanings. By adopting a phenomenological approach, Lewerentz recognises prayer as an individual, meditative activity.[16]

Caruso suggests that *haptic* experience of materials is subjective, and whilst he quotes Heidegger he seems to misconstrue phenomenology to mean "individual subjectivity". As we have seen, and I will demonstrate further, this is a misunderstanding of Heidegger's thinking on spatiality and creativity. Anyway, Caruso contradicts then his claim that experience is subjective, in claiming that a "phenomenological approach" to building materials might provide the basis for something objective, ie "form". This is a classic example of an intelligent and talented architect confusing the design process with criticism. We sort-of know what he means, in the way in which you sort-of know what someone is saying in a foreign language without being able to speak it, but you might as well say instead: "Sigurd Lewerentz and a Subjective Basis for Form". However, this also would teach us nothing, nor bring us any closer to the building or to the architect's intentions, and would further obscure Lewerentz's great ability to situate tradition in the modern world. In sum, it is simply a mistranslation of his aims and achievements, and no guide to anyone interested in learning from Lewerentz's example.

Whilst there isn't otherwise a great deal written about St Peter's in English, Lewerentz continues to attract critical attention from practising architects.[17] Yet the most informative essay remains Colin St John Wilson's "Sigurd Lewerentz: The Sacred Buildings and The Sacred Sites" published in various formats from the 1980s onwards.[18] Wilson offers us the compelling image of a "hidden lake" beneath the church, and he also emphasises the importance of the "Lutheran Mass", and by implication the Catholic nature of the services that St Peter's was designed to house. Wilson may have met Ridderstedt, as he mentions his involvement in the project. There is no mention of this in the biographical monograph of Ahlin. Wilson also suggests a series of connections to both ancient Greek and modern poets—in particular

he mentions somewhat suggestively the poetic theory of TS Eliot, who was a touchstone for Anglo-Catholics like Wilson.[19] Eliot defined himself as a Catholic because he was a modernist, which for him meant someone who believed in the transformational power of tradition. Wilson attempted elsewhere to consider the architectural implications of Eliot's essay "Tradition and the Individual Talent" (from *The Sacred Wood*, 1921),[20] straining to relate the poet's criticism to the work of Alvar Aalto, and ultimately to attempt to redeem what he calls the other tradition of modernism.[21] Wilson's essays on Lewerentz and Aalto have been described as attempts to define an authentic Protestant architecture, from which England can learn. They could also be said to reveal not only the deeply ambiguous nature of his definition of modernism as a form of tradition—evolved from what he calls nineteenth-century "English Free School", but also of the ambiguous character of his High Church Socialist Anglicanism. Without elaborating beyond introducing Ridderstedt as a protagonist in the drama of the creation of St Peter's, Wilson touches upon the complex nature of Lewerentz's commissions within the milieu of the ambiguously "conservative" and modern Swedish High Church Movement.

Similarly, Peter Blundell-Jones claims that St Peter's darkness is "not Puritan clarity", without elaborating on this claim.[22] He attempts to construct a tectonic-programmatic reading of the detail of the doors and gutters and downpipes that suggests that the ritualistic use of the building is articulated in its ironmongery and joinery. This reading doesn't become fully iconographic since it is not his intention to do so, nor part of his functionalist-tectonic heritage (established alongside Wilson at Cambridge beside Sir Leslie Martin). Wilson refers directly to Ridderstedt in passing, but neither he nor Jones mention in detail Ridderstedt's role in the project. Although their insights are at best quasi-poetic or quasi-intuitive attempts to decipher the mystery of the architecture, Wilson and Blundell-Jones nonetheless make suggestive and intriguing readings of St Peter's without managing to reveal the depth of the urban and architectural problems that Lewerentz engaged with. This claim is made not to discount their contributions, but to suggest that Ridderstedt's description of site meetings with Lewerentz—and of their creative discussions— sheds direct light upon the liturgical and architectural task he faced and thus upon the design as a response to this. I will attempt to reveal the profoundly urban character of this task—the reconciliation of landscape and architectural design with an ornamental and programmatic depth.

More recently, Nick Temple attempts to deepen our understanding of the architectural intent and meaning of St Peter's in invoking the iconography and morphology of baptisteries in the early church, suggesting that St Peter's can be seen as an invocation and representation of the original sacrifice myth of Christianity.[23] This is not specifically proven in

16 Caruso, Adam, "Sigurd Lewerentz and a Material Basis for Form", *OASE*, no 45, 1997.

17 There are two graduate dissertations of note, both of which approach the building with a phenomenological interpretation. Nicholson, Gordon A, "Drawing, Building, Craft: Revelations of Spiritual Harmony and the Body at St Petri Klippan", unpublished MArch dissertation, McGill University, 1998, looks at the significance of the Lutheran Mass upon the design of the architecture. As the title suggests, the "poetics of silence and darkness" and a sort of superstition about the significance of brick construction as metaphor (craft=faith; an unwitting Free Masonry) clouds an otherwise insightful contribution. This tendency is shared in Patterson, Paula Anne, "The architecture of the poetic image: the visible and the invisible in the sacred architecture of Sigurd Lewerentz", unpublished PhD thesis, University of Washington, 2009, in which St Peter's is briefly referred to as "profound silence".

18 Wilson, Colin St John, "Sigurd Lewerentz: The Sacred Buildings and The Sacred Sites", *Sigurd Lewerentz 1885–1975*, Nicola Flora, Paolo Giardiello, Gennaro Postiglione eds, Milan: Electa, 2001; Ahlberg, *Sigurd Lewerentz 1885–1975*; also published in Wilson, Colin St John, *Architectural Reflections: Studies in the Philosophy and Practice of Architecture*, Oxford: Butterworth, 1992; Manchester: Manchester University Press, 2000.

19 See Spurr, Barry, *Anglo-Catholic in Religion: TS Eliot and Religion*, Cambridge: Lutterworth Press, 2010.

20 Wilson, *Architectural Reflections*.

21 Wilson, Colin St John, *The Other Tradition of Modern Architecture: The Uncompleted Project*, London: Academy Editions, 1995; London: Black Dog Publishing, 2010.

22 Blundell Jones, Peter, "Sigurd Lewerentz: Church of St Peter Klippan 1963–1966", *ARQ*, vol 6, no 2, 2002.

23 Temple, Nick, "Baptism and Sacrifice: Cosmogony as Private Ontology", *ARQ*, vol 8, no 1, 2005.

Above: All Saints Margaret Street by William
Butterfield, 1859, with views of exterior.

Right: All Saints Margaret Street by William
Butterfield, 1859, with views of interior.

24 Ridderstedt, *Adversus Populum*, p 343.

Ridderstedt's description of the evolution for the project, although the intention was to recover the atmosphere of "holiness" of early Christian "catholic churches".[24]

Yet Ridderstedt describes a project that was much more ambitious and pragmatic than any one could have guessed. My method will again be to describe the process of design and to seek to amplify the importance of the decisions that Lewerentz made; and then to place Ridderstedt's theological text into an architectural discourse. Despite his erudition and humour, Ridderstedt's field was liturgy. St Peter's is not simply a built liturgical programme, but a highly useful and witty response to a set of particular and universal architectural problems and themes, problems that are specific and also typical of the modern urban situations where architects are called to work.

In the case of Klippan, architecture was not the first thing that the Swedish government thought about when it considered founding a town. My thesis is that despite this situation, Lewerentz's architecture—in concert with other arts—enabled the re-establishment of the town in a meaningful way: as a recognisably

modern habitat, part of both the natural world, and the modern and traditional modes associated with Swedish life. The Swedish situation, as we have seen, was an interesting if self-congratulatory and slightly complacent admixture of political and social forces intent upon a somewhat smug compromise between history and action. For example, the trade unions had a voice in the governance of both businesses and the state. Alongside a hereditary monarchy, the Church of Sweden was at once High-Church Lutheran in liturgy and socially minded in everyday practice.

If this sounds familiar to readers in England, it is because Sweden and England experienced quite similar reactions to church reformation and to the modernisation of the state. Both countries experienced a political reformation in which monarchs broke with the Church of Rome and ultimately established a national church as a means to further their own ambitions. Unlike England, the Swedish Church's liturgy was directly shaped by Lutheran theological teachings. Calvinism was considered alien, and up until the eighteenth century it was illegal. The Church

Rudolf Schwarz, illustrations from *The
Church Incarnate*, 1947.

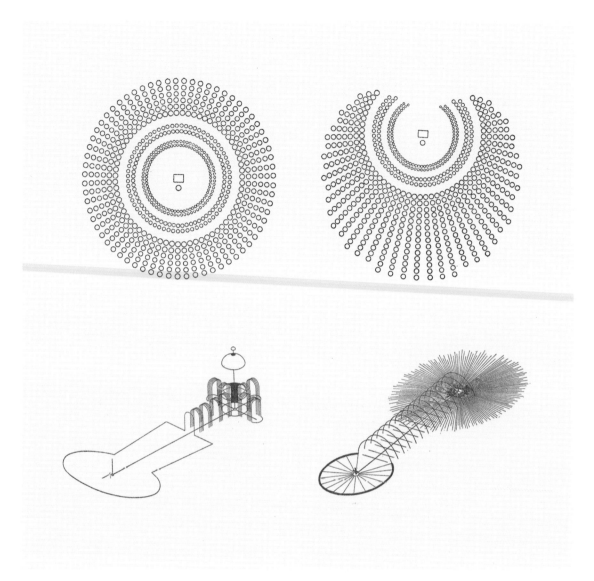

of Sweden was disestablished in 2000 and whilst
church attendance is as low as 2 per cent, the majority
of Swedes (73 per cent) recognise their membership
and pay a church tax. However, the High Church or
Anglo-Catholic movement in the Church of England,
the Tractarian movement or Oxford Movement, was
highly influential upon the Church of Sweden in the
late nineteenth and early twentieth century, Lars
Ridderstedt claims.[25] In England, the rediscovery of
the Catholic origins of Anglicanism occurred at exactly
the same time as the industrialisation of the country—
nineteenth-century Medievalism was a reaction to
and rejection of this industrialisation, and religion
was one means by which political resistance was
manifest. This led in England to the oppositional
paradox of High Church Anglican priests operating
in working-class parishes in sympathy with the
poor, and in concert with Labour groups, against
the establishment that they were intrinsically part
of.[26] In Sweden this conflict seems to have been
less extreme. In part this was because the country

adopted industrial working processes relatively later
than England. In the early twentieth century, the
population became urbanised, and the creation of
consensus governance established both continuity
with traditional ways of life and belief and enabled
modern visions of social welfare to grow naturally
from the charitable foundation of Christian worship.

Nonetheless, the High Church Movement in Sweden
grew in part in response to social critics alarmed that
industrialisation and rapid urbanisation were stripping
society of its symbolic common ground. In "the Swedish
model" of social governance the church was another
voice to be listened to, but it was not represented in
government in the way that the Anglican Bishops
sit in the House of Lords. In fact, the growth of the
economy and the generally smooth transition from
agrarian to industrial economies led to a lack of
conflict in Swedish society, and the role of the church
diminished with the development of urban capitalism
and what the Bishop of Lund Frantz Wormordsen
called "rationalism".

25 Ridderstedt, *Adversus Populum*,
    pp 333–334.

26 Spurr, *Anglo-Catholic in Religion*;
    see also Yelton, Michael, *Anglican
    Papalism: An Illustrated History*,
    Norwich: Canterbury Press, 2005.

27 Ridderstedt, *Adversus Populum.*

28 Ridderstedt, *Adversus Populum.*
    Curiously, perhaps, there is no
    mention of William Lethaby being
    a direct influence on Swedish
    architecture, although one could
    arguably extrapolate an imaginative
    if unsubstantiated lineage from his
    Architecture, Mysticism, and Myth
    (1891) and *Mediaeval Art* (1904)
    to Lewerentz's work. In particular
    Lethaby's response to Ruskin, "the
    temple idea", demonstrates ways
    of seeing mythic man's inherent
    engagement with nature and the
    translation of this into the architecture
    that echoes Lewerentz's own
    contribution in this field.

29 Schwarz, Rudolf, *The Church
    Incarnate: The Sacred Function of
    Christian Architecture*, English
    translation, Munich: Puset 1958,
    pp 220–227.

30 Ridderstedt, *Adversus Populum*,
    p 335.

31 See Ridderstedt, *Adversus Populum*;
    and also Wang, Wilfried, *The
    Architecture of Peter Celsing*,
    London: Inferno Books, 1996.
    Celsing's son Johan Celsing is
    also a very good church architect,
    and in fact he recently completed
    a new crematorium chapel at the
    Woodland Cemetery.

Ridderstedt suggests that in response to the intense and rapid industrialisation of Sweden at the end of the nineteenth century, the theologian UL Ullman and the art historians Sigurd Curman and Johnny Roosval "tried to awaken interest, in Sweden, for Medieval churches and art". For Ullman "solemnity" ("*högtidlighet*") "was a key-word having a distinct theological content". Ridderstedt links this in part to what he calls "National Romanticism and Mysticism",[27] "the most prominent exponent" of which was the architect Lars Israel Wahlman who "had been inspired by the English Arts and Crafts movement and had been impressed by the traditions of John Ruskin and William Morris".[28]

Wahlman "emphasises the importance of the Byzantine Heritage in the creation of church space" and his two concepts of 1920, "sincerity and truth", Ridderstedt suggests, "came to leave a lasting mark on the churches of Lewerentz and Celsing". Similarly, the liturgy and in particular the role of communion was seen as central to the sacramental character of the Swedish Lutheran *Mässe*. However, the High Church Movement, with its sympathy towards greater solemnity—generally a movement within Protestant national churches (Sweden and England etc)—was countered from within the Roman Church and Protestant churches in Germany. On the one hand, the influence of Rudolf Schwarz's 1923 book *Vom Bau der Kirche* (translated as *The Church Incarnate: The Sacred Function of Christian Architecture*) emphasised the communicative nature of the Eucharistic celebration, and in his designs the priest faced the congregation over the altar, prefiguring the changes of the Second Vatican Council by 30 years.[29]

Härlanda Church, Gothenburg, by Peter Celsing, 1958.

Alongside this Catholic influence from Germany the chapels of Matisse at Vence and of Le Corbusier at Ronchamp and the *Art Sacré* movement generally was profound. In Swedish this led to the publication in 1962 of a study of the history of church architecture, "*Domus Ecclesia*", written by the priest Dean Axel Rappe, which Lewerentz read whilst he was working on the designs for Klippan.[30] On the other hand, the Low Church Calvinistic-Lutheran tradition that developed

under Friedrich the Great in Prussia continued to challenge the idea of the church as a House of God (*Domus Dei*), in favour of the idea that instead what was needed was a Parish House—a hall that could also be used for religious services (*Domus Ecclesia*).

Peter Celsing recommended Sigurd Lewerentz to the church committee of Klippan.[31] At this time the Lutheran community met in a local school, and as I mentioned before, initial plans were for something that Ridderstedt calls a building type akin to "The Working Church", or at best what Wahlman called a "church with appendices". In the most extremely Protestant case this meant in effect a parish hall that could also be used as a chapel; at the high end of Lutheranism there was quite a lot of theory about what modern "catholic" churches should be like, but without referencing that many actual examples. Thus Lewerentz began with a not particularly promising brief, but on the other hand it was a situation with possibilities. Once the parish committee visited Lewerentz's St Mark's Church in the Stockholm suburb Björkhagen, they were convinced that he was the architect for them, and also that their project could be architecturally and socially ambitious. This model, of a church with ancillary social buildings, satisfied the local SDP politicians and the Low and High parts of the church commission and the local population, and a design competition was initiated with Lewerentz's St Mark's in part forming the model for the design brief.

Lewerentz submitted a scheme that is very close to what was ultimately built, proposing an assemblage of a central block with a threshold oriented towards the road, and with an L-shaped block creating a cloister between the sacred and social parts of the church complex. In the competition brief a site was identified on the corner of the town park, at the crossroads of two major roads. Unlike the other entrants' designs, Lewerentz did not propose to place the buildings on this corner. Instead, he proposed to site the church 200 m to the east of the crossroads, aligning the entrance directly across from the entry to a large detached timber suburban villa. He seems to have done this in order to isolate the church somewhat from the crossroads, protecting it from exposure to any future development there. This was prudent. Today there is a large petrol station-cum-convenience store diagonally across from the church-park corner, creating the most extremely banal form of suburbanism.

I suggest that Lewerentz wanted to provide a counter example to this, to create sufficient terrain around the church—a landscaped threshold—that established a different mood to the road-based town planning that dominates Klippan. He achieved this through the creation of a fruiting hedge upon a 2 m tall mound that shelters the church complex from both an existing fast food shack and the roundabout crossroads. The earth for this was spoil dug to form a large pool that sits between the church and the crossroads, establishing a series of landscaped thresholds within which the church sits.

Left: View of St Peter's, Klippan, by Sigurd
Lewerentz, 1963, from the town park,
with the community wing on the left and
the chapel in the background.

Above: Views of farm houses and castles
in Skåne.

The intention seems to have been also to unite it with the pattern of the domestic settlement of the town, and to infer that the villa has grown up around the church. This tactic is intrinsic to the architecture itself, which appears strikingly primitive and anachronistic within the modern setting of the new town of Klippan, strongly reminiscent of Skåne brick farms and manor houses.

From the exterior, the church complex appears older than the neighbouring buildings, suggesting that Lewerentz was attempting to retrospectively re-establish the town as something that has grown up around a farm or manor in a traditional or vernacular fashion or form of urban development. This conceit works well in the sense that one does not notice the church as something that was planned after the park was established. In fact, the park now appears as part of the extended landscape of the religious complex, and is also articulated as part of the town by the church.

In creating a particular and special character of place around St Peter's for highly pragmatic reasons, Lewerentz succeeds in uniting the road system with the town's open spaces, via the church. A car park for parishioners sits behind the southern sweep of the mound beside the kiosk, and from this approach the first sight you have of St Peter's is of a tall brick chimney rising like a kiln on axis with the path. A large notice board announces the church of St Peter and the town's park, adorned with the crest of Klippan, a cliff and falling water.

It seems that in taking seriously his brief to create a "community centre" and a church, he understood

that what was at stake in this architectural problem was something profoundly urban. Lewerentz had the wisdom and ambition to attempt to solve more than the immediate "problem" of the design of a building, and he did this in a witty and erudite manner that revealed that the problem of designing a church in the modern world has as much to do with the world as it does with immaterial matters.

The church at Klippan reveals also the deeper problem of modernity with which architects grapple—banal briefs, clients who lack cultural ambition etc and the essential architectural tasks that have always existed—the resolution of mundane and ideal problems and the transformation of these into geometrical, tectonic and representational coherence and order. Lewerentz transformed the functional requirements of his brief into a representational programme that transformed use into action, exposing the drama of city life to public witness.

In the case of Klippan, the particular architectural problem was the foundation of the town itself—which originated as a hamlet (originally called Alby)—which lacked the status of traditional Swedish and indeed all European villages and towns. It lacked a proper name that anyone understood to have any meaning; it lacked a parish; and it lacked a deep connection between the land from which it sprang and the history and culture which sustain human settlement. The creation of the new town, "Klippan", derived its name from a local geographic feature, but, of course, this was not enough to situate life there in a meaningful manner. In actual and

Google Earth view of St Peter's, Klippan,
showing the pre-existing town park, the
villa opposite, the roundabout and garage.

Site plan of St Peter's, Klippan, by Sigurd
Lewerentz, 1963, final revision 27 May
1966. From the Swedish Centre for
Architecture and Design's collections.

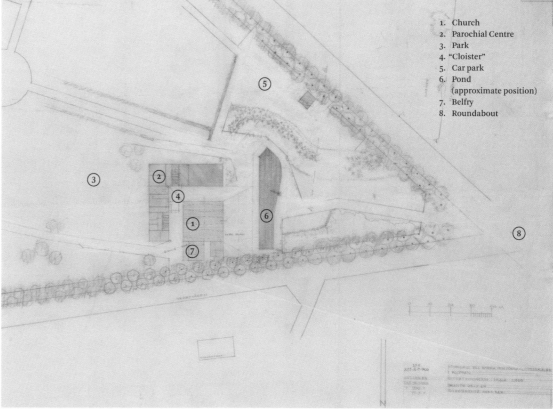

1. Church
2. Parochial Centre
3. Park
4. "Cloister"
5. Car park
6. Pond
   (approximate position)
7. Belfry
8. Roundabout

View of St Peter's, Klippan, from the
roundabout on Klosterhagen showing
the fast food kiosk on the right and the
church set back on the left.

View of north facade and entrance of
St Peter's, Klippan.

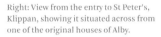

Left: View of west facade of St Peter's,
Klippan, looking towards the path to the
car park, with the pond hidden beneath
snow on the right.

Right: View from the entry to St Peter's,
Klippan, showing it situated across from
one of the original houses of Alby.

Left: View in the cloister looking towards
the pond.

Right: View of the cloister in-between the
chapel, on the left, and the community
centre, on the right, looking north.

Sigurd Lewerentz, design development
drawing, ground plan of St Peter's,
Klippan, 18 May 1966. From the
Swedish Centre for Architecture and
Design's collections.

metaphorical terms, Lewerentz succeeds in refounding
and alluding to an alternate founding of the town as a
place with meaning and significance for its inhabitants.

How does he achieve this? St Peter's isn't just a
metaphor of a rock: a church houses many uses
beyond the weekly or everyday worship of believers.
Of course, across the world, chapels and synagogues
and mosques act as the focus for local communities
of course, providing a location for the rites of passage
that characterise the public nature of our lives. At
Klippan, the church and community centre form a
coherent urban ensemble, united by the rhythm of
situations accommodated there, set into a quasi-natural
setting oriented by a rhythm of brick boxes (and also
by the spaces in-between these structures); and made
up of "terra cotta" (ie, bricks).

The ground is formed from a series of excavations,
and by assemblages of chthonic settings. Earth dug

to form the pond forms the berm that shrouds the
western edge of the site from the roundabout. The
altar and baptismal font are complementary echoes of
void and mass. A series of settings are defined by brick-
formed mounds, and in use they describe a journey
from earth to light, from mundane to sacred territory,
situating the town as a fragment of a profound
civilisation. Generally, this movement is between
earth and light, and the material hierarchy set up from
the site-location (roundabout—park): pool, berm,
cardinal orientation, sculptures, street furniture,
ironmongery, architecture. This then extends within
the buildings:

A   boxes of baked-earth with openings
B   altar and baptismal font (both these settings and
      the structures themselves are analogous of hills
      with pits filled with water)

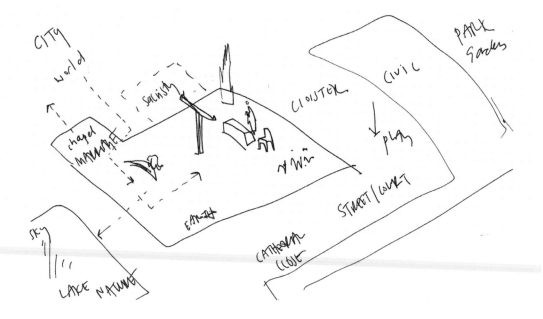

Patrick Lynch, sketch showing
the movement of a worshipper at
St Peter's, Klippan.

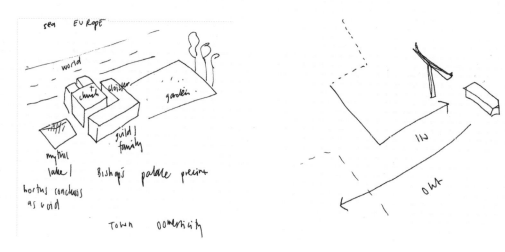

Left: Patrick Lynch, sketch showing
St Peter's, Klippan, as an urban ensemble.

Right: Patrick Lynch, sketch showing
the movement of a worshipper at
St Peter's, Klippan.

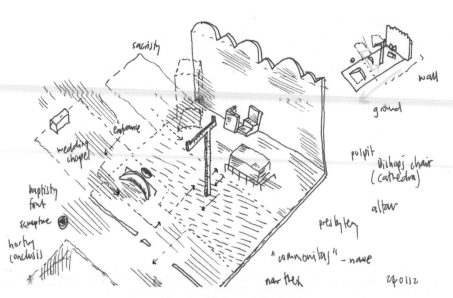

Patrick Lynch, sketch showing the spatial
settings of worship at St Peter's, Klippan.

32 Falkfors, Lars, *Sankt Petri Church
in Klippan: A Masterpiece by Sigurd
Lewerentz*, a pamphlet printed by
Sankt Petri Church, Klippan. Neither
the maker nor designer of the cross
is named.

C   steel "cross" and steel font structures (with a
        conch shell supported on the latter)
D   timber furniture
E   light
    i   existing everyday natural light
    ii   oriented daylight and shadows
    iii   candlelight
    iv   electric lights

The brick whole also comprises a series of settings
laid out in accordance with the order of liturgy, and
set beneath the movement of the sun across the sky.

The representational and actual activities of
Christian worship are organised together in rhythmic
harmony as parts of the church complex, and as a
fragment of an actual and symbolic landscape. St Peter's
is made up of a series of powerful spatial images that
invoke other places and actions, whilst grounding one
strongly in Klippan.

I am now going to present a phenomenological
description of the experience of moving through
the church, and in particular of visiting it in use one
Sunday morning in February 2012. I will then attempt
to reveal the hermeneutic significance of the various
situations encountered along this route or journey.
I hope that the repetition captures some of the rhythm
of one's encounter with the various spatial settings
at St Peter's, which changes quite dramatically from
shock to pleasure, and from bewilderment towards
orientation. My aim is to juxtapose an individual
experience of the building at various times of the
year and over a decade, with the public aspects of
participation in the *Mässe*, in order to try to reveal the
great visual intelligence and wit at play at St Peter's.

The entrance to the church is first a descent, followed
by ascension. Bells hang in a hollow roof to the left of a
low timber door. The door is pressed deep into a brick
opening, and is adorned with a curious cross; its "four
ribbons symbolise that our way forward and upwards
leads through the four evangelists".[32] Entry is a step up.
One is immediately presented with a small model of a
boat that appears to float in a brick vault of light. The
narthex of the church is in fact a small wedding chapel.

Ahead, to the left, an opening breaks through a
cliff of bricks. This is the entrance at the corner of what
in contrast is a very large, very dark, almost black room.
Four high windows pierce the darkness, two on the right,
two ahead. High windows on the right cast light down
onto a small brick mound; the emphatic brick-ness of
the space is cut by reflecting and intermittently
moving water.

In the background a large brick table seems to
hover. Something tall and thin lurks in the middle of
the room, deeply in shadow. Initially, all is mass and
matter. Bricks predominate above, below and beside
one. Slowly one becomes accustomed to the lack of
light, and things begin to register as such. It slowly
becomes apparent that there is equipment in the room,
awaiting use. The space seems to pulse like an empty
stage, tense, apparently resting, but ready, awaiting action.

Immediately on the left, a conch shell sits in a black
steel shelf, held above a shallow pool that appears as a
deep cut in the brick mound. Water drips from a thin
metal pipe into a shallow smear of water held within
the shell. In turn, this drips out down into a culvert in
the brick ground: drip, drip. Immense and quite loud
in the room, it is as if one had forgotten the sound of
water, and the rhythm of a heartbeat.

Above: View of the entrance of St Peter's,
Klippan.

Left: Photograph of the model boat
hanging in the marriage chapel at
St Peter's, Klippan.

Right: Sigurd Lewerentz, section through
marriage chapel in the vestibule at St
Peter's, Klippan, looking east towards the
entrance doorway, 4 October 1965. From
the Swedish Centre for Architecture and
Design's collections.

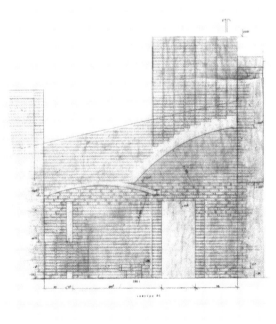

During *Mässe* a horizon of candles marks out the room above head height. Light bulbs hang from the gloom, creating a field of light. Balls of light reveal the fall of the floor, like an orchard planted on a slope. The altar table is set out lower in the space. Pale timber and woven straw chairs sit in rows marked out by the brick floor, somewhat askance to the walls and yet intently focused upon the altar. Deep on the left, a large blonde timber and reflecting steel organ steps out from the dark. The back wall seems to sit backwards, receding into darkness.

After an hour into the 11 o'clock Sunday service, in spring and autumn, the sun suddenly enters in through the two south-facing windows to the right of the altar. Two things suddenly become clear. Directly in front and very close, a massive steel cross becomes visible silhouetted against the sudden light that enters through the west-facing doors. The tall steel column is holding aloft huge, high steel beams. Above them, brick clouds seem to roll over the steelwork, tensed like brick muscles in motion, echoing and inverting the profile of the conch shell. The space of the church is held in between these two profiles.

The massive steel cross dominates the centre of the room, penetrating the horizons of light that define up and down. Outside, three lamps hang their heads like figures crucified upon Calvary, and the nave of the church is suddenly revealed as the Way of the Cross. This spatial type is part of Swedish Lutheran tradition (it is an example of *imitatio Christi*)—and formed the basis also of Lewerentz's design for the landscape of the Woodland Cemetery. Originating with St Francis of Assisi, it is paradigmatic of pilgrimage, which was, to St Augustine, paradigmatic of Christian life more generally.[33] Pilgrimage is both a horizontal movement that involves the body in a form of sacramental spatial rhythm (walking); and is also a form of contemplative action that is oriented by and focused upon the soul's movement vertically. At St Peter's these two forms of movement are united in the re-enactment of the sacred mystery in the Mass, and specifically at the Eucharist; at which point the horizontal and vertical elements of the space can not only be seen but can be understood, ie one experiences the "communicative movement" of the space through the rhythm of worship.

A few things need to be explained to account for this effect. Firstly, as one can see from the image of the young girl at the font, seen from her height (or when genuflecting or praying), the interior of the church is dominated by the image of a cross on a hill. One is not directly aware of this as an adult, or as a non-participant in the Mass, or during a casual visit to St Peter's. It only becomes evident, like the way in which the Way of the Cross defines the spatial rhythm of

33 See MacCulloch, Diarmaid, *A History of Christianity: The First Three Thousand Years*, London: Penguin, 2010. For a general recent discussion of the relationships between theology and church architecture in traditional and modern settings, see Seasoltz, R Kevin, *A Sense of the Sacred: Theological Foundations of Christian Architecture and Art*, New York: Continuum, 2005.

Right: Sigurd Lewerentz, section east-west through St Peter's, Klippan, last revision, 14 June 1965. From the Swedish Centre for Architecture and Design's collections.

Below: Sigurd Lewerentz, section south-north looking towards the internal elevation of the west facade, last revision 4 October 1965. From the Swedish Centre for Architecture and Design's collections.

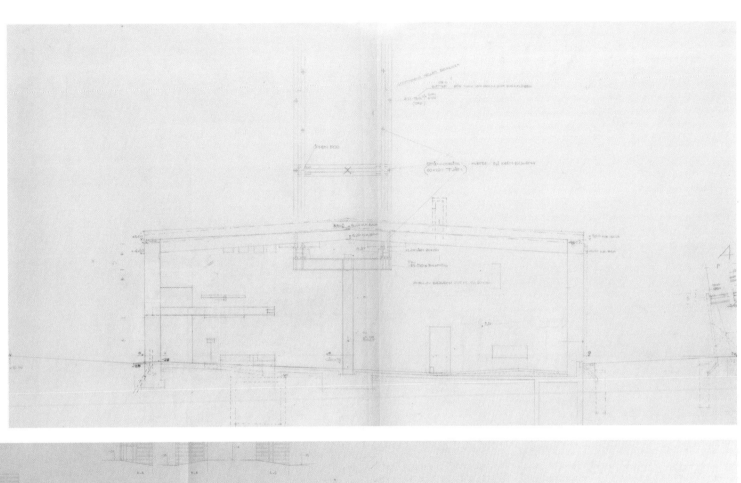

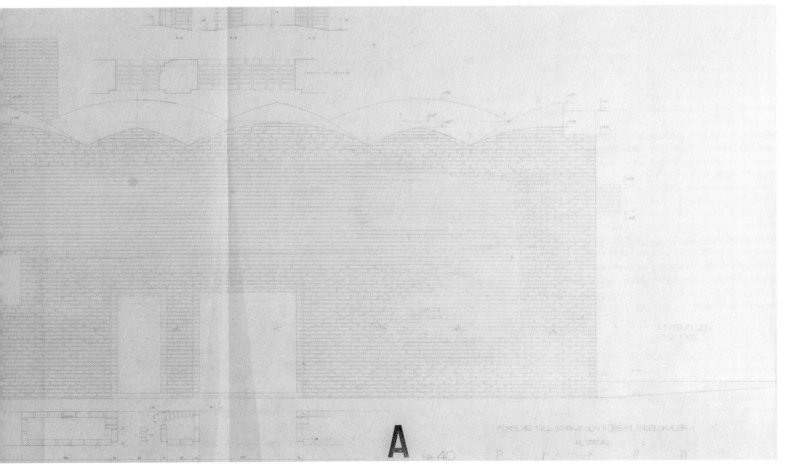

Detail of staining from the copper roof
on the west facade.

the nave, via participation.[34] Over time, as one adjusts
to the extreme shadows, it becomes evident that a
number of things are placed directly onto the brick
surfaces of the church. Metal numbers on the walls
announce the hymns.

At the font, a brick cross is inlaid in the floor to
describe the position of the initiating priest, making
the sacrificial nature of Christian baptism evident.
As the material details of the church become clear, a
number of situations are revealed. These situations
accommodate the sacramental and non-sacramental
rites recognised by Lutherans. In order of appearance
they are Marriage, Baptism, Eucharistic Communion
and Confirmation (the *Cathedra* is evidence of the latter).

Whilst there are no "pictures" in the building, there
are in fact a number of very memorable spatial images.
A very large table, a cross on a hill, a river cut into this,
a cave whose door is opened; Golgotha, Calvary, Jordan
and the Holy Sepulchre are evoked and elide to bring
the Holy Land into close resonance with the church and
with the town of Klippan. As in the churches of Rudolf
Schwarz, the Last Supper, the Crucifixion, Christ's

Baptism and the Resurrection appear at once; Maundy
Thursday and Good Friday appear together.[35]

The Christological aspects of the Mass are set out
in a series of sacramental settings that allude to the
actual and poetic landscape of a universal church,
situated in a continuum of places and in a continuum
of events.

Arguably, all Christian churches are recreated
images of Golgotha, Calvary etc. At Klippan the
referential and androgical character of the spatial
situation is articulated as architecture, sculpture and
ground. The garden and pool beyond are approached
from an intense experience of darkness. The resultant
disorientation is confusing, physically shocking and
intellectually shocking. In inferring and evoking some
sort of space beyond comprehension, an allusion is made
to the Edenic paradise of a monastic *hortus conclusis*.

An imageless image appears, making doubly
present the rhythm of clouds and sunlight. The natural
conditions of the site are brought to appearance with
phenomenal intensity, and at the same time images of
early Christian cloisters echo around the site. What is

34 We know from Lewerentz's drawings
of the cemeteries, and from
Ridderstedt's account of the design
of St Peter's, that these traditional
religious spatial typologies were
central motifs in his architecture.

35 See Kieckhefer, Richard, *Theology
in Stone: Church Architecture from
Byzantium to Berkeley*, Oxford: Oxford
University Press, 2008, p 238.

Patrick Lynch, sketch of the Christological
and Apophatic aspects of St Peter, ie
rhythm of situations (Christ as man) and
rhythm of armature (God as light).

Patrick Lynch, sketch plan of St Peter's
indicating orientation of spatial types.

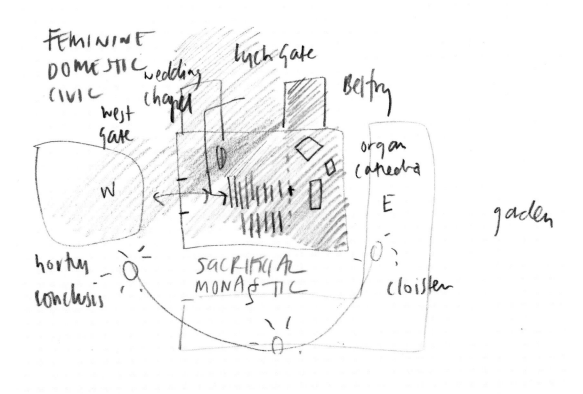

View of St Peter's, Klippan, looking
towards the altar just before the
beginning of *Mässe*. Note that from a
child's height one sees a cross on a hill.

revealed in the pond is the central tenet of Christian belief—that heaven and earth were reunited when God became man.

Whilst the Reformation of the church led to the removal and mistrust of images, in Luther's Catechism Christ's demand to the apostles at the Last Supper to "do this in remembrance of me" meant exactly that.[36] Luther insisted that participants witness the Mass as if they were seeing it for the first time, and thus the use or "*usus*" of bread and wine and a table should be exactly that. However, Luther was emphatic that the act of communion should remind communicants that the "*actio*" that they are witnessing is a representation of something.[37] Fully incarnate and also embodying an image of an event, the Mass needed no other mysteries, no relics, no painted images, no candles for the dead. For Luther, Mass was a sacred theatre. The priest and congregation re-enacted the Last Supper and the Crucifixion and the Resurrection. At St Peter's a tapestry hangs from the ceiling intensifying the

atmosphere of "Eucharistic Sacrifice". Lewerentz has achieved a powerful—almost Baroque—synthesis of the arts, creating a syncretic moment in which art and architecture combine to articulate each other. At St Peter's, abstract art is reconciled with use. The rhythm of the liturgy, and the time it takes one's eyes to adjust to the gloom, synchronise one's movements within an orchestrated experience of art and architecture—one united to reveal the dramatic temporality of worship as re-enactment.

Lewerentz and Ridderstedt added allusions to the universal, ie Catholic nature of the church of St Peter, placing a *Cathedra* into a Swedish Lutheran Church "for the first time since the Reformation", Ridderstedt claims.[38] In this way, a continuum of historic time is suggested in a shockingly subtle image. The floor of the church appears to be crimped and to fold up the eastern wall to form the *Cathedra* and the clergy bench. This mirrors the mound of earth outside that hides St Peter's from the crossroads, creating an intense

36   *Handbook for the Proper Evangelical Mass*, Malmö, 1539; echoed in the twentieth century in another conservative Lutheran handbook *The Proper Communion Vestments*, "De rette Messeklaeder", 1924.

37   Luther, Martin, *The Large Catechism*, F Bente and WHT Dau trans, Pennsylvania: Pennsylvania State University's Electronic Classics 2005: "However, it is not enough for them to comprehend and recite these parts according to the words only, but the young people should also be made to attend the preaching, especially during the time which is devoted to the Catechism, that they may hear it explained and may learn to understand what every part contains, so as to be able to recite it as they have heard it, and, when asked, may give a correct answer, so that the preaching may not be without profit and fruit. For the reason why we exercise such diligence in preaching the Catechism so often is that it may be inculcated on our youth, not in a high and subtle manner, but briefly and with the greatest simplicity, so as to enter the mind readily and be fixed in the memory. Therefore we shall now take up the above mentioned articles one by one and in the plainest manner possible say about them as much as is necessary." (p 11)

38   Ridderstedt, *Adversus Populum*.

Left: View of the altar at St Peter's,
Klippan after *Mässe*.

Right: The organ sitting unaligned with
the brick ground but aligned with the
diagonal of the square plan of the church,
angled to catch the sunlight entering the
chapel from the south at noon.

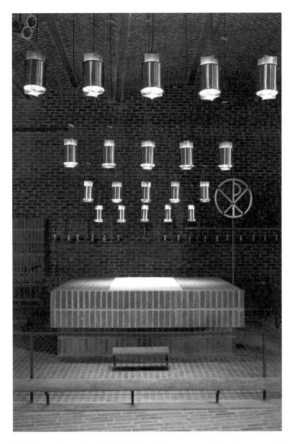
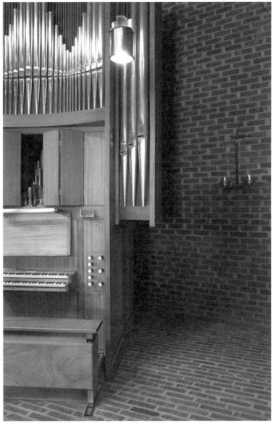

Left: Hymn books at St Peter's, Klippan,
after *Mässe*.

Right: View of interior looking south.

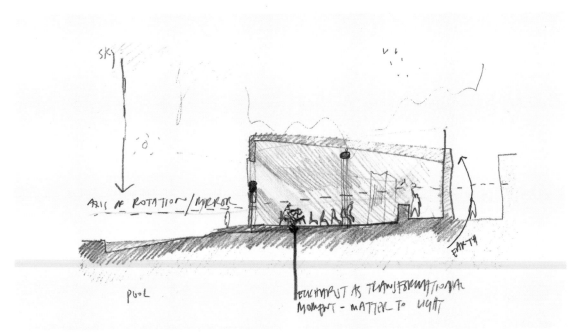

Patrick Lynch, sketch section west-east showing iconographic spatial relationships between the pond and the ceiling of St Peter's, Klippan, oriented around the horizon of sight at the altar.

Left: Column-beam connections.

Right: View of brickwork wall and floor.

View of interior looking west with the west gate open after *Mässe*.

Patrick Lynch, sketch of St Peter's, Klippan, showing the spatial settings of the sacraments as a series of types.

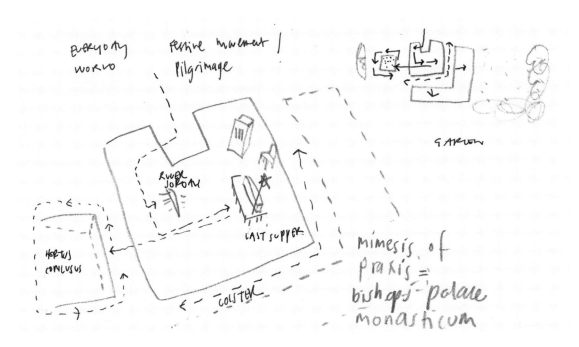

39 See Sedlmayr, Hans, "Zur Charakteristik des Rokoko", *Manierismo, Barocco, Rococo*, Rome, 1962. See also Miller, Naomi, *Heavenly Caves: Reflections on the Garden Grotto*, London: Allen & Unwin, 1982. Jose de Paiva notes: "The connection of Mary and [water and specifically] the sea has, in a sense, always been there, though of course historically it is entirely based on wordplay. We see this throughout the Middle Ages in the Latin play between the word *mare, -is,* and in the plural *maria* (literally 'seas') and *Maria*. The connection to water is there too in Medieval iconography either relating to Mary, or the baptism of Christ. This develops with the multiplication of Medieval pilgrimages to Marian shrines—finally coming to identify the pilgrim himself with the shell, under the protection of Mary. In the fifteenth century, this takes a turn with the maritime expansion, under the patronage of Henry the Navigator; and by 1500 we are dealing with churches like Santa Maria de Belém, the foundation of which is availed by the Papal *bula inter cætera*, and built for mariners as they arrived in Lisbon from the expeditions to the indies. The aim of the sea expansion was made explicit in the sails bearing the cross of the Order of Christ, and could be described as religious, political and commercial. In the *Lusíadas*, a Renaissance epic poem published in 1572, Camões describes it as "the expansion of the empire and the faith'. In line with Franciscan interpretation, the expansion was now seen as leading potentially to a fifth empire, in this case a Christian one, following the empires of Antiquity." Email to the author, 8 March 2014.

40 Leatherbarrow, David, "The Sacrifice of Space", *Common Ground: A Critical Reader*, David Chipperfield, Kieran Long and Shumi Bose eds, 13th International Architecture Exhibition, La Biennale di Venezia: Marsilio, 2012, p 12.

41 Appia, Adolphe, *Texts on Theatre*, Richard C Beacham ed, London: Routledge, 1993, p 74.

juxtaposition between the church and the town—a landscape of thresholds is articulated between them. The centre line about which the mirroring of mound and bench occurs is the west gate.

Similarly, the transformational moment of the Eucharistic sacrifice occurs at noon. At this point in the Mass sunlight floods the raised Host, and the huge, dark steel cross is revealed as the centre of the church. At this moment the brick floor appears to mirror the sky, and both are held together and apart by the steel crucifix. Immediately after this the west gate opens, flooding the space beyond with daylight. As one's eyes adjust to this sudden convulsion the pond reflects the sky. It is not otherwise visible from the interior. Mirrored planes exist about the vertical axis of the west gate and about the horizon of the raised Eucharist, situating the church in relation to the town and to the sky.

Implicit in the geometric order is the central importance of the Crucifixion to Christian worship, around which the movement of the worshippers literally revolves. Nick Temple's plan drawing demonstrates that the steel cross sits at the centre of the plan form, central both to the chapel and also to the church complex (see p 129). The quartering of the space into distinct territories recalls a traditional Greek cross church plan. In both cases one cannot easily sense the spatial type, and at St Peter's one cannot actually see the centre of the space, nor in fact occupy it. However, it is possible to come very close to the centre at the moment when the Crucifixion is celebrated at the Eucharist.

The baptismal font takes the place of the traditional site of a statue of the Virgin on the gospel side of the altar. A conch shell is of course a symbol for Venus and also for the Virgin Mary in Renaissance paintings, and this symbolism is of central importance for Marian worship and for Rococo architecture generally.[39] Whilst Mary is absent as a statue at St Peter's, she is present in

spatial and temporal terms—in the image of a pregnant mound, and in the wedding chapel, and in the baptism of children.

To the liturgy side of the church high windows block the sound and sight of "youths on motorbikes", Ridderstedt claims. On this side, light also fills the space at noon, transforming what cannot be seen into something whose effects can be. The absolutely mundane yet situational aspects of the architecture transform the space from dumb brickwork to a participatory communicative realm (what Schwarz and Ridderstedt both call "*commonitas*").

At St Peter's the visible and invisible swell and recede in the focus of the mind's eye. Metaphors and situated events coalesce and dissolve into actual useful things, and everyday events take on significance. This "ontological movement" is achieved within an atmosphere of silence and darkness. In *Architecture Oriented Otherwise,* David Leatherbarrow suggests that:

> Perhaps the greatest challenge for designers is to work through the non-expressivity required for this sort of dialogue; the communication I have in mind arises instead out of a tacit form of presence. Articulation in architecture presupposes reticent receptivity, the silence that architects such as Loos, Le Corbusier, Kahn, Peter Zumthor and Ando have recommended in their writings and cultivated in their projects.[40]

Perhaps it is exactly this quality of potential that enables Lewerentz's building to articulate something that cannot be approached directly? Appia called this quality "expectancy", and a profoundly communicative architectural imagination is present at St Peter's".[41] This was formed, I suggest, not only by the Reformation, or by the High Church Movement in Sweden, or by the

Sandro Botticelli, *The Birth of Venus*, 1486.

View of the font at St Peter's, Klippan,
from the priests' side.

Left: View of the font at St Peter's,
Klippan.

Right: The font from the east side.

42 Marion, Jean-Luc, *The Idol and
Distance: Five Studies*, New York:
Fordham University Press, 2001, p 78.
As many commentators have noted,
Nietzsche's direct philosophical
confrontation between man and
God led indirectly, largely through
misunderstanding, to the rise of
fascism, which was typified also by a
lack of distance between life and myth.

architect's devout Christianity, but also in Lewerentz's acknowledgement of the conditions of modernity. Lewerentz's cemeteries are "new types", I suggest, in a similar way that Rykwert describes Borromini's Oratory. Lewerentz's imagination is also oriented towards *decorum,* and the rhythmic orders of time and geometry in his work reveal the natural conditions that lie beneath the appearance of modern urbanity.

I would like to suggest that it is also a response to the twentieth-century condition generally, an architecture that acknowledges a certain distance from tradition, and also distance from the assumption that transcendence occurs directly via representation. Lewerentz grew up in a period that witnessed two world wars and one in which Nietzsche had claimed the "withdrawal of God" (in *Will to Power* and *The Twilight of the Gods* etc). Jean-Luc Marion believes that "Nietzsche transgressed the idolatrous relation to the divine" by coming "face to face with something finally living within the divine", and that this led to his descent into madness, "the plunge into darkness". This "patent contradiction" is explained by the fact that in *Man and Superman*, *Antichrist* and *Beyond Good and Evil*:

> Nietzsche believed himself to be advancing beyond or in the place of the idols, in order there to play a metaphysical role. But, as if sucked in through the idols as far as the divine itself, he there succumbed. Dionysus touched him. This is

perhaps because, without distance, a distinction can be made between the idols and God no more than the relation to the divine can be supported. Only the infinite separation of distance ensures one of subsisting within the infinite proximity of God. Conceptually idolatrous, too removed from the divine—too close, personally experienced with the divine: a double missing, lacking of distance, which brings together and separates at once, which in a word keeps the divine and man at a good distance—a distance of Goodness. Perhaps this is what Nietzsche teaches, at bottom, that is most precious.[42]

This distance, or "silence" enables the "at hand" aspects of St Peter's to "remain ready at hand", as Heidegger puts it, without becoming things that we can easily "pass-over" or consume, aesthetically or otherwise. They transcend consumption and resist appropriation, opening up a space for participation. Things in the world coexist for us along with relational associations in the same way that stories and myths and beliefs resist direct assimilation, and, as Alberti saw it, are aspects of the rhythmic transformation of natural conditions. Reality is not made up of distinct objects for humans, but is experienced by us via involvement and interest, and in participation. In the same way, classical and Christian cultures form a "cumulative, paradoxical and inaugural

Nick Temple, plan drawing of St Peter's, Klippan, showing the geometrical relationship between the chapel and the community centre complex as a square within a square with the steel column in the centre of the chapel.

1. Church entrance
2. Narthex/Wedding Chapel
3. Sacristy
4. Nave
5. Baptismal Font
6. Central X Column
7. Altar
8. Cathedra
9. Organ
10. "West gate"/Exit
11. "Cloister"
12. Parochial Centre
13. Stairs down to crèche

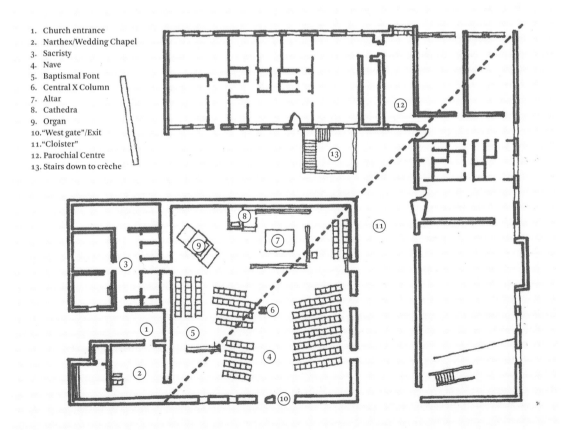

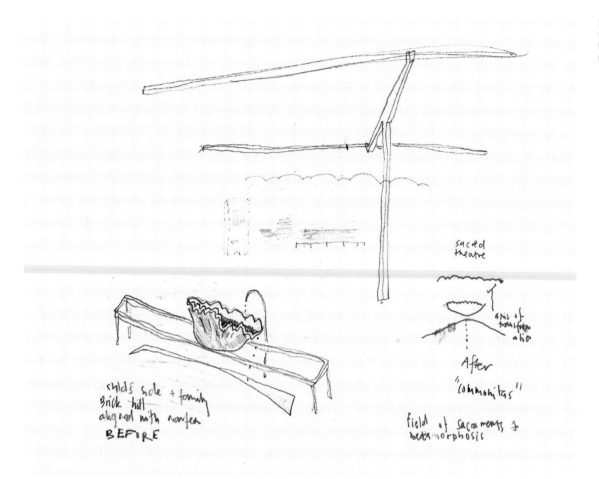

Patrick Lynch, sketch showing the relationships between the roof and the font as paradigmatic representations of sacramental territories.

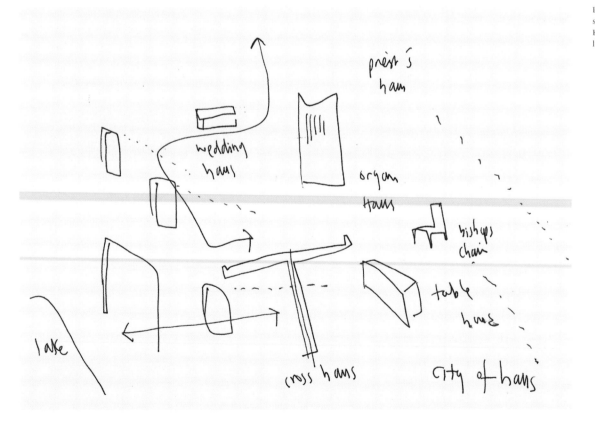

Patrick Lynch, sketch view of the various situations encountered at St Peter's, Klippan, seen as a series of aedicules or little houses.

A Cross on a Hill (baptism is death and renewal, initiation into eternal life, attained through death).

43 Marion, *The Idol and Distance*, p 213.

44 Merleau-Ponty, Maurice, *The Phenomenology of Perception*, London: Routledge, 2013, p 291; see also Vesely, Dalibor, "Architecture, Simulation and Reality", *Scroope: Cambridge Architecture Journal*, no 5, 1993/1994, pp 26–28.

45 Merleau-Ponty, *The Phenomenology of Perception*, p 265.

46 Short informal interview over coffee after Mass, 26 February 2012.

47 Arguably, the pastor has attempted to alleviate this condition in ways that are blasphemous from both a Lutheran and from an architectural point of view! For example, Luther believed that prayers for the dead were wrong, as doing so implied the possibility of human intervention beyond the limit of the temporal realm. This is why you do not find candles lit for the dead in Protestant churches, although it has recently become also fashionable in Anglican cathedrals to do so.

heritage for Heidegger", Marion claims—"the fraternity of Christ with Hercules and Dionysus" that he (and Hölderlin) both "understood".[43] St Peter's is a dark background presence inviting imaginative use. Whilst the equipment in the chapel and the rhythms of use and action there "de-severs" distance, its powerful spatial presence maintains a distance between ritual and everyday life, reminding us of Merleau-Ponty's assertion that "what protects the sane man against delirium or hallucination, is not his critical powers, but the structure of his space".[44] Whilst it might be tempting to describe spatial qualities in terms of complexity or simplicity, these aesthetic criteria fail to reveal the relational character of spatial situations. Leatherbarrow is adamant that "talk of space will always be distracting if it is seen as a neutral or homogenous field in which independently conceived objects are placed". Rather, "space", he insists, "must, instead, be seen as a field of variations".[45] The referential field of variations at St Peter's is topological (geometric) and topographical (both rhetorical and material), and somewhat shadowy, thick and mysterious.

The current pastor thinks that the chapel is "too dark" in fact, and he believes that "it does not welcome you".[46] Presumably in an attempt to make the church less "dark", he has recently installed supplementary lighting. A black plastic spotlight has been attached to the column, illuminating the candles.[47] I attended the confirmation of the children of the parish. The priest preached with a PowerPoint presentation projected onto a plastic screen fixed above an empty *Cathedra*. No one processed with the cross of St Peter. A piano was used rather than the organ.

Perhaps the pastor's claim that the chapel is "too dark" is correct; perhaps it is too much like a force of nature to be reassuring, or simply enlightening. It is a national monument and cannot be harmed too much by changes in the fashion of worship, or by brief appearances of new technologies. Whilst it is the fate of churches today to be venerated mainly as the settings for artworks—nonetheless they remain a horizon of sorts. All of the equipment necessary for the traditional life of a parish are in place in Klippan. St Peter's resists; silent, waiting, open like a book, or like a stage anticipating action.

Patrick Lynch, sketch of St Peter's,
Klippan, looking towards the west gate
just after *Mässe*.

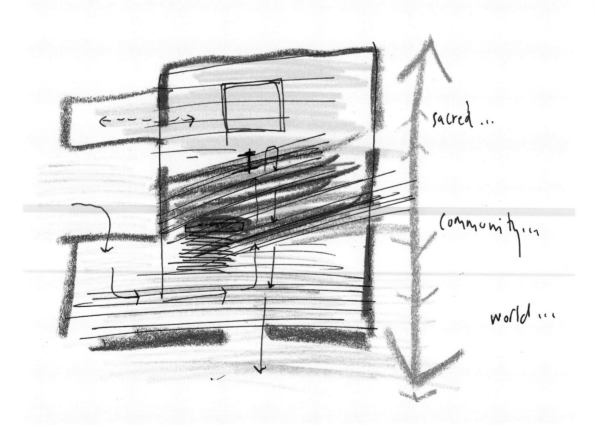

Patrick Lynch, sketch of St Peter's,
Klippan, looking towards the west gate
just after *Mässe*.

Patrick Lynch, sketch showing the relationship between the material and immaterial aspects of St Peter's as experienced in the "ontological movement" of a worshipper's experience of *Mässe*.

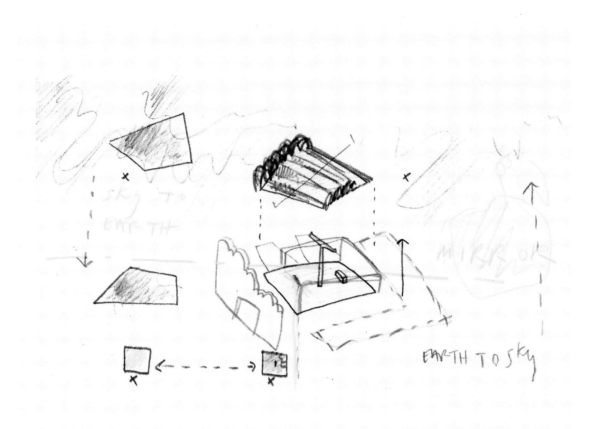

Patrick Lynch, sketch section through St Peter's, Klippan, from east to west.

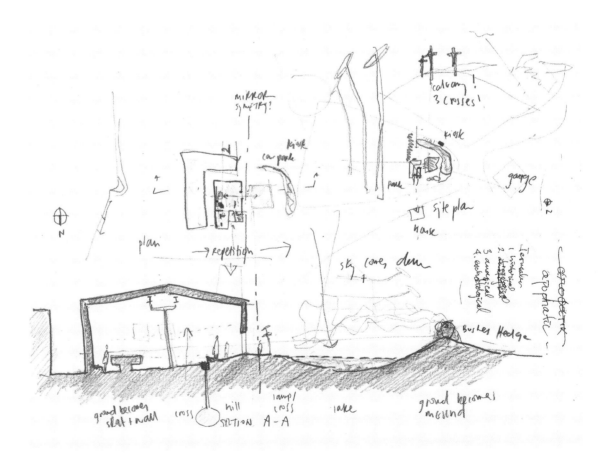

Patrick Lynch, sketch showing the relationships between the rocks of St Peter's, Klippan, and water.

sculpture = Rock with hole
architecture = cave with holes

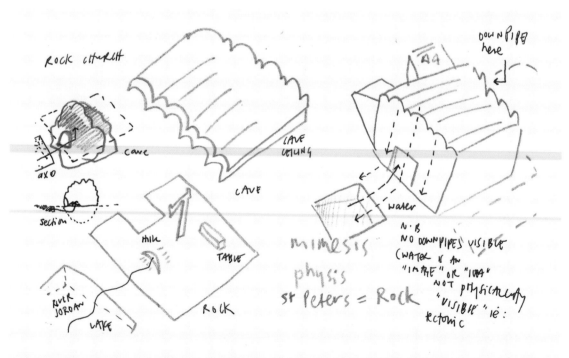

Patrick Lynch, sketch showing the symbolic role that water plays at St Peter's, Klippan.

Patrick Lynch, sketch showing the
relationships between the roof and the
pond as paradigmatic representations
of celestial realms.

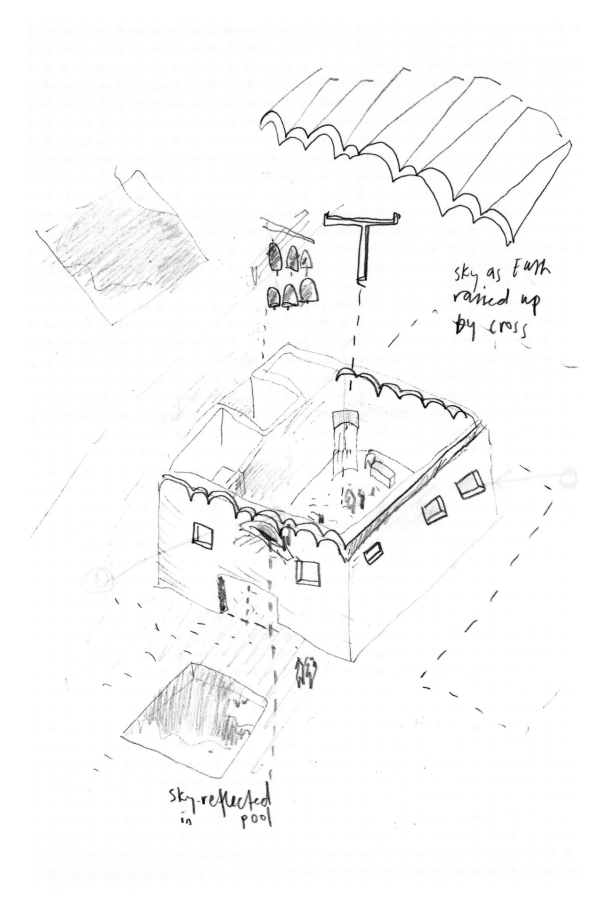

sky as Earth
raised up
by cross

sky-reflected
in pool

Left: View looking west of the "Sacrifice" side of the tapestry designed by Sven Erixson and woven by Barbro Nilsson for St Peter's, Klippan.

Right: View looking east of the "Redemption" side of the tapestry designed by Sven Erixson and woven by Barbro Nilsson for St Peter's, Klippan.

View of vaulted ceiling and steel structural beams with central "Cruciform" column.

Left: Windows from the inside looking out.

Right: View after *Mässe* of the pastor and congregation leaving via the west gate.

Left: Sigurd Lewerentz, photographs of an Italian journey, 1909.

Right: Christian Berg, *The Bowls of Grace*, 1963: "The turned up bowl: we receive God's Grace. The turned down bowl: we give people what we have received from God."

48 Vesely, Dalibor, *Architecture in the Age of Divided Representation: The Question of Creativity in the Shadow of Production*, Cambridge, MA: MIT Press, 2004, p 58.

49 Carl, Peter, "City-image versus Topography of Praxis", *Cambridge Archaeology Journal*, October 2000, p 328.

50 Ridderstedt, *Adversus Populum*.

Perhaps the best way to describe the church is as a heuristic landscape. Its landscape of images is a catechistic device, a theatre of memory, a Sunday school made flesh. It has something in common with the primitive qualities of a child's drawing. Lewerentz seems to have been aware of the profoundly image-like character of memories.

Lewerentz's photographs of Italy, made at the end of the second decade of the twentieth century, reveal that he composed spatial images as fragments.

St Peter's, Klippan, carries the emotional violence of dream-like fragments into the waking world, reclaiming for it—in the fecundity of images—the profound power of situations. It situates what we might call the positive aspects of Vesely's fragments, what he calls "the reciprocity of the actual and the possible".[48] The sculptures at Klippan transcend formalistic and subjective readings of them, and distinctions between use and meaning seem specious.

St Peter's exemplifies Peter Carl's assertion instead that "there is no such thing as an absence of content, no gap between the practical and the symbolic, only progressively more explicit modes of symbolic representation".[49]

In Lewerentz's work, *pathos* is leavened by wit, and St Peter's is a *Spielraum* for the serious games of religion and art.

Ridderstedt claims:

That the name of the church became St Petri depends of course on the allusion to the name of the town and the connection to Jesus" words in Matt 16:18 : "And I tell you that you are Petrus, the cliff (rock), and on this cliff I will build my church."[50]

Klippan means "the cliff" (or the rock), Ridderstedt reminds us, and not only does the church appear as a cave, but also the naming of the church and the town is inscribed in the most rhythmic parts of the building.

Ridderstedt takes delight in telling us about the process of naming the bells:

By tradition, church bells were usually provided with a text stating when and by whom the bell had been cast as well as providing information about the current acting bishop, priests, etc. A hymn often complemented this list. In Klippan, Pastor Gustafsson made contact with Poet Bo Setterlind, who early on had taken an interest in this particular poetry art form. In an undated letter (probably written in spring-winter 1966) Setterlind thanks Gustafsson for "the study material about the church and its architect! Very rewarding. I found quite soon, that there existed a friendship, not unsubstantial, between the architect and the poet, also professionally—we are both romantics", Setterlind writes. In a letter dated 19 April 1966, he proposes that the church bells would be named after the apostles Petrus, Andreas, Paulus and Tomas, "the largest to the smallest". It is hardly surprising from a theological point that the big bell was named Petrus, but Setterlind gives the

View of the west facade of St Peter's,
Klippan, reflected in the pond in summer.

View out of the west gate towards the
pond in summer.

Overleaf: Views of the interior of
St Peter's, Klippan.

Left: View up into the belfry at
St Peter's, Klippan.

Right: Setterlind's "bell-poems" texts, cast
in a bronze plaque mounted across from
the entrance to the church.

View of the three "crucifixion lights",
Mount Calvary/Klippan.

51 Ridderstedt, *Adversus Populum*.

52 Vesely, *Architecture in the Age of
    Divided Representation*, p 84.

53 As in Heidegger's image from Goethe,
    cited at the conclusion Heidegger,
    Martin, "Art and Space", *The Heidegger
    Reader*, Günter Figal ed, Charles H
    Seibert trans, Bloomington: Indiana
    University Press, 2007, p 8.

apostle's name a local connection: EVERYTHING
EARTHLY ESCAPES—ITS GLORY DISAPPEARS—
BUT THE LORDS CLIFF STANDS—FOREVER.[51]

At St Peter's the topography of Klippan is brought
into the church and blessed and named. Lewerentz
commingles the River Jordan and the Klippan river,
united in a common image. Thus the stories associated
with St Peter act as topic, common ground, or
rhetorical *topos*, onto which various meanings can
be set in play in order to refound the town of Klippan
as a legitimate place oriented within a deep context
of history and geography. Lewerentz managed to
retrospectively insert the church into the history of
the foundation of the town, placing it into the centre
of the town like a ruin, a ruined cathedral complex,
a *cloistered monasticum* or even a renovated one.

In this audacious act, the town is recuperated,
brought back to consciousness after its premature
birth as an accidental consequence of technology.
The town and the park are re-presented in the
mirroring windows of the church and community
centre. It appears as if the sky comes to earth when
it is reflected in the pond, suggesting that "it is in the
dialectics of imagination and its hidden content that
our vision becomes an on-going and inexhaustible
process", revealing, as in a "mirror, the hidden content
of pre-reflective reality".[52] When the bells ring out, and
the sky is reflected in the pond, the world is converted
into pure rhythm, fulfilling Heidegger's description in
"Art and Space", of art's role in "evoking harmony".[53]

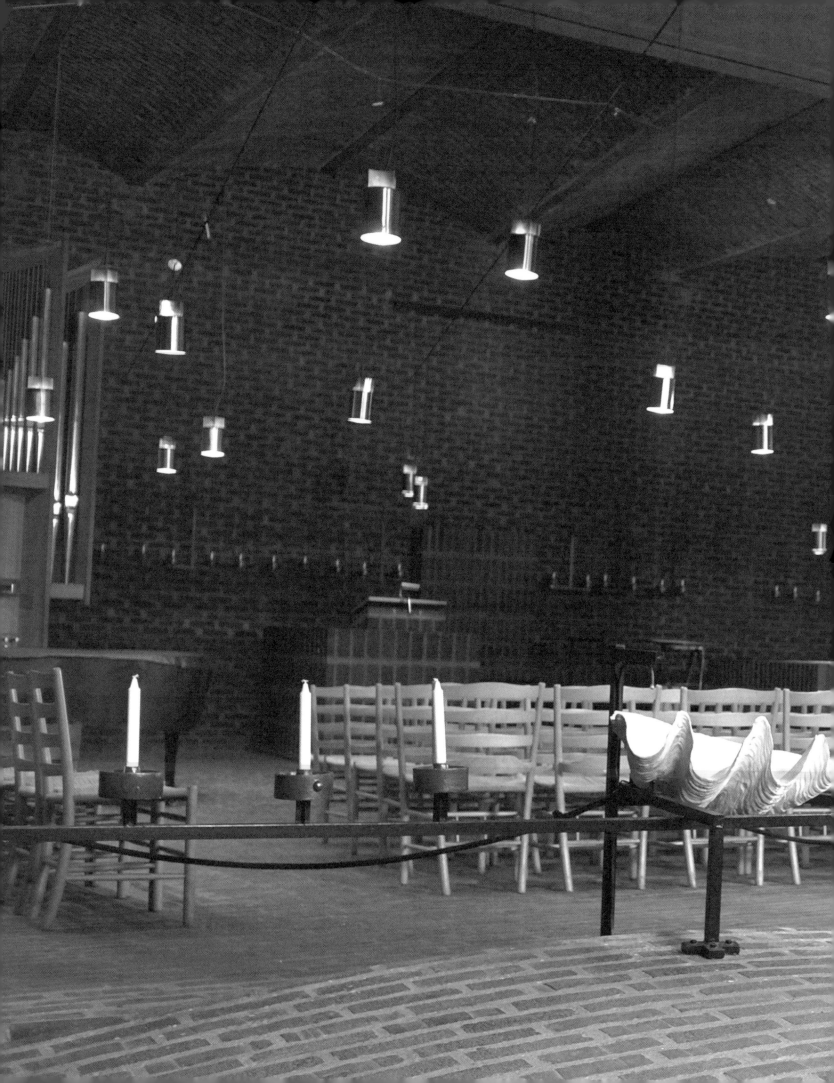

Álvaro Siza and Santa Maria at Marco de Canaveses

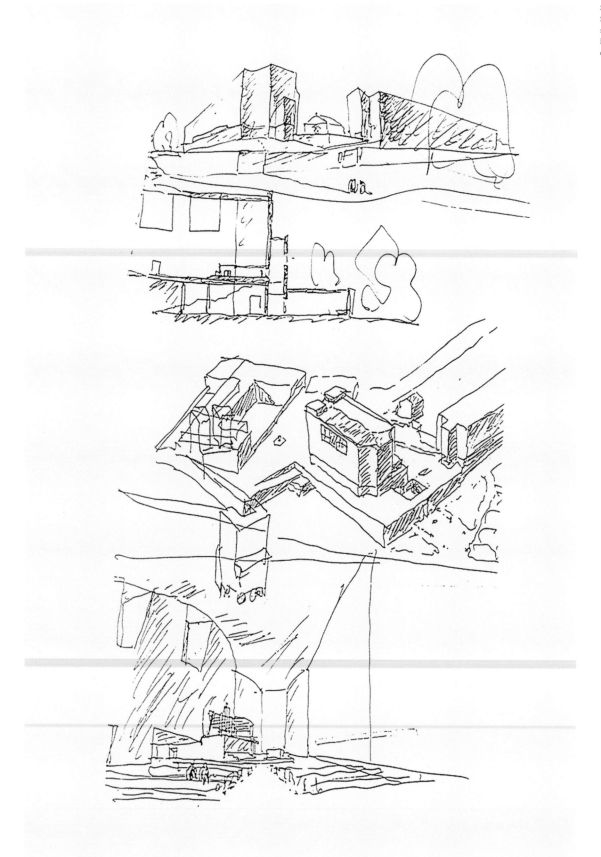

Sketches of Santa Maria by Álvaro
Siza showing the architect thinking
simultaneously about the role of the
horizon and topography in the design
of the church and parochial centre, 1990.

Top left: Site plan.

Top right: Upper level plan (nave).

Below: Section west-cast.

1   Higino, Nuno, *Garden and Mortuary: Church of Saint Mary: Álvaro Siza Vieira*, Cenateca, 2001, p 44. Higino was a priest, is now an academic, and was Siza's client for the church.

2   Bauer, Hermann, *Barock: Kunst einer Epoche*, Berlin: Dietrich Reimer Verlag, 1992, p 9. Bauer writes: "*Der Ausdruck kommt nach einigen vom portugiesischen barocco (rohe, ungleich geformte Perle)*". For a discussion on the role of rhetoric in Baroque style, see Lynch, Patrick, *The Theatricality of the Baroque City*, Saarbrücken: Verlag Dr Müller, 2011. This text was originally my Master of Philosophy dissertation in the History and Philosophy of Architecture, Cambridge University, 1996. José de Paiva suggests that the first mention of baroque is indeed in relation to pearls: "*Tudo pode ser verdade porque ho aljofare que de cà vai, e as perolas he groso, e redondo, e em toda perfeiçam, e o que della vem das indias sam huns barrocos mal afeiçoados, e não redondos, com agoas mortas*", Orta, Garcia de, "Da Margarita", *Coloquios dos simples*, Goa: Ioannes de endem, 1563, colloquy *35*, fol 139v.

3   José de Paiva notes: "The connection of Mary and the sea has, in sense, always been there, though of course historically it is entirely based on wordplay. We see this throughout the Middle Ages in the Latin play between the word *mare, -is*, and in the pl. *maria* (lit. 'seas') and *Maria*. The connection to water is there too in medieval iconography either relating to Mary, or the baptism of Christ. This develops with the multiplication of Medieval pilgrimages to Marian shrines—finally coming to identify the pilgrim himself with the shell, under the protection of Mary. In the fifteenth century, this takes a turn with the maritime expansion under the patronage of Henry the Navigator, and by 1500 we are dealing with churches like *Santa Maria de Belém*, the foundation of which is availed by the Papal *Bula inter cœtera*, and built for mariners as they arrived in Lisbon from the expeditions to the indies. The aim of the sea expansion was made explicit in the sails bearing the cross of the Order of Christ, and could be described as religious, political and commercial. In the *Lusíadas*, a Renaissance epic poem published in 1572, Camões describes it as 'the expansion of the empire and the faith'. In line with Franciscan interpretation, the expansion was now seen as leading potentially to a fifth empire, in this case a Christian one, following the empires of Antiquity", email to the author, 8 March 2014.

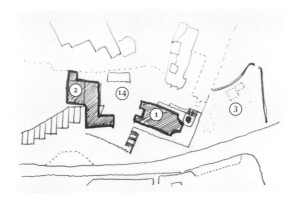

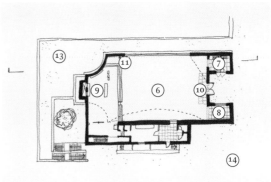

1. Church
2. Parochial Centre
3. Old farmyard
4. Courtyard
5. Crypt
6. Nave
7. Belfry
8. Baptistry
9. Presbytery
10. Narthex
11. Statue of the Virgin
12. Organ shelf
13. Plinth
14. Public square

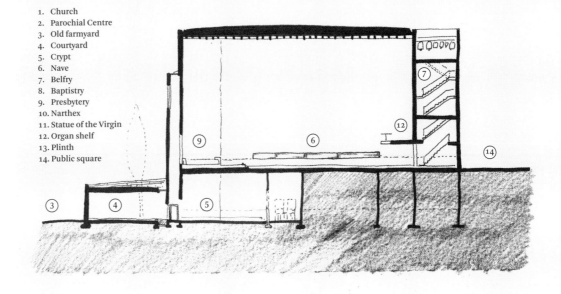

At Marco de Canaveses, 40 km east of Porto, Álvaro Siza's church of Santa Maria (1997) sits within the garden of an old farm, beside an ancient chapel. The farm's spring feeds a fountain that fills the courtyard beside the crypt with the loud crash of water, and the violent disruption of broken splashes of light.[1] A cypress tree sits forlornly in the lower courtyard, around which steps rise, creating an informal route up to the church above. The lower ground floor crypt-story is faced in granite and seems to grow out of the topography of the site, fusing the farmyard walls into a rocky plinth.

Santa Maria, Marco de Canaveses, Álvaro Siza, model by the architect.

From outside, the eastern end of the church is defined by two concave curves. From the inside these compress the view towards the presbytery, focusing one's attention upon the tabernacle; they act as a form of natural perspective whilst also recalling the baroque churches that originated in seventeenth-century Portugal. Baroque, of course, is a derivation of the Portuguese term *barocco*, originally used to describe a misshapen or deformed pearl.[2]

The crypt sits within the battered granite base. It is lit from above with a pale steady light, and from without by the rhythmic oscillation of a broken column of water. The crypt is subtly reminiscent of a Rococo chapel—a sophisticated cave—and the role that water plays is surely not accidental, recalling as it does the tradition of Marian chapels in Portuguese Baroque architecture,[3] and their fusion of Christian and pagan symbolism with Neo-Platonic Humanism. Principally, the Virgin Mary is associated in Baroque culture with the sea (*maria-mares*), with sea caves and with grottos.

Maria is typically depicted in "rocky" chapels as if she is (pearly) light, falling onto and emerging from a grotto. She is symbolic in Renaissance painting of

Left: François Boucher, *The Triumph of Venus*, 1740.

Right: View of the interior of Santa Maria de Belém.

4   See Sedlmayr, Hans, "Zur Charakteristik des Rokoko", *Manierismo, Barocco, Rococo*, Rome, 1962. See also Miller, Naomi, *Heavenly Caves: Reflections on the Garden Grotto*, London: Allen & Unwin, 1982.

divinity, and of the fecundity of the natural world.[4] The elision of light and water is evocative in Marian symbolism of both the sea (*mares-marias*), baptism and the church itself. Each individual baroque church is seen—both literally and figuratively—as a protective (oyster) shell. Pilgrimage and refuge also typify Marian devotion, as well as the simultaneity of death (crucifixion) and life (baptism). These extreme contrasts typify the material and spatial hierarchies of Baroque décor; they are fused into highly theatrical images of the ground and the sky—painted, plastered and carved spatial thresholds mediated by the rhythmic movements of pilgrims, and by the musical devotions of worship. This dramatic spatiality resonates in the material iconography of death-earth-darkness, and in the counterpoint of life-water-light; its recuperation in modern architecture is particularly clear in Siza's church at Marco de Canaveses.

A change in level situates the entrance to the church on the crest of a hill, one story above a garden and the crypt. This difference is articulated also in the contrast between the white stucco render on the outer and inner faces of the nave, as well as in the contrast between the rough exterior walls and the smooth, slick light of the interiors, which are predominantly lit from above. Visitors find themselves precisely situated between a lambent ceiling and a rocky ground.

The church is accompanied by a two-story parochial centre that sits facing the west doors of the church, forming a series of deep thresholds between the dusty piazza and the variously scaled rooms within. Discrete spatial volumes and definite, more or less specific situations are established in shadows and niches; territories are implied by kinks in the walls, variations in the borders of horizons and a stepped internal ground plane.

Freedom of movement between the buildings continues within the anterooms of the parish centre, which are generally freely accessible when the centre is open in the summer months. The co-existence of defined spaces is at once clear and also intimated and sensed, rather than absolute. A double-height meeting room is announced by changes to the

height of the marble skirting boards, which rise to become wainscoting. Doors rise up and step back from the common parts of the plan, away from the staccato rhythm and movement implied by the staircase. The desert-like piazza is common ground, and the beat of a football often marks time on weekday afternoons.

The tall oak doors of the church are opened at funerals, enabling the western afternoon sunlight to reach in and touch the altar. Inside, the church is cool, the nave a simple rectangle. A baptismal font sits to the left of the west gate, beneath a tall roof light. This massive shaft situates the font beneath a tower of air and light. Similarly, a bell tower sits on the other side of the tall entrance, forming a seemingly solid shaft of space that echoes and inverts the baptistry. Above head height in the nave, the north wall billows outwards like a broken pearl, cut by two clerestory windows.

One is struck by the extreme contrast between the abstract material qualities of the space and the figural material qualities of the equipment within it. At two places this contrast comes together to provoke movement of thought from contemplation towards comprehension, resonating without ever fully resolving itself into an image. Reflective, polished oak floorboards direct one's eyes towards the sacristy. Oak chairs sit on this oak ground like coiled, reclining figures.

A tall processional bronze cross sits on the northern Gospel side to the left of the altar, and a *Cathedra,* or bishop's chair, sits to the right. There is a strong contrast between intricate timber furniture and the scale-less, waxy light of the upper curved surfaces, so that the latter dissolve into shadowy and cloudy peripheral focus; meanwhile, the furniture seems to become extensions of one's body, a rhythmic armature of postures and gestures. The timber floor strongly emphasises the traditional nautical character of a "navis" (nave) suspended above water. Siza has avoided all explicit religious symbols, he claims, although one can see small crosses in some of the handmade tiles marking the sites of each sacrament.

Behind the altar two pale, weak columns of light appear in the gloom, and one realises or remembers that they drop light down onto the face of someone in a coffin in the crypt below. A faint sound of splashing

Opposite: Santa Maria at Marco de Canaveses, Álvaro Siza, 1997. View of the east facade showing the nave of the church sat on a granite plinth, with the old farm yard to the right.

Left: View of the old farmyard to the east of the church.

Right: View of the "common ground" in between the church, seen on the left, and the parochial centre on the right, looking south.

Left: View of the courtyard with pool and window to the crypt.

Right: View of the south facade looking west towards the parochial centre with houses beyond.

Left: View of the south facade of the church with the parochial centre on the left.

Right: View of the interior of Santa Maria showing the baptismal font.

View of the south facade of the church (1997) before the construction of the parochial centre with the old chapel in the distance.

Left: Interior view of the parochial centre.

Right: View of the interior of Santa Maria showing the baptistry to the right of the tall doors, and the belfry to the left, with the organ shelf in the foreground.

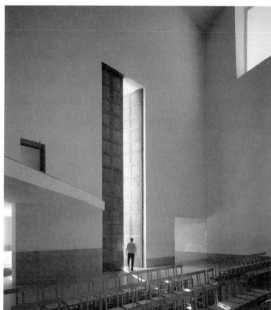

Left: View of the interior of Santa Maria looking south.

Right: View of the interior of Santa Maria looking up towards the north-facing clerestory windows.

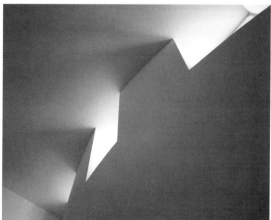

View of the interior of Santa Maria
looking east, showing the presbytery.

water rises up from the pool beyond the crypt. A body on
a cross is implied by the absence of matter each side of
the thin vertical shafts of light.

At the moment in the Mass when one first kneels,
attention is almost always upon the altar, the Eucharistic
prayer, and the actions of the priest. At Santa Maria,
however, attention towards the Sacred Mysteries is
balanced by a peripheral sensation of light entering from
the south. The source of this light reveals itself to be an
enormously long horizontal slit window, set 1.2 m off
the ground. Midday sunlight falls in through this long
slot. A northern Portuguese landscape—of arid hills and
scrubland, cars, petrol stations and small houses—comes
into view.

At the end of this very long window, Siza placed an old,
paint-flaking half-scale statue of the Virgin Mary holding
the infant Christ. Maria is of course patron of the church
and, for worshippers, the human link between numinous
and the material realms, something that Christian belief
co-laminates. Traditionally, statues of the Virgin Mary are
set within a niche, or held above head height on a shelf
or bracket. Here, she looks at the congregation at their
eye height, sat exactly at the threshold between the sacred
topography of the presbytery and the body of the church;
prayer and worship are situated in a frank encounter
with the fragile actuality of the everyday world beyond the
church. The Gospel is read from a simple oak lectern that
appears to grow from the timber floor of the church.

View of the interior of Santa Maria
showing the statue of the Virgin
and Child at the threshold to the
presbytery with the south-facing
window on the right.

Sketch of Santa Maria showing the church sat within the landscape oriented with the solar symbolism of the Christian liturgy.

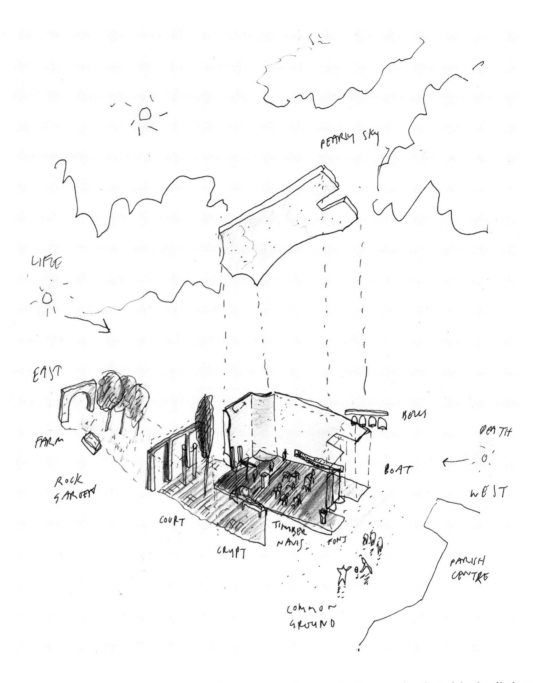

5   Leatherbarrow, David, *Architecture Oriented Otherwise*, Princeton: Princeton Architectural Press, 2009, p 11.

In contrast, the golden cross sits upon the presbytery floor, hovering between matter and light.

At Santa Maria, the horizon of ritualistic worship is counterpoised with a worldly horizon that is shockingly close by. The immateriality of light above and beyond the altar is counter-poised with the rhythm of sunlight, and one's view of the material world beyond the chapel. In experiential and geometric terms, its centre is displaced.

Siza's liminal placement of the statue of the Virgin Mary reminds us that the relationship between architecture and sculpture continues to refer us to spaces beyond their immediate location, and that "orientation", as Leatherbarrow suggests, "is nothing other than the acknowledgement of this ecstasis or alliocentricity".[5]

Communicative space is oriented, in ritualistic and everyday terms, towards situating particular historical circumstances (political conflict, human suffering, human hopes etc) with respect to the conditions that are common to all. A rhythm of associations and spatial counterpoints is established at Santa Maria in such an orchestrated manner as to suggest that architects' and sculptors' work might be understood as something fundamentally spatial, and essentially communicative. It reveals, in other words, the primary conditions of urbanity.

Axonometric sketch of Santa Maria
with the old farmyard on the left and
the new public square to the right of
the church.

Sketch section through Santa Maria
west-east showing the movement of
sunlight across the interior throughout
the day—the coincidence of solar
symbolism with water—and the role
of both in sacramental use.

Sketches of Santa Maria examining the significance of its iconographic civic topography in the context of the town and Christian liturgical symbolism.

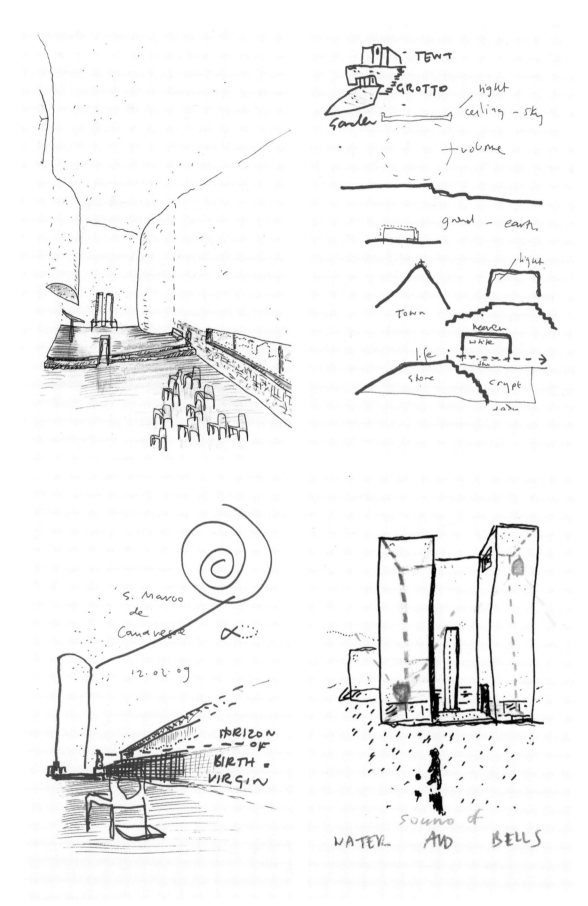

Overleaf: Views of the interior of Santa Maria.

Rhythmic Spatiality and the Communicative Movement between Site, Architecture and Sculpture at Victoria Street

The Problem of Civic *Decorum* and the Disunity of the Arts in Victorian London

In his report to the Office of Works in 1905, Aston Webb proposed a series of decorative stone figures arranged on the Victoria and Albert Museum in London, so that:

> The Painters would occupy the central curtains of the Cromwell Road front, while the Sculptors would have the West and the Architects the East curtains of this front, the Craftsmen occupying the whole of the Exhibition Road front.

In effect, the attempt to unify the arts and to house their fruits together at the Victoria and Albert Museum was arguably undone at the moment in which their accommodation was conceived—the architect placing his work amongst the "other" artists and separating these from craftsmen.[1] The placement of statues depicting "Knowledge" and "Inspiration" on either side of the main entrance typified the curious situation that Aston Webb was trying to work in at the beginning of the twentieth century—one which Peter Eisenman's recent advocacy of "the new subjectivity" seems unconsciously to reflect.[2]

Whilst the late nineteenth-century city is often typified by the alienated figure of the flâneur, the other figure that haunts it is the craftsman. A fundamental tension existed in the nineteenth century between the ideal of an artist as a free—if poor and often mad—genius, and the counter reaction to this, which took the form of attempts to revive the Guild tradition, eg the Art Workers' Guild was founded in 1884. What was at stake in these diverse images of the artists was the quality not only of art but, I suggest, the public value of this art. For the flâneur, the city is a finished artefact that has no need of any creative contribution (the flâneur's view is essentially Hegelian, accepting his argument for the death of art). Creativity for the flâneur is instead a form of criticism, a pessimistic commentary upon a state of abandonment— what Charles Baudelaire called a struggle between "spleen" and "ideal" in *Les Fleurs du Mal*, 1857. In contrast, the Victorian neo-Guildsmen were embedded in culture, responsive to economic and civic needs, socially active and devoted to improving the worst aspects of industrialism. It is not an exaggeration to describe William Morris's Christian socialism as the counterpoint to twentieth-century Situationism—whilst both share a profound antipathy towards capitalist industrialisation and the spectacle of the modern city, Morris's position was both active and contemplative— a proto-modern embodiment of Alberti's pragmatic and socially active Civic Humanism. In contrast, Eisenman's position can be said to be always to try to de-situate Alberti and Palladio from the conditions that their imaginations encountered, and similarly to attempt to escape from architecture and *praxis* generally, into literary theory or art practice. Contra this, Leatherbarrow's description of the loggia of Palladio's Palazzo Chiericati situates it exactly in the civic topography of sixteenth-century Vicenza as well as its current status as both grand entrance and public short cut.[3] Increasingly, it is not the areas of interest to which Eisenman directs us to that are uninteresting or irrelevant, but rather that his attempts to claim autonomy for these architects and artists and critics that is misleading. It is a symptom, I suggest, of the various dualisms between practical knowledge and theory that typified nineteenth-century culture. Eisenman sees that something is at stake, but cannot identify what this *topos* is, and so everything is reduced to a fight between a neo-liberal notion of the individual genius versus the everyday world, and their hunt for autonomous rules and orders. The irony of this paradox should be amusing, but is somehow not.

I would suggest that what was at stake, in Victorian Londoners' attempts to house the arts and sciences together at Albertopolis—and in Webb's efforts to represent the unity of progress and tradition in sculptures set into facades—was not simply the neuroses of architects, nor the credibility of architecture as an intellectual discipline, but its contribution to the public good, which means its role in a modern city. Architecture is obviously a discipline with a history, but it is dependent and contingent rather than autonomous in character, and the architectural imagination—if one can use such a loose term—flourishes in confrontation with the negotiations that typify urbanity.[4] The role of the architect is at stake in this confrontation—are we "free" like modern artists, or bound not only by the character of specific commissions, but by the broader ethical ambit of civic architecture?

Despite the art historians' attempts to reduce nineteenth-century civic architecture to a question of styles, this civic topography is largely what we inherit in European and American cities. Victorian civic architecture in Britain was largely the result of the Municipal Reform Act—or Municipal Corporations Act— of 1835, after which properly elected and accountable municipal governments were formed in Manchester, Birmingham, Bradford and Leeds. From these grew the drive to make these productive landscapes into proper cities. There were roughly four stages in the development of civic pride in Victorian England.

The Industrial Revolution created profits but also misery—the moral crisis signalled by Engels in his study of working conditions in Manchester in the 1830s.[5] Previously provincial centres of production— factory-towns—sought to transform themselves into "proper" cities after 1835. For this to work, an appeal to high culture was required—which of course industry was not.[6] Asa Briggs documents the growth of the so-called "civic gospel" of Birmingham, in his book *Victorian Cities*.[7] In terms of buildings, this took the form of institutional monuments, from town halls to educational bodies to charitable organisations, along with the urban planning necessary to make visible their proper functioning, which one might call, after Briggs, the topography and architecture of "civic pride". In this context, "art" was the mark of a cultured society, and the municipal art schools were among the institutions

1 In conversation with Melissa Hamnett, Director of Sculpture at the Victoria and Albert Museum (V&A), and Kieran Long, Director of Architecture and the Digital Arts at the V&A, in July 2013, I suggested that instead of a new sculptural programme for the new courtyard, an annual symposium might be a better way to connect the building to the city. The first of these was in spring 2014 celebrating the life and work of Joseph Rykwert. An annual festival each summer will help to animate the new courtyard. The architect of the V&A's refurbishment, Amanda Levete, seems to be strangely resistant to the project's use as a sculpture court.

2 See Interview with Peter Eisenman by Iman Ansari, "Eisenman's Evolution: Architecture, Syntax, and New Subjectivity", *Architecture Daily*, 13 September 2013.

3 Leatherbarrow, David, "The Sacrifice of Space", *Common Ground: A Critical Reader*, David Chipperfield, Kieran Long and Shumi Bose eds, 13th International Architecture Exhibition, La Biennale di Venezia: Marsilio, 2012.

4 See Till, Jeremy, *Architecture Depends*, Cambridge, MA: MIT Press, 2009.

5 See Engels, Friedrich, *The Conditions of the Working Class in England*, London: Panther, 1891.

6 See Arnold, Matthew, *Culture and Anarchy*, London: Smith, Elder & Co, 1869.

7 Briggs, Asa, *Victorian Cities*, London: Pelican, 1963, p 184.

"Knowledge" and "Inspiration" figures
by Alfred Drury, RA, on either side of the
main entrance of the V&A designed by
Aston Webb.

8   Gunn, Simon, *The Public Culture of
the Victorian Middle Class: Ritual and
Authority in the English Industrial City
1840–1914*, Manchester: Manchester
University Press, 2007, p 178.

9   Gunn, *The Public Culture of the
Victorian Middle Class*, p 178. See
also Cunningham, Colin, *Victorian
and Edwardian Town Halls*, London:
Routledge & Kegan Paul, 1981.
Victorian history painters, such as
Lord Leighton, were particularly
interested in processions, eg
*Cimabue's Celebrated Madonna is
carried in Procession through the
Streets of Florence*, 1853–1855.

10 Gunn, *The Public Culture of the
Victorian Middle Class*, p 179.

11 Gunn, *The Public Culture of the
Victorian Middle Class*, p 178.

12 See Rykwert, Joseph, *The Judicious
Eye*, Chicago: University of Chicago
Press, 2008.

by which cultured civic pride could be communicated to the unlettered masses, in effect creating a properly "cultured" constituency via civic art and ornament, and of course a new mode of *decorum*.

These newly civic cities (Liverpool was a village at the beginning of the nineteenth century) enacted the representational tropes of earlier forms of corporate power. These were "inscribed in the public rites and in the published funeral addresses, which sought to recreate a life devoted to beneficent exercise of power and to place the individual into a long line of patrimonial duty".[8] In a recent study of the public culture of the Victorian middle class, Simon Gunn notes how the "shared modes of ritual expression" in Victorian "processional culture... offered rich resources for the display of civic pride and community, and of authority, social order and identity".[9] Local worthies—as they became known—aspired to patriarchal values ("he lived and died like a patriarch" was a common claim) and "municipal leaders" saw in the public spectacle of funerals ways to sanctify their newly found "civic virtues". Architecture was not only key in the creation of buildings to house civic virtue, but was also seen as an essential part of the foundation of new universities. The Roscoe Professorship at Liverpool University was the first chair in architecture at a British university, and is still funded by the Leverhulme Trust (who of course also owned Port Sunlight and made soap). The elision of great wealth with civic virtue is most evident in the cities created in North America in the nineteenth century, of course (Pittsburgh's Carnegie Mellon University etc). Munificent cultural patronage also created new forms of social life and the establishment of municipal public art galleries (the Walker, the Tate etc) by industrialists, who "had the capacity to transform evanescent authority into something resembling the permanence of power", Gunn believes.

However, "the illusion of power embodied by mid Victorian civic ritual" was "transitory", he concludes, and "the sheer number and scale of public spectacles in the second half of the nineteenth century gradually satiated the appetite of observers for such events".[10] Enthusiasm for representational structures and rituals went somewhat against the august puritanism of the northern merchant class, who were almost entirely Methodists and Quakers, and the "evangelical" wing of the Church of England struggled to represent and to accommodate these tensions within the establishment.[11] "The Battle of the Styles" was not simply a matter of taste of course, but of denominational definitions, and these were closely related to perceived political status and the closeness or not of provincial cities to a national or international sense of modernity. Arguably, the port cities of Liverpool and Glasgow saw themselves as part of the wider Atlantic context that included North America. The Enlightenment, and Whig politicians favoured Greek architecture to the ultramontane position of the Oxford Movement.[12] The sudden appearance of Anglo-Catholic rituals alongside the rebirth of pseudo-Medieval traditions (the grand funeral parade etc) and Neo-Gothic architecture was an attempt to save England from the dangers of rapid industrialisation. The immense wealth necessary to imitate Medieval culture meant that Neo-Gothic architecture is at once strangely anachronistic and innovative. This contradiction is clear in the ways in which architects sought to reconcile technological innovations with the bizarrely arcane notions of late Medieval train stations. Stations tended to be either triumphal arches (Euston, King's Cross, Gare de l'Est) or hotels (Victoria, Liverpool Street). The spires and loggias of St Pancras Station and Hotel by Giles Gilbert Scott embody both types.

London was somewhat different to the northern British cities, of course, and its aspiration to be the centre of the British Empire meant that it did not have to borrow "culture" in the way in which provincial cities imitated ancient Greece or Rome. However, Albertopolis was, in effect, an attempt to transpose a Victorian version of ancient Alexandria to London, with the Victoria and Albert Museum the site where two conceptions—of craft and industry—met. Another way of understanding this is as a matter of making culture through making artefacts of a certain quality (for which the organisation by period and locale as the "styles" was crucial). Industrial production had supposedly triumphed at the Great Exhibition of 1851. A counter reaction was made in attempts to claim for "culture" a greater degree of authenticity. Everybody involved in commenting upon "culture", from John Ruskin to Matthew Arnold, saw craftsmanship embodying not only artistic values, but also greater moral worth than mass labour. For Marx, the division of labour resulted in inequality; for Morris this was a form of spiritual and material deprivation also.[13]

Whilst it is tempting to focus our attention solely upon grand civic buildings as representations of this or that style or as the manifestation of genius, what must be acknowledged is that architecture arises out of the dynamic forces that shape a city. Victorian cities often have some beautiful buildings, but the major achievement was the creation of safe, sanitary and recognisably urbane habitats. Victorian civic culture's greatest contribution and innovation is the high street, transforming the villages of Georgian London into a series of town centres within a metropolitan whole. This enabled the creation also of distinct districts represented by football teams, as well as the possibility of civic representation at local political level. One legacy of this diversity is the influence that Borough Councils have upon development and which local planning policy has upon architectural culture.

A high street brings together all of the representational buildings that we now recognise as the *topos* of the modern city: accommodating libraries, town halls, churches, banks, pubs etc, in a recognisable and coherent image of a city, but at a coherent and local scale. Its distinct character can still be sensed in Rathmines in Dublin, at Deptford High Street or on Upper Street in Islington, and at a larger scale the city centres of the great English northern towns are marked by the integration of cultural buildings and commerce. What makes these places valuable, in almost every sense, is the connection that the largely anonymous background of housing has with the high street. For example, it is very hard to argue that the destruction of the nineteenth-century streetscape and its replacement with road engineering has not damaged both Liverpool city centre and Charles Cockerell and Harvey Lonsdale Elmes's magnificent St George's Hall. The grand civic buildings of nineteenth-century cities seem to emerge from "background" topography.

The Problem of Urban Infrastructure, Civic Depth, Rhythmic Spatiality and the Disunity of Victoria Street

The original foundation of Victoria Street as a street can still be sensed, even if its formation was initially also technological. Victoria Street is constructed on marshland that was drained as part of the creation of the Victoria Embankment, built ostensibly to commemorate the Queen's Silver Jubilee in 1860. At the same time, the Victoria Embankment was designed by Joseph Bazalgette to distribute effluent away from the Thames, which by 1858 had become a fetid mass. "The Great Stink" was powerfully obvious to politicians in Barry and Pugin's new Houses of Parliament, and led MPs to debate the problem of the Thames. Sir Edwin Chadwick was able to create the Metropolitan Commission of Sewers and then the Metropolitan Board of Works in 1855, which led to Bazalgette's almost invisible but profound contribution to London—the creation of a centralised drainage system for human waste.[14]

Chadwick was a utilitarian, and under his guidance the ancient image of the city as a body (with the king at its head) was transformed so that "the metropolis had transformed into a machine". Utilitarianism defined virtue as "the most good for the most people". The metropolitan sewerage system was suddenly of crucial importance for all, and not only to solve the problem of the unpleasantness of human waste. It was necessary because John Snow had shown in "On the Mode of Communication of Cholera", 1854, that infected potable water supplies killed people. Snow proved that an infected parish-pump on Berwick Street in Soho was the cause of the spread of cholera there. From this discovery sprang the urgent need to create a "metropolitan" system of fresh water and drains and sewers.

Section through the Victoria Embankment.

Bazalgette's network of invisible pipes led him eventually to his proposals for a new embankment, cutting Somerset House off from the Thames and unifying modern infrastructure into one landscape. The Victoria Embankment houses sewers and what was originally called the Metropolitan District Line, as well as forming a road viaduct enabling vehicles to by-pass central London. Leo Hollis is clear that this development meant that "London was now the city of engineers".[15]

13 See Morris, William, *News from Nowhere and Other writings*, London: Penguin, 1994.

14 Hollis, Leo, *The Stones of London: A History in Twelve Buildings*, London: Weidenfeld & Nicolson, 2011, pp 264–297; see also Hunt, Tristram, *Building Jerusalem: The Rise and Fall of the Victorian City*, London: Phoenix, 2005; and Nead, Lynda *Victorian Babylon: People, Streets and Images in Nineteenth-Century London*, New Haven: Yale University Press, 2000.

15 Hollis, *The Stones of London*, p 269.

William Daniel, *Somerset House from the
River Thames*, 1805.

16 Hollis, *The Stones of London*, p 269.
Sadly there seem to be no images of
these proposals.

17 Ward-Jackson, Philip, *Public Sculpture
of the City of London*, Liverpool:
Liverpool University Press, 2003,
pp 227–282.

Bazalgette's plans included also a proposal to create
a series of terraced garden plots connecting the Strand
to the Thames, but this failed to convince a number of
private landowners, so was never instigated.[16] Instead,
Middle Temple and Somerset House have had their
river frontages cauterised, and the subsequent pattern
of development saw a line of semi-classical Portland
stone office blocks sat somewhat awkwardly on the
new ground.

The construction of the Victoria Embankment.

At what was the confluence of the River Fleet and the
Thames, on the corner of Farringdon Road and the
Victoria Embankment, raised up 9 metres from the
water levels at low tide, Unilever Houses (Sir John
Burnet and Partners, 1920—Burnet's practice went
on to become Burnet, Tait & Partners, the architects
of the original Kingsgate House and Westminster City
Hall) illustrates the difficulty of any authentic response
to the new relationship between architecture and
nature. The battered base is an awkward attempt to
allude to the nautical origin of the site, but stuck three
storeys above the river; the building seems to lack any
connection with the ground. It appears overly defensive
and yet marooned amongst roads and tunnels that
undermine the credibility of architecture there.
The heavily rusticated ground floor is windowless,
apparently to reduce traffic noise inside the building.[17]
Sculptures are used to try to communicate some
relationship between architecture and site, and the
corners are marked by entrances surrounded by large
plinths on which are placed sculptures of human
figures restraining horses called *Controlled Energy*
by Sir William Reid Dick. In addition, there are also
merman and mermaid figures by Gilbert Ledward.

This new, engineered ground is riddled with holes.
The river is damned at this point, accessible only
intermittently, and seems to pass by like a panorama
or a film. Cars surge by, on two-minute sequences of
red and green traffic lights. Sometimes between the
rhythm of din and emptiness you can hear the river
lapping the wall and smell its presence.

Bazalgette was a brilliant engineer, and he
also seemed to have understood the architectural
consequences of his work. This is limited to the George
V Archway on the Embankment, which borrows from the
iconography of Somerset House—and its now occluded
river gate—in depicting Father Thames, although the
river is now obscured from view by a small plinth.

The creation of the Embankment led, arguably, to
the destruction of a visible link between the tides of the
Thames and London, and this has led to the loss also of
the vital role that ornament played in its architecture, as
representations of nature, which traditionally formed
the mediating border between river and city. Sculptural

settings attempt to mediate between nature and city, and nature remains present analogically in sculptural settings, albeit transformed into "geography", or "archaeology", "myth" or "agriculture".

At the point that one crosses the buried River Fleet on the Holborn Viaduct, four sculptures remind you forcibly of the Victorian sense of *decorum*; Commerce, Agriculture, Science and Fine Art are depicted in four statues that define Victorian civic virtues, and confirm the bridge as a new mode of an ancient type—a version of a grand civic portal. Pseudo-classical gatehouses sit in two corners of the viaduct, and connect the upper and lower levels of the Victorian city. Its riverine origins are both buried and revealed at this point. The river is alluded to if not made visible in actual or metaphoric terms in both the iconographic content of the figures, and in the extreme topographical junction made by the viaduct. This is a mode of modern *decorum*, one in which man celebrated his victory over the natural world, which is represented now in its "produce" and in the industrial character of modern modes of production. It is a form of "third nature", divorced from the primary field of representational reference. The long tradition of civic bridges is evoked.

Modern architecture refers, if it refers to anything at all, to the history of architecture (echoing the way in which modern man refers to his own achievements).[18] The Houses of Parliament embody all of the tensions of Victorian civic culture, and yet transform the technological and artistic demands of a modern democratic representational structure into an image of continuity and invention. It is full of quotations of semi-mythic, semi-historical veracity, and Barry and Pugin retrospectively invented heraldic crests for Edward the Confessor in order to create visual consistency across the facades of their Palace of Westminster. It is at once a grand infrastructure project and a series of rooms. The building can be said to be "anachronic", renewing and embedding new traditions in the city and reviving and re-establishing the tradition of them there.[19] This term implies that something that appears to be anachronistic, in terms of style, might in fact be something like a type or an archetype in spatial terms. In the case of the creation of the Houses of Parliament, this was not so much the case of inventing a new type or copying an established one, but of reusing certain spatial typologies. This was a particularly sensitive approach I suggest, since a debating chamber that was based upon a former chapel represented well the inherent tensions between the crown and the state, and between democratic and monarchic power, that typify British governance.

18 A strange anomaly is 55 Broadway (1927–1929), by Charles Holden, which houses St James's Tube Station (although it is not in St James's!). Built to house the offices of what is now called London Underground Limited, 55 Broadway was conceived of as a "cathedral of industry". Its cruciform plan form is extruded to define a sort of urban block that is decorated with a number of sculptures, which attempt to embed technology within a pseudo-mythical relationship with the natural world. These are: *Day and Night*, Jacob Epstein; *North Wind*, Alfred Gerrard; *North Wind*, Eric Gill; *East Wind*, Eric Gill; *East Wind*, Allan G Wyon; *South Wind*, Eric Gill; *South Wind*, Eric Aumonier; *West Wind*, Samuel Rabinovitch and *West Wind*, Henry Moore (see Aumonier, William ed, *Modern Architectural Sculpture*, London: The Architectural Press, 1930). The function suite on the tenth floor of the building was originally set up as a dining room for the chairman and senior executives, in the manner of the grand civic patriarchs of provincial England, and of course the merchants of Florence and Venice. At this level there are also two roof gardens, one of which was dedicated to the wife of a former managing director. Apparently this is in recognition of her enthusiasm to encourage this early form of environmental work. Any link between the analogical structure of gardens and their unity with sculptures is sadly absent in this "recognition". Similarly, there is no spatial relationship between the building and the surrounding representational structures. It is almost impossible in fact to view the sculptures as this entails stepping into traffic. Instead, it is possible to suggest something of a mechanical sort of patrician sensibility at play, a hangover of Victorian civic pompousness, crossed with awareness of the death of natural conditions (ie faux Medievalism). Holden seems to have intuited the imminence of the modern sensibility that the futurists et al evolve from industry, ie electricity as god, speed as ecstasis (see McCarthy, Tom, *London*: Vintage, 2011). I would tentatively suggest also that the intellectual and "poetic" climate of England at this time is echoed in the various attempts by people like TS Eliot (and Holden) to fuse modernity with myth. Eliot's great London poem is *The Wasteland*, and according to CK Stead, the structure is based on: 1) The movement of time, in which brief moments of eternity are caught; 2) Worldly experience, leading on to dissatisfaction; 3) Purgation in the world, divesting the soul of the love of created things; 4) A lyric prayer for, or affirmation of the need of, intercession; 5) The problems of attaining artistic wholeness which becomes analogue for, and merges into, the problems of achieving spiritual health (*The New Poetic: Yeats to Eliot*, London: Pelican Books, 1969). This structure fits somewhat too neatly into a reading of the Tube station as an example of a sort of Dante-esque mediation between heavenly gardens and an infernal pit, of course, to be true.

19 See Nagel, Alexander and Christopher Wood, *Anachronic Renaissance*, New York: Zone Books, 2010.

Holborn Viaduct with the four statues
representing "Agriculture", "Commerce",
"Science" and "Fine Art".

Opposite page:

Left: View of Unilever House, London,
by Sir John James Burnet, 1933, at the
corner of Farringdon Street and the
Embankment.

Top right: Sir William Reid Rick,
Controlled Energy, 1933.

Bottom right: Unilever House, London, by
Sir John James Burnet, 1933.

In response to pressing economic and social problems—and the threat of more civil unrest, the politicians' commission to the architects was opaque. Barry won the commission by solving functional problems of the site, retaining the river edge and orchestrating the twin houses of British democracy in such a way as to enable security and ventilation etc. He also resolved the representational problem of the three-tiered hierarchy of British government in the unusual situation where the monarch is also head of the church. The twin towers of Big Ben and Victoria Tower house chimney flues that originally heated the structure, but they also have iconographic significance, suggesting the origin of democratic debate in St Stephen's Chapel. The debating chamber of the House of Commons is in fact based almost exactly on the spatial type of St Stephen's. This was retained and inverted, forming a point of orientation between the topographic and geometric contingencies of the new river wall and the cardinal orientation that the old palace shared with Westminster Abbey. This insistence upon continuity enshrined a crude mode of dialectical confrontation and arguably supports what is now a rather fictional tradition of a two-party political system. Somewhat anachronistically, the image of democracy originating in a monastic context is retained and amplified in Barry's plan and Pugin's facades. Similarly, Nicholas Hawksmoor's anachronistic Neo-Gothic towers at the Abbey are arguably yet another example of an attempt to heal rifts between tradition and history at Westminster. In both instances, architecture is deployed to remake broken traditions, to reassemble an image of continuity, and to accommodate almost unbearable tensions between inherited tradition and political change.

In direct and immediate contrast to these courtyards of power and mythic Englishness, Victoria Street was born from a systematic suppression of history by ingenuity and technology. Unlike the Palace of Westminster and the Abbey, the architecture of Victoria Street ignores the natural world, banishing it and any civic representation to the disconnected background of schools, hotels, private gardens and the Royal Parks. The morphology of Victoria Street is defined by three things: at the eastern end the most important buildings in England sit around Parliament Square—a quasi-public space-cum-garden—and arguably a street, Whitehall, fulfils the role of a "piazza". At the western extreme, Victoria Station sits at the head of what was a canal basin. The canal that fed the Stag Brewery was filled in with train lines once Snow made the connection between the dangers of standing water and cholera. Advances in medical science and transport technology shaped the formation of the new area known as Victoria, as much as the attempt to create a new civic quarter linking the courts of Belgravia to Parliament.

Springing seemingly fully formed from the minds of the Cubitt brothers in the 1820s, Belgravia was developed as a ready-made fashionable residential district, close to the court of St James's and to Buckingham Palace, which had recently become a Royal Residence. Along with Regent Street, Belgravia is a typical example of large-scale Georgian town planning from a single developer-architect-client. It was conceived almost entirely as residences, and whilst it imitates in part the "public squares" of Italy, Belgravia lacks urbanity. Thought of in terms of typology, Georgian squares have affinities with the sorts of places that

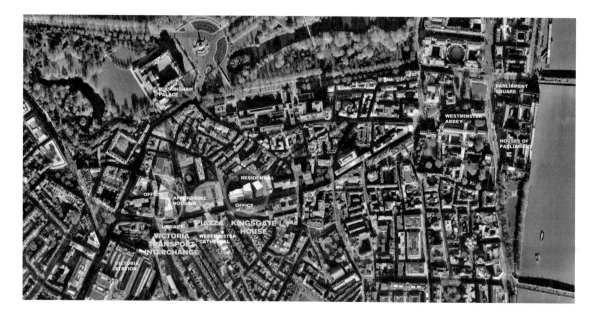

Collage showing Lynch Architects'
projects on Victoria Street.

English architects and patrons visited on their Grand Tours. Both lack the vital element of spontaneity that comes from the mixture of different activities that characterise the life of a city.

In contrast, Victoria Street lacks a clear geometric order—it is not a boulevard drawn as a straight line on a map. The third influence upon its formation was the introduction of underground trains. The Tube network occurred without a central plan, once railway entrepreneurs realised the limits of building dormitory suburbs and constructing train lines to bring people from the countryside into town. The limit being commuting time, specifically the time necessary to traverse, on foot or by horsepower, the largest city in the world.[20]

Victoria Street was really founded because of the creation of Victoria Station, and ostensibly it triangulates the station with Buckingham Palace, and also with Westminster Abbey and the Palace of Westminster. Yet, not only is there no regal route that would justify the street being named for the Queen, nor was it ever used for the sort of victory parades that inspired Haussmann's boulevards in Paris or Schinkel's work in Berlin. Victoria Street also kinks roughly at its centre, as the District and Circle Lines peel away to avoid drifting into the water table.

Despite its formal architectural shortcomings Victoria Street was thought of by the engineers who worked upon and named it and established their offices there (on what became known as "Engineers' Row") primarily as a street. As such, Victoria can be thought of as exhibiting the characteristics of a high street in a town, or as a town within a town—as a typical London district. Until recently "civic depth" of Victoria Street was obscured.[21] This background depth is partly a non-systematic "network" of institutions whose layering reflects the typicality of almost all European city quarters. Yet this urban order was until recently impossible to traverse, and it was impossible to "see" the rich background that is supported by Victoria Street.

Spatial continuity between the urban hinterland and the "high street" was blocked by large slab-blocks.

Acknowledgement of the latent urbanity of Victoria Street and the problematic character of rhythmic and communicative space in Victorian London has been the basis of my approach towards the series of architectural interventions that we have proposed there over the past ten years. The architectural task then was not only to situate new buildings in relation to old ones in terms of form and style—or "mass and bulk", if one prefers planning terminology—it is also to try to resituate the existing civic structures in relation with each other in such a way that the latent urban order and the submerged natural world can be sensed, if not always directly seen.

Our design insertions at Victoria Street are made into a nineteenth-century topography that is latent with a spatial richness, but this richness was previously obscured by buildings that denied any "communicative movement" between site, architecture and sculpture. Our insertions need therefore to be similarly rich enough in order to fill out the lack of mediation between the upper symbolic levels of life represented by the Cathedral, the Abbey, Parliament and City Hall, and the vacuous blocks of information processing represented by conventional office buildings.

In viewing the City of Westminster as a series of spatial settings, or "urban rooms", the latent "communicative movement" between them becomes clearer. In this way, the "style" of the architecture that houses these is not as important as the depth of reciprocity between the internal and external spatial settings that accommodate the life of a city. This is territory that has been traditionally also mediated by sculpture, often within as well as in between buildings, and often at the threshold between private and public realms. For this reason, the formalist, art-historical cliché of "The Battle of the Styles" in Victorian architecture is unhelpful to describe the actual achievements of, say, Cockerel at Liverpool

20 White, Jerry, *London in the Nineteenth Century*, London: Vintage, 2008, pp 37–65.

21 See Carl, Peter, "Civic Depth", *Civic Architecture: The Facades, Passages and Courts of Westminster*, Lynch Architects exh cat, New London Architecture Gallery, The Building Centre, November–December 2014; see also Lynch, Patrick, *Mimesis*, London: Artifice books on architecture, 2015.

22 See AW Pugin's *Principles of Gothic
Architecture*, Matthew Arnold's *Culture
and Anarchy* etc. Arguably, the
tendency to confuse aesthetics with
ethics—and advanced technology
with progressive politics—are
examples of Victorian puritanical
intellectual habits that continue to
"haunt" architectural theorists today.

Model photograph showing Victoria
Street looking east towards Parliament
Square with Lynch Architects' projects
in pink.

or Waterhouse at Manchester. Both St George's Hall
and Manchester Town Hall are fundamentally civic
buildings, settings for artworks and city life, and in
both cases the art of architecture is indivisible from
the art of city-making. Victorian architecture, regardless
of what one thinks of its quality or its style, is almost
always civic architecture, even if this notion was often
confused with religious or nationalistic themes, and
with confused questions of morality.[22]

Iridescent Architecture

The client for our recent projects in Westminster, Land
Securities, is in the unusual position of owning most
of the land and buildings on Victoria Street, and so has
the opportunity to act as a patron of architecture in the
tradition of the great estates of Georgian London. Our
task has been to respond to their ambitions to create
a new city quarter that resolves some of the problems
associated with a major urban transport hub. This
task might be called civic architecture. Despite their
excellence at railway design and sanitation technology,
and the quality of their churches and town halls,
Victorian patrons could not always reconcile civil
engineering with *civilitas*. Certainly, Victoria is not
synonymous with great buildings, nor is it known as a
pleasant part of the city—despite its proximity to parks
and national monuments, the river, Belgravia, St James's,
Pimlico etc. The road engineers of the 1960s seemed
to scorn civic culture. In the 1960s, Land Securities
constructed a number of mediocre modernist pastiches
on Victoria Street, eg Portland House is a not-so-distant
echo of Gio Ponti's Pirelli Tower in Milan, itself copied
by Belluschi et al for the Pan Am building in New York.
EPR Architects built a series of buildings from the 1960s
to 2005, and Burnet, Tait & Partners were behind
the creation of a series of mega-blocks from the late
1950s onwards.

Land Securities are also developing projects at
Victoria by David Chipperfield, PLP (formerly KPF),
Benson & Forsyth, HHbR (formerly Buschow Henley)
and Lynch Architects.

Victoria Street has always resisted attempts at
imposing an overarching aesthetic master plan.
Conceived, originally at least, as a typical Victorian
high street, until recently the rich hinterland of Victoria
Street—its schools and housing—has been obscured
by some very large and very monotonous twentieth-
century buildings that (unwittingly perhaps?) denied
its civic presence. Recent attempts by architects
including Hopkins, Allies and Morrison and PLP to
seek within this submerged urban richness a singular
visual order seem in retrospect perhaps always to have
been doomed to be defeated by the fragmentary and
episodic character of Victoria Street. What is emerging
instead are a number of buildings that address specific
situations. In particular, buildings that seek to heal
certain rifts in the civic structure, revealing connections
between the train station and the palace; reconnecting

the Cathedral and Victoria Street; opening up
pedestrian routes between City Hall and the urban
grain to the north and south; and reinforcing the
density of uses and urban forms that one expects to
find on a typical high street.

The large urban estate developments of London
over the past 200 years are typified by a number of
buildings by different architects, and also by a number
of different buildings by the same firm of architects,
and Victoria Street is no different.

Lynch Architects have been involved in the process
of the transformation of Victoria Street since 2006,
and are now realising a number of urban blocks, each
of which responds very precisely to its immediate
context. Kings Gate and The Zig Zag Building replace
one third of the mega-blocks that previously sat each
side of the tower of City Hall, the other one being
recently replaced by César Pelli's 62 Buckingham Gate.
The residential building, Kings Gate, defers to the civic
importance and scale of City Hall, stepping back in
plan to address its previously underplayed entrance
colonnade. In the process, the tower's slender, elegant
silhouette is revealed alongside its quiet authority as
arguably the most "public" building on Victoria Street.
In particular, the view from Wilcox Place now reveals the
presence of the St James' Court Hotel in the background
of Victoria Street, and the creation of new pedestrian
passages emphasises the hitherto obscured civic depth
of Victoria. Similarly, The Zig Zag Building seeks to
create a good background context to John Francis
Bentley's masterpiece, Westminster Cathedral, as well
as amplifying the pedestrian's experience of the high
street, whilst creating state-of-the-art offices.

Until recently, the high-quality buildings on Victoria
Street were neither complemented by good neighbours
nor cherished. Frank Matcham's robustly civic and
charming Victoria Palace Theatre was abutted by
domestic properties. Now it will be accompanied by
another "palace"—this time a palace of books. Victoria
Library will be noticeably more flamboyant and "public"
than Lynch Architects' other buildings, creating a
counterpoint to the theatre and the grand stone portico
of Victoria Station. These will together form a "stone
urban room" towards the western end of Victoria Street
to echo the stone piazza at its eastern end, Parliament
Square. This local version of a national civic quarter
will consolidate the setting of the listed theatre and
emphasise the scale of the high street. Nova East will
act as a refined and subtle "medium-scale" building,
mediating the extreme contrast in scales between
Portland House, the Duke of York, the theatre and
PLP's very tall office buildings. These buildings, along
with Nova West, will be the dominant architectural
figures on the skyline and the streetscape. In contrast,
Lynch Architects' projects are largely quieter in tone
and more demure in architectural character, acting
as the links between the large-scale new projects and
the existing local buildings, enabling a potentially
disparate series of buildings in a fragmented urban
setting to together form a coherent place.

Left: Westminster Abbey at the extreme
eastern end of Victoria Street.

Right: Courtyard of the St James' Court Hotel
off Victoria Street and Buckingham Gate.

Left: Westminster Cathedral from
Westminster Cathedral Piazza.

Right: View of Castle Lane off Buckingham
Gate, north of Victoria Street.

Kingsgate House (site of The Zig Zag
Building and Kings Gate by Lynch
Architects), photographed in 2010.

Left: Kingsgate House (site of The Zig
Zag Building and Kings Gate by Lynch
Architects), photographed in 2010 from
Wilcox Place.

Right: View of Seaforth Place looking
south towards Westminster City Hall.

171

Left: Patrick Lynch, sketch of
Civic Ground at Victoria, 2018

Right: Patrick Lynch, sketch of
Victoria Library, 2018

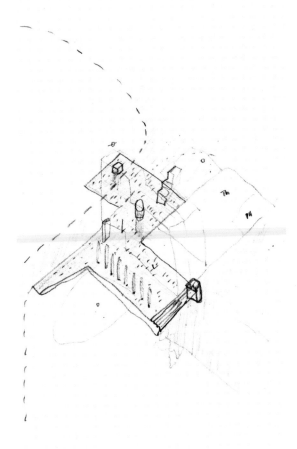

Victoria Library forms the "setting of a listed building", Frank Matcham's pseudo-Renaissance Victoria Palace Theatre. It is the Section 106 part of a much larger development that has been called variously Victoria Transport Interchange (VTI), Victoria Circle, and at the moment, Nova (North Victoria). Large developments inspire complex taxation (known in planning law as Section 106 agreements) that stands in for, and in many ways replaces, if not replicates, the welfare state. The Library sits above a sewer built by Bazalgette in 1865, following his work on the draining of the marshland upon which Victoria was originally constructed.

In-between the library and the sewer runs the Victoria Line, and in particular a new ticket hall is currently being built beneath our project, and its ventilation towers will be incorporated into our building. The presence of major subterranean technological infrastructure, and its submergence and taming of the natural world are primary themes in our Victoria projects. It is also the principal inspiration for the iconographic programme of sculptures that we have devised with the artist Hilary Koob-Sassen.

The other major influence upon the design of the building is its southerly aspect and the need to limit solar gain and thus to limit the running costs of the library. Ventilation shafts represent the presence of the underground system and its reliance upon fresh air,

and our project is in a crude sense a decorative carapace around this. Earth, air, sunlight; these are the primary ingredients of the decorative programme. Koob-Sassen sees the screen facade as a trellis upon which the cultivated natural world blossoms into an expression of the fruits of culture, revealing the constant presence of the natural world and of the implicit tensions within technological infrastructure and public life.

In urban terms our project is a mixed use, L-shaped edge to a city block, and we have tried to consolidate and to emphasise the primacy of the block in this location in contrast to the neighbouring existing and proposed buildings whose forms are generated almost exactly as a correlation between the shape of sites defined by roads and the economic imperative, which ordinarily leads architects to build to the limit of the plot boundary.

The library is pre-let to Westminster City Council at a "peppercorn rent" for 20 years. In programmatic terms, the library is accompanied by a mixture of "market" and "social needs rented" apartments that sit partly above its lower floors and to the north beside it on Bressenden Place. Accompanying these uses, a small office building will sit perpendicular to Bressenden Place along Allington Street at the rear of the site, behind the Victoria Palace Theatre's planned new fly-tower. The small office will incorporate the reconstructed facade and ground floor of Sutton House,

1/3 scale engineered timber model
of Victoria Library constructed by Eurban,
for Lynch Architects' installation
"Inhabitable Models", part of Common
Ground, the 13th Venice Architecture
Bienale, 2012.

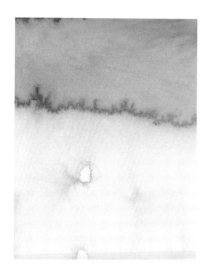

Hilary Koob-Sassen, watercolours for
the ornamental glazing at the top of the
staircase of Victoria Library, 2015.

a 1930s "moderne" pawnbrokers, which used to sit 200
metres away on Victoria Street.

Despite its niches and statues, Frank Matcham's
frons scenae facade of the Victoria Palace Theatre is
uninhabited and shallow. In contrast, our urban
palace can operate not only as an allusion to a classical
architectural trope analogically, but its use as a library
enables us to inhabit the facade with real bodies.

The ground floor of the library will be entered—
during library hours—at the southeast corner of the
building, and after-hours the upper-floor restaurant and
bar can be entered from the secondary entrance beside
the theatre.

Theatre and library are established in continuity
with each other both as urban figures on the streetscape,
and as a series of territories held and defined by their
theatrical facades and one's ascent through them; these
are penetrated by a landscape of staircases. One ascends
from foyer to theatre bar to stage on the one hand,
and from library lobby to cafe bar to public meeting
room next door. The large stair at ground floor resolves
a practical problem by creating a territory between
the children's library—necessarily situated at ground
floor—and its proximity to the main entrance. This
solution avoids the need for walled barriers, but also
creates a shared theatrical, civic *topos* for book readings,
performances by the actors next door and for more or
less structured children's play.

The library also has a side entrance, sat against the
party wall with the theatre, to be used in the evening
when the reading rooms are closed but the upper
parts remain open. Entrance is prefaced by a bas-relief
sculpture sat on the flank wall of the lower colonnade
to the Victoria Palace Theatre. This is best revealed
in light falling onto it from above. Seen as you
ascend the staircase looking back down towards the
street, the sculpture establishes a spatial thematic of
depth—heightened by Koob-Sassen's allusions to the

presence of an underworld beneath Victoria Street.
His sculpture alludes (in its implied material depth and
chiaroscuro emphasis upon light and dark sections of
ground) to the murky past and to the complex depth
of the street beneath you; to what Peter Ackroyd calls,
in *London Under*, "darkness visible".[23]

In this vein the ascent through the library
corresponds with an archetypal journey from matter to
light, from opacity towards transparency.

Ascending to the fourth floor, past and through
three floors of reading floors, one emerges past, and
as if through, a translucent red glass wall, arriving in a
cafe and onto a south-facing roof terrace framed by a
row of giant-order stone columns that form a parterre
overlooking the long sweep of the railway tracks towards
the river. These establish an analogue between the gallery
of a villa or a palace, and its garden or loggia.

The red glass panes are part of a single image
that appears as a layer of watery light when viewed
from afar—a sort of miniscus or horizon that you pass
through in order to reach the upper public rooms of
the library. Red afternoon and early evening sunlight
falling through these red glass walls will emphasise
your experience of these rooms at the end of the day,
when the library below is closed. At night, and on
winter afternoons, the red glass will glow from within,
complementing the theatrical signage and lighting of the
theatre next door, and establishing the library as part of
the upper horizon of the night-time city.

From the "urban room" of the fourth-floor cafe and
its terrace, one ascends further, arriving ultimately at a
double height public meeting room above. The meeting
room is open to the east and the south, taking in views
of the cathedral and the river beyond. Evening sunlight
enters this room from a small, high, west-facing red
coloured window, situating the planning committees
and the other municipal events that will take place there
in an explicit relationship with both the city beyond and

23 Ackroyd, Peter, *London Under*,
London: Vintage, 2012, pp 1–13.

Patrick Lynch, axonometric of south
facade of library.

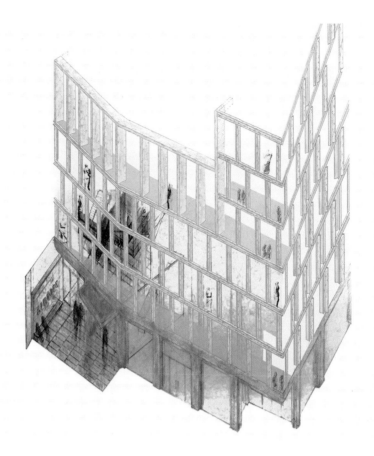

also the natural world. The horizon of the civic actions to be enacted within is literally above, but not aloof or distant from, the life of the city.

The theatricality of the cafe terrace below—its character as a grand urban garden balcony—works in concert with the dramatic performances of local government and its everyday passions, to situate civic life in relation to the natural world. The cycle of political life— bi-weekly planning meetings, monthly council meetings, local committees, AGMs etc—will be complimented by secular marriages and parties of all sort: the drama of civic life juxtaposed with the rhythm of the seasons.

The urban institutions of Victoria were present but hidden from each other by the domination of traffic-determined architecture, and Victoria Street became typified in the 1960s by very long, monotonous, monolithic office buildings.

The construction in 1975 of Ashdown House, designed by EPR Architects, led to the creation of Westminster Cathedral Piazza and to the opening up of the Cathedral facade to Victoria Street. Up until then, the Cathedral had no space in front of it for processions. Cardinal Manning was able to consecrate the building in 1910 by blessing the Cathedral precinct, but until 1975 it was impossible for Palm Sunday processions or any other civic displays to occur there. Various legal covenants were in force, however, limiting commercial use at the base of the buildings facing the Piazza, and as a consequence it is somewhat lifeless and prone to occupation by rough sleepers.

In 2011, Westminster Council held a design competition for Westminster Cathedral Piazza, in concert with the Cathedral and Land Securities, who owned the commercial buildings facing it. The brief was quite vague but called for a project that addressed the material and social conditions of the Piazza, and architects were invited to submit initial concepts for its refurbishment.

Lynch Architects were shortlisted, and we proposed that a structure was required to establish a transitional territory between some new shops and the Cathedral, acting also as an external baptismal font, and as a drinking fountain for the homeless. This would take the form of a *baldacchino*, whose height and location is set up by the rhythm of the colonnade within the Cathedral, one bay of which was to be projected out into the piazza.

Westminster Cathedral was designed by JF Bentley following a trip to Venice, from where his trip to Istanbul was curtailed by a cholera outbreak. Bentley's intention was to visit early Christian, Byzantine churches and to base his design upon these precedents, feeling that the Gothic style had been appropriated by the Church of England and that nothing could compete with Westminster Abbey. He was also looking for an ecumenical architecture, something that could re-establish continuity following the break with tradition symbolised by the English Reformation. His Venetian visit was fruitful, however, and the Cathedral was certainly influenced by St Mark's. What is lacking

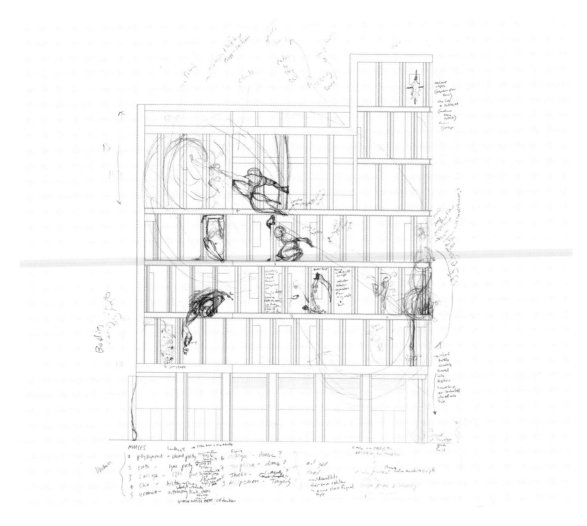

Patrick Lynch and Hilary Koob-Sassen, exploratory drawing of the south facade of the library showing the nine muses arranged thematically in relation to the architecture, natural phenomena and the city.

at Victoria, though, is the Piazza San Marco and the Piazzetta San Marco. At Venice, this *topos* holds the competing demands of temporal and divine power in a balanced equilibrium and tension; the Cathedral, the Doge's Palace and Sansovino's library combine together to articulate a representational spatial realm. This is achieved through the rhythm of the spatial settings and through the repetition of spatial proportions and volumes within the facades of the various building types and in the measure of the volumes that connect them. The markings on the ground at Venice enabled Napoleon to regulate the market traders, creating what he called "Europe's drawing room". Our design for Westminster Cathedral Piazza takes the idea of a city of urban rooms as the basis for a spatial proposition that sees rhythm as a mode of *decorum*. Our plan is to introduce these two types of spaces to Victoria, creating a strong rhythmic connection to Westminster City Hall in a way that is analogous of the civic territory of Venice.

Furthermore, Westminster Cathedral is built upon the foundations of a prison, which sat in the former marshland, and so, unlike traditional Christian churches, it does not face east. Our proposed white *baldacchino* would sit on cardinal orientation within the piazza, beside a mature plane tree; acting as a threshold, orienting the space towards cosmic and mundane time, and marking a limit to ritualistic and everyday uses of the site.

We also suggested an iconographic programme for the *baldacchino*, working again with the sculptor Koob-Sassen. We proposed that only one of the columns would be carved, and that only one of the sides would depict a figure. This image would depict the face of the Blessed John Henry Newman (which was said to have been as white as milk), who is on the way to becoming the first English saint for 400 years. The *baldacchino* would be made of fine, white pre-cast concrete, parts of which would be inlaid with white marble, enabling the likenesses of future English Saints to be carved into the structure. Obviously, it would take a very long time to complete this project. Sadly, in 2015, Westminster Council announced that none of the shortlisted entries deserved to be built.

Westminster City Hall is housed within a 19-storey office tower built as a speculative development in 1960–1966 to a design by Burnet, Tait & Partners, and the council rent it from Land Securities. On either side of it the same architects built two 135-metre-long slab blocks called Kingsgate House (to the west of City Hall) and Selborne House to the east. The latter was

Lynch Architects, collage showing
proposed *baldacchino* in Westminster
Cathedral Piazza, 2010.

Left: Plan showing the position of the
proposed *baldacchino* in Westminster
Cathedral Piazza, generated from the
continuation of the geometric rhythms
of the internal structural order of
Westminster Cathedral.

Right: Photograph of 1/25 scale plaster
model of the *baldacchino* by Hilary Koob-
Sassen and Lynch Architects, 2010.

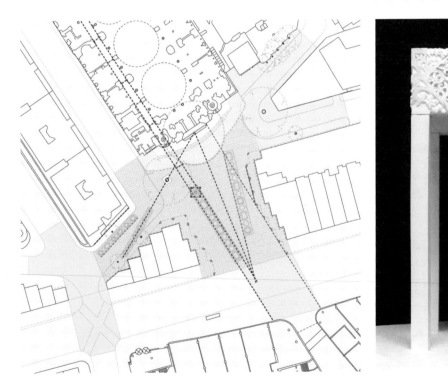

View of Kings Gate and Westminster City
Hall looking north across Victoria Street
from Wilcox Place.

demolished in 2009 and is now replaced with a new office building by César Pelli. My practice's other building site on Victoria Street comprises two new buildings and three new public spaces next to City Hall. The District and Circle Lines run to the rear of our site forming the northern edge, cutting off Westminster City School and the St James' Court Hotel from Victoria Street.

The original Kingsgate building echoed this divisive condition, acting as wall between the south side of Victoria Street and the north. The land between the Tube line and Kingsgate House was used solely as a service road for City Hall and the retail units that faced Victoria Street. Despite these twin boundaries and the resulting apparent "rifts" in the urban topography, alleyways such as Seaforth Place to the north of Victoria Street are still used.

The service road was a pedestrian alternative to Victoria Street enabling passage across it to Westminster Cathedral to the south or east-west from Cardinal Place towards Christ Church Gardens past the Korean Embassy. A network of civic institutions existed, but they lacked any architectural articulation or civic presence. Tube and road infrastructure cut off the two sides of Victoria Street at the very moment that it was created.

Our project is based upon a grand conceit that seeks to draw out the latent urbanity of Victoria as a city quarter. Our aim is to create a situation in which it appears as if we have simply taken away a twentieth-century building, enabling "once again" connections across Victoria Street.

Our new office block, known as The Zig Zag Building, has a solar-gain protecting layered facade that opens for ventilation, and the concrete ceilings can help cool the office floors (via cold water pumped into the concrete floor slabs). The development should avoid technical obsolescence and remain a useful part of the city when fossil fuels become depleted or ridiculously expensive, and conventional ways of cooling modern buildings via air conditioning become difficult if impossible.

The residential building is shaded by a stone filigree screen that acts as a brise soleil. As well as cutting solar gain, the screen enables large south-facing domestic balconies to take their place on the street in a discreet, civic manner. The sun's movement across the building reveals its spatial and material depth. Deep stone piers cast shadows onto inhabitants' balconies, commingling the private and public aspects of these thresholds. Similarly, metal fins cast shadows across the surface of the glass facades of the offices, so that the presence of figures within the building will be revealed to the street. The deep window reveals situate the human figure within the facades of large buildings giving scale to the structures. This ambition is inspired by Joseph Rykwert's statement about architecture: "The metaphor with which I have been concerned is more extended—a double one—in that it involves three terms, a body is like a building and the building in turn is like the world".[24]

Our aim is to make architecture that confirms Alberti's description of design as *natura naturans* or "second nature"; architecture that elaborates upon and extends the presence of the natural world in everyday life; architecture as mediation between nature and culture, forming the face and ground of the city. On the northwest side of the building, the layers of the facade are reduced, creating a different rhythm.

24 Rykwert, Joseph, *The Dancing Column:
On Order in Architecture*, Cambridge,
MA: MIT Press, 1996, p 373

Model photograph of Kings Gate and
The Zig Zag Building.

Plan of The Zig Zag Building and Kings
Gate showing the proportional rhythms
of the buildings and the public spaces
between them.

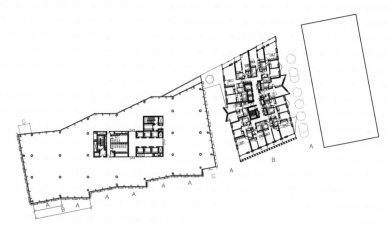

Left: View looking west down Victoria
Street with Westminster City Hall in the
foreground.

Right: Drawing of Kings Gate south
facade showing compositional rhythms
and proportional relationships.

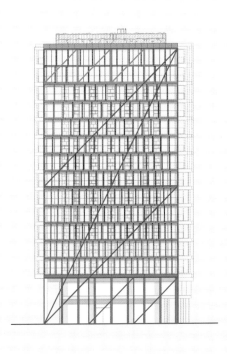

Rut Blees Luxemburg and Lynch
Architects, *Silver Forest*, Kings Gate,
Victoria, 2016.

View from above of Angela Hooper Place
in between The Zig Zag Building and
Kings Gate.

View of *Silver Forest* on the side of
Westminster City Hall.

View of *Silver Forest* in Kings Gate Walk,
looking south towards Victoria Street, with
Westminster City Hall on the left, from the
entrance colonnade of Kings Gate.

In this situation—an office block and an apartment block—our buildings lack explicit representational "civic" programmes, and are conceived of as background to the neighbouring buildings that do: Westminster Cathedral and City Hall. The former exhibits strong urban characteristics, whilst City Hall is really only civic in the sense of being the tallest building in the middle part of Victoria Street. Its previous neighbours each side did not emphasise the urbane character of a tower structure. Our new buildings step up the street beginning with a contextually deferential stance towards the Cathedral to the west. The office building is composed of what appear to be three blocks, whose scale, form and massing echo directly the apartment buildings that neighbour Bentley's Cathedral quarter. In planning terms we form "the setting of the Cathedral conservation area" and "the setting of a listed building". Our residential building continues this stepped composition in plan and section, and is angled to align with both the front and rear faces of the ground floor colonnade that forms the entrance to City Hall, bringing its threshold into play as part of a rhythm of spaces.

This colonnade is the only example of architectural rhythm on this side of the street, and the only thing that could identify City Hall as anything other than a tall office building. Looking east up Victoria Street from the edge of Westminster Cathedral Piazza, Westminster City Hall now appears as a distinct urban figure.

A quiet "court" is being created between our new residential building and City Hall. Lined with trees and without any public seating, this passage provides entrance to the apartments and is conceived of as

a route connecting to the Medieval alleyways to the north and east. It is a version of the courts typical to Westminster, something like a Venetian or Portuguese *largo*, a route and a civic space, but not a piazza. Our public art strategy for the project includes a number of other artists working in a variety of different media with the common theme of "second nature". The two-storey sidewall of City Hall has been revealed by the demolition of the old Kingsgate House. This is now filled by *Silver Forest*, a shallow bas-relief artwork 30 metres long and 8 metres tall by the photographic artist Rut Blees Luxemburg, cast into glass-reinforced concrete, and broken into panels formed by thin pilasters forming a faux colonnade. A path in a forest is revealed when viewed from the entrance of the apartment building, through a gap in a line of trees. At this point, the entrance to the residential building is marked by a pattern carved into a cruciform granite column, an artwork designed by the textile artists Timorous Beasties that fuses architecture with nature as ornament. The tree-crucifix-column, known as *Birdstane*, is based upon an eighteenth-century French chinoiserie toile.

Kings Gate walk is both a green space and also an image of an urban garden, one situated on a newly opened route between the river and the nearby Royal Parks. The static components of the architecture are juxtaposed with the conditions of Victoria Street, sunlight, weather, traffic, pedestrians etc combining to articulate an exaggerated experience of temporal and spatial civic depth. Kings Gate Walk was almost immediately appropriated by the council, who, in spring 2017, installed a war memorial designed by

Left: Detail view of the west facade of The Zig Zag Building.

Right: Detail view of the south facade of Kings Gate.

Top: Isometric drawing of the lower floors of The Zig Zag Building.

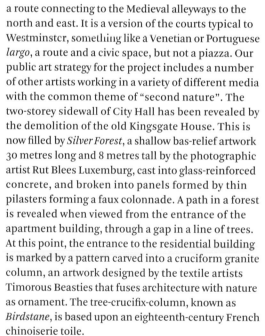

Bottom: Patrick Lynch, sketch of Kings Gate, The Zig Zag Building and Westminster City Hall.

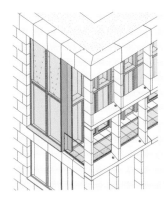

Top: Isometric drawing of the upper floors of Kings Gate.

Bottom: View of a south-facing Kings Gate roof terrace looking west towards Westminster Cathedral.

Right: View of Kings Gate and The Zig Zag Building from within the portico of Westminster City Hall.

25 David Evans, co-director of Lynch Architects, in conversation with the author, 2010.

26 Vesely, Dalibor, *Architecture in the Age of Divided Representation: The Question of Creativity in the Shadow of Production*, Cambridge, MA: MIT Press, 2004, p 106.

pp 184–193: Various views of The Zig Zag Building and Kings Gate, Angela Hooper Place, *Silver Forest* etc.

Lee Simmons, dedicated to the staff of Westminster City Council who gave their lives in the First World War.

The spatio-temporal characteristics of the artworks, and their dramatic combination with architecture, is continued in one's experience from the street of the staggered stone piers on the residential facade above. These reduce each floor (by a ratio of n–1) to restrict views and to protect the privacy of occupants on the lower floors, acting also as a solar screen. Experienced as an extended body of stone clothing by the occupier, the balconies act as an extended threshold between the inner and outer life of the flats. The simple formula of the iteration of columns has a curious effect when viewed from the street. The reduction of a column per floor results in the surface appearing to form curves that appear and disappear when you pass underneath Kings Gate. This effect is revealed in movement, but also heightened by the sun's movement across the facade; in fact it

is present as a temporal phenomenon in the curved pattern that appears in the stone facade.

We have aimed to make architecture that is highly responsive to the rhythms of the seasons and to the daily life of Victoria Street: architecture that reveals the hidden topography and scale of the city. The hope is for "iridescent architecture" that is nonetheless silent.[25] This paradox is possible because "the silence of embodiment is always to a certain extent also a voice of articulation", Vesely reminds us, and "it is only under these conditions that we can understand the language and the cultural role of architecture".[26] My intention has been to try to articulate an ecological architectural aesthetic as a new mode of ornamental civic culture, both in representational terms via collaboration with artists, and as a latent, experiential aspect of spatiality. This might be summarised as rhythmic armatures housing rhythmic situations, in an attempt to reveal the conditions for a renewed poetics of architecture.

Conclusion:
The Civic Grounds for a Poetics of Architecture

In my approach, there is a point where the interpretation (hermeneutics) and the way of making (poetics) come so close to each other that they become fully reciprocal: what we know contributes to what we make, and what is already made contributes substantially to what it is possible to know.... The distance separating the instrumental and the communicative understanding of architecture represents a wide gap in our contemporary culture. Any serious attempt to bridge this gap requires a new kind of knowledge, that can indicate how to reconcile genuine creativity and creative spontaneity with the productive power of contemporary science (technology).... The framework in which the communicative role of architecture can be restored must allow, apart from any other role, the reconciliation of the abstract language of conceptual constructions with the metaphorical language of the visible world. This was a typical task of poetics, replaced in modern times by the science of poetics, known better as aesthetics, which left the creative principles of making unaddressed.... I have argued why it is important to return to poetics and why it can be, as a new poetics of architecture, together with contemporary hermeneutics, the most appropriate framework for the restoration of the humanistic nature of architecture. It is to this goal that the main part of this book is devoted, with the full awareness that the text, as it stands, is only a foundation and framework for such a goal.
—Dalibor Vesely, *Architecture in the Age of Divided Representation*[1]

Civic ground isn't simply a particular species of space. It isn't a description of a certain kind of material surface, a specific typology, or a place defined by a limited range of functions. Civic ground is rather the basis for city life, and it is the support for and expression of a certain way of thinking about and imagining civic-oriented architecture. In the instances offered in this book, civic ground articulates tensions between historical time and cosmic conditions.

The Platonic and Aristotelian traditions of philosophical enquiry that I have investigated in this book—and its modern legacy—confidently situate geometry alongside logic, poetics alongside rhetoric, and natural science alongside making in general (*poesis*). This tradition survived until quite recently even in the "natural sciences", and architecture is traditionally a discipline that attempts to embody the visible aspect of reality, and to represent its invisible aspects. In this regard, it is fundamentally poetic. Despite contemporary prejudice, poetics is not subjective expression, but something civic.

Aristotle's *Poetics* concerns the art of drama specifically, and in particular, the importance of mediation in theatrical presentation. Aristotle suggested that poetry and painting, as arts of imitation, should use the same principal element of composition (structure),

namely, plot (myth) in tragedy and design (outline) in painting.[2] Aristotle does not explicitly define the use of these terms with regards to architecture, but Gadamer and Vesely have together developed a way of discussing the poetics of architecture that suggest that there is an irrevocable link between use and appearance (ornament), and that this reveals its linguistic character and its capacity to contribute to civic order (*decorum*).

Vesely suggests that the silent character of architectural language might be compared to the role that music plays in explaining the "mystery of symbolization, mediated by communicative movement". Settings for music reveal, he claims, "that architecture contributes to the life of our culture as text does to our literacy".[3] He continues:

In a space of a church or a concert hall, where the silence of architecture is complemented by the sound of words carried in music, we can recognize a distinct mode of spatiality in the sphere of words, sung, as it were, from a page. Enhanced by music, the spatiality of language reveals the deep structure of articulation in which words are animated by the hidden communicative movement and meaning of gestures. The gestures themselves belong to a unified corporeal scheme, which not only is a source of order but also provides the structure and content of communication. As we have already seen in the case of a game, a corporeal scheme has the power to situate and structure the complex, changing world of the game in the framework of the playing field. If we extend the notion of the playing field to architecture, then it may be possible to say that what the playing field is to the game, architecture is to culture in its broadest sense. This structuring role of architecture is clearly displayed when the same piece of music is performed in different places— leading us to wonder how the architecture of a particular place contributes to the overall musical experience. A similar question can be raised in view of the changing nature of space in film, when the sound turns into silence. Less obviously, we are answering the same question each time we choose the most appropriate place for activities such as work, study, and conversation.[4]

Vesely recognised that *mimesis* was debased in architectural terms as "imitation of reified precedents, such as the primitive hut, the Solomonic Temple, exemplary buildings and so on, or to such generalised notions as 'the imitation of nature'.[5] Nonetheless, he held fast to the idea that the modern imagination draws inspiration from the tradition of poetic *mimesis*, and that this "poetic paradigm (or poetic *mythos*)"[6] has the power to overcome the distancing effects of "the science of poetics (known better as aesthetics)".[7] Poetic architectural work is still possible, he believed, because of the potential of each new commission to become part of a whole, since "each project, however small or unimportant begins with a program—or at least with an anticipated result. Such a program or vision is formed in

1   The passage cited is from an unpublished manuscript made available to me by the author via José de Paiva.

2   Aristotle, *Poetics*, 6.19–21. See "*ut pictura poesis*", a phrase originating from Horace, *Ars Poetica*, which is based upon a notion of *mimesis* as *decorum* in both painting and poetry. The idea that poetry and painting are similar was not Horace's discovery of course, and he probably knew of a more explicit earlier statement of Simonides of Keos (first recorded by Plutarch in *De gloria atheniensium*, 3.347a, more than a century after Horace's *Ars Poetica*): "Poema pictura loquens, pictura poema silens" (poetry is a speaking picture, painting a silent, mute, poetry).

3   Vesely, *Architecture in the Age of Divided Representation*, p 104.

4   Vesely, *Architecture in the Age of Divided Representation*, pp 104–106.

5   Vesely, *Architecture in the Age of Divided Representation*, p 366.

6   Vesely, *Architecture in the Age of Divided Representation*, p 368.

7   From the unpublished manuscript version see above; see Vesely, *Architecture in the Age of Divided Representation*, p 8.

8   Vesely, *Architecture in the Age of Divided Representation*, p 13.

9   Vesely, *Architecture in the Age of Divided Representation*, p 13.

10   Aristotle, *Poetics*, 1451b10, cited in Vesely, *Architecture in the Age of Divided Representation*, p 367.

11   See Carl, Peter, "Praxis: Horizons of Involvement", *Common Ground: A Critical Reader*, David Chipperfield, Kieran Long and Shumi Bose eds, 13th International Architecture Exhibition, La Biennale di Venezia: Marsilio, 2012, p 76: "Architectural design is not simply a talent or expertise; it is part of civic *praxis*. Drawing upon Aristotle's *Poetics*, Dalibor Vesely argues that architectural interpretation (*mimesis*) is a hermeneutics of typical situations."

12   Gadamer, Hans-Georg, "On the Contribution of Poetry to the Search for Truth", *The Relevance of the Beautiful and Other Essays*, Cambridge: Cambridge University Press, 1986, p 105.

13   Gadamer, Hans-Georg, *Truth and Method*, London: Sheed & Ward, 1993 (1960), p 490.

14   Gadamer, *Truth and Method*, p 490.

15   Gadamer, *Truth and Method*, p 124.

16   Gadamer, *Truth and Method*, pp 125-126.

17   Gadamer, *Truth and Method*, p 126.

the space of experience and knowledge available to each of us".[8]

Paradigm and programme are interchangeable with plot or myth for Vesely, and although he is exquisitely aware that whilst human relationships and situations might be continuous throughout the history of architecture, they are not open to direct imitation in a typological or formal sense.

Situation grounds abstractions, such as space or function, in a resolutely human world. Situations suggest their possible articulation in an architectural sense—but they continue to recur anyway, despite architects. The task of "restoring the practical nature of situations as a primary vehicle of design enables us", Vesely claims, "to move away from inconclusive play with abstract forms and functions" that usually just form a "contemporary version of poetics often reduced to technical innovation and aesthetics".[9] Sensing the appropriate way to accommodate the variety of situations that we encounter as architects is an act of poetic *decorum*, best drawn out of the possibilities of a situation, Vesely suggested, via gestures, bodily craft, poetic making: sensible imitation.

This imaginative search is comparable to a poet's quest for the right words; it involves rhythm, movement, work, drawing something forth. In order to emphasise the profound reciprocity of articulation and embodiment, Vesely suggested that artistic work is actually exactly like the search for a mislaid book; both succeed only when you actively reach out your hand for it. The spatial character of memory, and the dramatic nature of architectural performance, is one reason why, Vesely insisted, we can still "speak about poetic *mythos* as the soul of all the creative arts, including architecture".

Architecture is less the representation of anything else than itself the *mimesis* of *praxis* (and *praxis is the mimesis of praxis*, the essence of *praxis* itself,[10] as Peter Carl reminds us).[11] The commingling of poetics and *praxis* in the practical art of architecture points to its profound contribution to culture in general, and also to the profound role that poetics plays in daily life.

Gadamer's work also extends Aristotle's poetics into a discussion about contemporary *praxis*, reasserting its philosophical dimension. He begins his argument in "On the Contribution of Poetry to the Search for Truth" asserting that "it seems incontrovertible to me that poetic language enjoys a particular and unique relationship to truth".[12] He declares that this is despite "the old Platonic and naive objection to the trustworthiness of poetry and poets—'poets often lie'... for the liar wants to be believed". His faith in the performative nature of truth—as an aspect of dialogue and of participation with reality—is at the heart of his objection to claims for scientific method as the only mode of articulation of truth. Gadamer insists upon the role of "Language as Horizon" in *Truth and Method*, and of "language games" as an essential aspect of the relationship between Being and world.[13] In his essay on poetry and truth he contends that "language always furnishes the fundamental articulations that

guide our understanding of the world. It belongs to the nature of familiarity with the world that whenever we exchange words with one another, we share the world." Poetry's role in "making ourselves at home" in the world suggests a profound similarity with architecture of course. This similarity is suggested by Gadamer's insistence in the conclusion of *Truth and Method* upon the ludic character of discourse, interpretation and creativity in general. He emphasises the fundamental orienting role that play has in culture generally:

What we mean by truth here can best be defined again in terms of our concept of *play*. The weight of the things we encounter in understanding plays itself out in a linguistic event, a play of words playing around and about what is learnt. *Language games* exist where we as learners—and when do we cease to be that?—rise to the understanding of the world. Here it is worth recalling what we said about the nature of play, namely that the player's actions should not be considered subjective actions, since it is, rather, the game itself that plays, for it draws the players into itself and thus becomes the actual *subjectum* of the playing.... When we understand a text, what is meaningful in it captivates us just as the beautiful captivates us... what we encounter in the experience of the beautiful and in understanding the meaning of tradition really has something of the truth of play about it.[14]

Gadamer's thesis is that in comparing *Truth and Method* dialectically, scientific method is revealed to operate within the horizon of language. It is thus shown to be another aspect of play, and that in fact theory, as *theoria*, is ultimately a mode of playing with the possibilities latent within the order of the cosmos. This *play involvement* is not subjective, he contends, just as "the ability to act theoretically is defined by the fact that in attending to something one is able to forget one's own purposes".[15] Similarly, philosophical work (theoria) shares with festive engagement the active characteristic of intense participation, of really being there. In order to emphasise the philosophical value of these modes of being Gadamer insists that the character of art experience, "the true being of the spectator who belongs to the play of art, cannot be adequately understood in terms of subjectivity... being present has the character of being outside oneself".[16] He goes on to demonstrate that "being outside oneself" is anything but a "kind of madness" or "a privative condition", because "being outside oneself is the positive possibility of being wholly with something else... self-forgetfulness... arises from devoting one's full attention to the matter at hand".[17]

Gadamer persuasively suggests that participation in festive events is a "positive accomplishment". Understood as festival, art experience (poetics) is a mode of playful engagement with reality with serious consequences.

He goes on to suggest therefore that philosophical research is a mode of play itself situated in *praxis*. However, "naive Platonism" often obscures the reciprocity of action and contemplation today, and he distinguishes "practical philosophy" from modern "theory" in the essays collected in *Reason in the Age of Science*. Gadamer suggests, "Today practice tends to be defined by a kind of opposition to theory", and that in "technocratic societies" theory dominates *praxis*.[18] In "What is Practice? The Conditions of Social Reason", Gadamer compares the role of craftsmen in traditional societies to the dominant role of experts in "technological civilizations". Expertise now dominates all aspects of common practical life, he claims. This is troubling, he suggests, because it affects political life; when we cease to have practical knowledge we are not capable of participating fully in society. *Praxis* is a fundamental aspect of being human, Gadamer suggests, since Being is typified as involved in the horizons of reality.[19] *Praxis* is an exemplary mode of Being, he explains, because:

> [It] involves consciously intended purposiveness, in terms of which one understands oneself as humanly reasonable, because one has an insight into the suitability of any means of commonly willed ends, the realm of all that transcends utility, usefulness, purposiveness takes on a unique distinction. We call anything of this sort beautiful in the same sense in which the Greeks used the word *kalon*. This referred not just to the creations of art or ritual, which are beyond the realm of necessities, but encompasses everything with respect to which one understands without any question that because it is choice worthy, it is neither capable nor in need of a justification of its desirability from the standpoint of its purposiveness. This is what the Greeks called *theoria*: to have been given away to something that in virtue of its overwhelming presence is accessible to all in common and that is distinguished in such a way that in contrast to all other goods it is not diminished by being shared and so is not an object of dispute like all other goods but actually gains through participation. In the end, this is the birth of the concept of reason: the more what is desirable is displayed for all in a way that is convincing to all, the more those involved discover themselves in this common reality: to that extent human beings possess freedom in the positive sense, they have their true identity in that common reality.[20]

Gadamer makes a case for "practical philosophy" as *Hermeneutics*, noting that whilst modern "hermeneutics is understood (as) the theory or art of explication, of interpretation", it is in fact "old".[21] In eighteenth-century German the "expression for this *Kunstlehre* (a teaching about a technical skill or know-how) is actually a translation of the Greek *techne*", Gadamer tells us, noting that this points to the origins of Humanism in Aristotelian philosophy:

> It links hermeneutics with such arts as grammar, rhetoric, and dialectic. But the expression *Kunstlehre*

points to a cultural and educational tradition other than that of late antiquity: the remote and no longer vital tradition of Aristotelian philosophy. Within it there was a so-called *philosophia practica* (*sive politica*), which lived on right up to the eighteenth century. It formed the systematic framework for all the arts, inasmuch as they all stand at the service of the *polis*.[22]

Hermeneutics is a mode of what Gadamer describes as *theoria*, and in fact he extrapolates—from Aristotle's "splendid statement", in his *Politics*, that "we name active in the supreme measure those who are determined by their performance in the realm of thought alone"[23]—the shocking statement (to us moderns) that "*Theoria* itself is a practice".[24] This statement makes sense in the context of the ancient world but seems odd to us today when we are used to thinking of theory in terms of science, and of poetry as something that is impractical, and in fact of practice, in contrast to "theory and science", in terms of "impurity, haphazardness, accommodation or compromise".[25] It makes sense if we think of it in terms of politics, Gadamer suggests, and in particular in Plato's writing on the state that distinguishes between "purely ideal order" and the "soiled and mixed up world of the senses"; the tension between these typify the character of the *polis* as site of *agon*, conflict and participation, and, Gadamer claims, "the relationship between theory and practice in the Greek sense".[26] Practice is thus an attribute of social reason, just as theory is a matter of participation in what is acknowledged as common. Participation is the basis of political life, and the nature of city life is that it is there that we agree and acknowledge what it is that we disagree about.

Poetics is in fact much closer to *praxis* than we are led to believe today. Peter Carl claims that in fact poetics is the imitation of *praxis*:

> Aristotle separates mimetic discourse from the work of politics and logic, in his *Poetics*. At the same time, he makes the central thesis of his treatment (of, mostly, tragic drama) the proposition that poetics is a *mimesis* of *praxis*; and the basis of this *mimesis* is what he terms *mythos* (usually translated as "plot"). Accordingly, one can see that Plato and Aristotle are responding to the life in *logos* in different ways, but that the life in *logos* itself harbours a commonality that claims all speakers. One always finds oneself in an agonic movement between particular and universal, between concrete many and symbolic one, between dialogue and dialectic. As the very nature of "finding oneself", being, there-being, this *agon* would be reframed by Heidegger as one between earth (conditions) and world (possibilities), which points to the universal nature of "situation (all situations involve interpretation).[27]

Carl's emphasis upon interpretation suggests its central role in poetics. Poetics as imitation of *praxis*

18 Gadamer, Hans-Georg, "What is Practice? The Conditions of Social Reason", *Reason in the Age of Science*, Cambridge, MA: MIT Press, 2001, p 69.

19 Gadamer, *Reason in the Age of Science*, p 76. Peter Carl notes that *praxis* is characterised by "horizons of involvement".

20 Gadamer, *Reason in the Age of Science*, p 77. The ontological meaning of beauty in Greek culture is clear in the meaning of *kalon* as beauty, and moral beauty, or goodness. This duality is one reason for the importance of Hellenic culture to Romanticism, evidenced most explicitly in John Keats' poem "Ode on a Grecian Urn", 1820. One reason for this interest in the integrity of artefacts is that industrial production and the changes this entailed in the relationships between cities and natural world—and between mankind and nature generally—disrupted what was traditionally mediated by craft (poetics).

21 Gadamer, "Hermeneutics as Practical Philosophy", *Reason in the Age of Science*, p 88.

22 Gadamer, *Reason in the Age of Science*, p 88.

23 Aristotle, *Politics*, 1325b 21ff.

24 Gadamer, *Reason in the Age of Science*, p 90.

25 Gadamer, *Reason in the Age of Science*, p 90.

26 Gadamer, *Reason in the Age of Science*, p 90.

27 Carl, Peter, "Geometry and Discourse", unpublished essay, 2010. For further elaboration on the role of architecture as a mode of *mimesis* of *praxis* ("*mimesis tes praxeous*"), see Hvattum, Mari, *Gottfried Semper and the Problem of Historicism*, Cambridge: Cambridge University Press, 2003, pp 75–83.

28 See Norri, Marja-Riitta and Maija Kärkkäinen eds, *Peter Celsing: The Facade is the Meeting Between Outside and Inside (Fasaden ar motet mellan ute och inne)*: Helsinki: Museum of Finnish Architecture, 1992.

29 See Gadamer, *The Relevance of the Beautiful*; and Gadamer, *Truth and Method*, pp 123-126.

30 See North, Douglas C, John Joseph Wallis and Barry R Weingast, *Violence and Social Orders: A Conceptual Framework for Interpreting Recorded Human History*, Cambridge: Cambridge University Press, 2012. Their recent work on violence suggests a malign side to the notion of "open access order" that they presented over the past decade.

31 An observation made at Emmanuel College Cambridge on 11 April 2016 at The Cultural Significance of Architecture: A Conference in Memory of Dalibor Vesely.

Top: Political demonstration outside Westminster City Hall, May 2015.

Bottom: The Mayor of Westminster opening Angela Hooper Place, November 2015.

suggests that it is in fact a mode of *decorum*—and that interpretation concerns what is or is not appropriate in a situation. In terms of architecture I would suggest this is not a matter of either the introverted nature of functionalism on the one hand, nor the extroverted character of formalism on the other. Rather, *decorum* is the communication between both the interior and exterior of buildings, people and the world. We see this most clearly illustrated in the role that facades play as spatial thresholds between interior and exterior rooms—indeed, the facade was itself understood as a type of space in Baroque architecture. This notion still has currency in modern architecture, I believe.[28]

In urban settings the role of the facade is key to establishing urbanity itself. This is because there is a certain degree of typicality both to spatial situations, (or "programmes"), and to urban contexts, which the facade of a building negotiates. This is the most obviously "ornamental" aspect of architecture. The central role that ornament and facades play in mediating between building and city, and its contribution to *decorum* generally, is a vital aspect of civic ground.

Civic ground is therefore not only a material phenomenon, but is fundamentally a spatial temporal aspect of existence. Certain conditions of Being are revealed in spatiality, and are made thematic in the conditions of rhythm. A pause in a dance, or space in between things, is like the *time-out-of-time* of festival etc, with obvious links to philosophy.[29] It is only in these gaps in everyday time that the fundamental conditions of Being become thematic, making Being as such "conspicuous".

In rhetoric, and all modes of play generally, what Dalibor Vesely calls the "communicative movement" (or "ontological movement") inherent in one's experiences of art and architecture are fundamentally specific. The "specific" qualities of artworks are something which late twentieth-century sculptors recovered from the wasteland of nineteenth-century Romantic egoism.

The architecture of Lewerentz and Moneo is undeniably site-specific, it should also be seen as typical of the tradition of a spatial dialogue between sculpture and architecture, inherited from the Greeks and which, I hope is now clear, has proven capable of regular renewal. This tradition is analogical: it represents some of the topics of Platonic and Aristotelian philosophy that unite rhetoric and poetry, dance with geometry and rhythmic spatiality. Traditionally, architecture is the setting for this unity; and the site of this unity I have called civic ground.

We have seen how architects have articulated the dialogue between sculpture and the natural world over the past 500 years, and that this is not a matter of form or style, but of rhythmic spatiality. Whilst the functional programme of a concert hall is distinctly different to a church and superficially the architecture of Moneo and Lewerentz is diverse, the quasi-operatic performances at the Roman Oratory indicate that the difference is not as great as between either of these and, say, a petrol station. Arguably, these modern examples are also exemplary of a late twentieth-century context in which a weakened mode of welfare state modernism encountered traditional culture on the one hand ("the Church", local politics etc), and neo-liberal capitalism on the other (social democratic governments, private-public finance etc).

This is largely the context in which any European architect will be lucky enough to be still working today. In an "open access society" we supposedly all have access to communication, and yet communicative space has become something that is now elusive if not impossible to encounter.[30] Vesely's phrase "communicative movement" seems to require a degree of participation and involvement that "open access" seems paradoxically to deny—since there can be no movement or transformation if *everything* appears open, yet in fact is already mediated, but lacks hierarchy. This leads to the attempt to define everything as a system: all the ethical and political good intentions of an architect are impossible to reconcile with a purely systematic or formal order.

We do not experience anywhere as architects that is not a mediated encounter: and as Peter Carl points out, "the earth is already architecture".[31] What we sometimes blithely call "the site" cannot be simply reduced to a redline boundary defining a building plot; when this happens, the Frankenstein architecture of "icons" emerges from the alienated imaginations of narcissistic architects. Peter Eisenman called for "critical site-specific architecture" 30 years ago, and yet immediately recoiled from the possibilities of this into the vacuum of "autonomous architecture".

The ghost of nineteenth-century architecture haunts the work of Colin Rowe and Peter Eisenman—it haunts us all. My argument is an attempt to recognise and to exorcise the ghost of the infamous and pointless notion of the Victorian "Battle of the Styles". Over insistence by historians on this alleged battle—for example between the Gothic decoration of Pugin and the Classicism of Barry—obscured the profound contribution that nineteenth-century architecture made to the creation and articulation of civic ground. The over-emphasis on stylistic warfare in early twentieth-century history is arguably one reason why modern architects saw in technology a way and means to avoid the question of ornament altogether.

Arguably, in comparing Le Corbusier's buildings to Palladio's via an analysis of their "mathematics", ie proportions stripped of ratio and analogue, Colin Rowe completed the task of providing a pseudo-historical justification for modernist architects' abandonment of *decorum* and rhetoric in favour of analysis and formalism.

This is perhaps why what we now call "theory" in architecture is incapable of bearing its traditional meaning, or of providing any practical guidance about anything that might be communicable to clients, planners, the public, our colleagues in other disciplines etc.

We have inherited civic ground from the Victorians that is incomplete. Aspects of rhythmic and communicative space survive but also its lack; or rather, we lack continuity between traditional and modern settings. The city itself, its urban rooms and routes, seems to be still largely obscured by the collision of social engineering with transport engineering in the domain of appearance.

We experience civic ground as a shock today, something unexpected in the interrupted topography of modern cities. Yet we recognise it as both the memory of typical situations, and as something paradoxically refreshing, a renewed, recognisable quality of civic life. Civic ground is similar to art in general in this regard, and Gadamer captures this paradox neatly in *The Relevance of the Beautiful*: "Art is the creation of something exemplary which is not simply produced by following rules."[32] In a very similar way to orienting oneself in the world in general, creative design, like the interpretation of a building or a typical situation, involves an act of imagination as much as memory.

There is a fundamental problem for urban *praxis* when architects crib methods from modern experimental science or from fine artists, and arguably "scientific method" per se is an inappropriate way to investigate architecture; since it is not an activity undertaken in an artist's garret nor in a laboratory.

Architectural *praxis* entails acknowledging "the reciprocity of the actual and the possible", and civic ground manifests "the reciprocity of necessity and freedom, where 'necessity' represents a given reality—the inevitable, necessary condition of our freedom and creativity".[33]

We learn from the resonance of site, architecture and sculpture—civic ground—that aesthetics are relational. "Beauty", Eduardo Chillida suggests, "is always mixed up in issues."[34] Civic ambition is inevitably oriented towards establishing the possibility of "the good life"; this helps explain why so much philosophy in Classical culture concerned cities.[35] This did not entail, however, attempting to create an ideal city or society, but, rather, revealing those aspects of conduct and ethics that manifest goodness. Plato saw, in the search for truth, goodness manifest as beauty, and whilst "Plato linked the idea of the beautiful to that of the good, he was still aware of the difference between the two and this difference involves the special advantage of the beautiful", Gadamer claims.[36] The advantage it has is that:

> The beautiful is distinguished from the absolutely intangible good in that it can be grasped. It is part of its own nature to be something visibly manifest. The beautiful reveals itself in the search for the good.[37]

Gadamer claims in fact that "beauty has the most important ontological function: that of mediating between idea and appearance", stating that this "is the metaphysical crux of Platonism". This "finds its concrete form in the concept of participation

(*methexis*) and concerns both the relation of the appearance to an idea and the relation of ideas to one another".[38] Participation lies at the heart of Plato's demonstration of the beautiful—as that which is visible to all (just as participation is the basis for Gadamer's own concept of art as festival): "However much beauty might be experienced as the reflection of something supraterrestrial, it is still there in the visible world." Yet "the beautiful appears not only in what is visibly present to the senses", Gadamer claims, because "it does so in such a way that it really exists only through it—ie emerges out of a whole".[39] Traditionally, *theoria* was a means to share in the full richness and diversity of the *kosmos*, acknowledging the complex hierarchies of relationships between the material and invisible aspects of reality. Poetics was the means to reveal the *harmony* that is latent within the cosmos.

Poetics is a quality that we find in visible, audible and comprehensible well-made things, what Aristotle called "well-formed works".[40] It enables beauty to "emerge as a harmonious whole that is proportioned within itself". Poetics plays a central role in the disclosure of truth, Plato believed, "which is part of the nature of the beautiful".[41] Gadamer reminds us that "the sensible mean, exactness of proportion is part of the oldest definition of the beautiful. We need only think of the sensitivity to the tonal harmonies from which music is constructed".[42] Beauty is manifest in material things, but it is better, Gadamer suggests, to describe it "not as simply symmetry but appearance itself... related to the idea of 'shining'.... Beauty has a mode of being of *light*."[43] Poetics embodies and articulates beauty, that which is "most radiant" (*to ekphanestaton*). Because it is "radiant", Gadamer suggests, beauty—like civic ground in general—is something that illuminates and makes beautiful the things that surround it.

The reappearance of civic culture in the modern city, despite everything that threatens to obscure it, suggests the grounds also for the renewal of poetic architectural *praxis*: in other words, a civic architecture, oriented, ecstatically, beyond itself.

32 Gadamer, *The Relevance of the Beautiful*, p 21.

33 Vesely, *Architecture in the Age of Divided Representation*, p 58.

34 Chillida, Eduardo, *Eduardo Chillida: Writings*, Dusseldorf: Richter Verlag, 2009, p 98.

35 A notable exception is Ábalos, Iñaki, *The Good Life: A Guided Visit to the Houses of Modernity*, Barcelona: Gustavo Gil, 2001. For an elaboration of the notion of goodness and beauty into ecological design, see also Ábalos, Iñaki, "Thermodynamism and Architecture", *Ábalos+Sentkiewicz, 2G 56*, Barcelona: Gustavo Gil, 2011. See also Fernández-Galiano, Luis, "Thermodynamics and Architecture", unpublished lecture at the Academia Real in Madrid 2012; see also Mallinson, Helen, *Aer to Air*, forthcoming; and "From city air to urban space: passion and pollution", in which she makes explicit the connections between "bad air" pollution and Platonic notions of civic good in sixteenth-century English thought: "Shaftesbury did not compete with Newton's mastery of space but instead tried to solve the epistemological problem of how the mind learnt about truth and beauty. He suggested that man possessed a moral sense rather than innate ideas. Locke himself had suggested there might be more than the traditional five senses and Shaftesbury took the opportunity to expand the repertoire. He reworked Platonic ideas about soul into a faculty of moral sense that could work with the good and the beautiful in the same way that the mind was able to work with the data provided by vision through sight and light. Shaftesbury's new faculty gave credence to the strong moral and educational agenda that developed in eighteenth century aesthetic theory. The problem of identifying 'the good' unfolded new horizons. Shaftesbury broadened the argument around enthusiasm by moving away from the issue of authenticity, focusing instead on issues of context and judgment. Both humour and imagination were essential to the new 'civility'. The material air, meanwhile, was slowly becoming associated with physical health rather than moral character", *Journal of Architecture*, vol 19, 2014, p 10. See also Mallinson, Helen, "Weather Dissidents: From *Natura Naturans*, to 'Space' and Back Again", *Architecture and the Paradox of Dissidence*, London: Routledge, 2013.

36 Gadamer, *Truth and Method*, p 480.

37 Gadamer, *Truth and Method*, p 481.

38 Gadamer, *Truth and Method*, p 481.

39 Gadamer, *Truth and Method*, p 482.

40 Aristotle, *Nicomachean Ethics*, ii: chpt 6, 1106 b 10.

41 Plato, *Philebus*, 51d.

42 Gadamer, *Truth and Method*, p 482.

43 Gadamer, *Truth and Method*, p 482.

View of Kings Gate with Angela Hooper
Place on the left.

Index

A

acceptera 107–109
Ackroyd, Peter 174
aediculae 79
aesthetic consciousness 67
agon 18, 62, 98, 198
Ahlin, Janne 111–112
Alberti, Leon Battista 12, 26–27, 69–71, 131, 162, 178
Albertopolis 162, 164
Alby 110, 116
All Saints Margaret Street 113
ambiguity 28, 53, 76, 79
anachronic 166
analogy, *analogia* 5, 12, 23, 25–26, 43, 46, 48–49, 57, 61, 70, 83, 98, 100
Anderson, Ross 99–102
Anglican 40, 111–112, 114, 133
Anglo-Catholic 112, 114, 163
aphasia 43, 48
Appia, Adolphe 52–54, 60, 129
Aristotle 5, 9, 12, 19, 46, 48, 62, 70, 76, 78–79, 97–98, 101, 196–198, 200
Arnold, Matthew 162, 164, 169
art experience 61–62, 67, 95–96, 197
Art and Space 76–78, 80, 96–97, 141
Art Sacré 115
Art Workers' Guild 162
Asplund, Gunnar 107–109

B

Bachelard, Gaston 9, 56, 83
baldacchino 175–177
Bataille, Georges 109
barn 80–83, 100
Baroque 54, 59–60, 67, 106, 126, 149, 151, 199
Baudelaire, Charles 162
Bazalgette, Joseph 164–165, 172
beautiful, beauty 5, 18–19, 30, 40, 43, 47, 49, 59, 62, 69–70, 72, 83, 92, 164, 197, 198, 200
Being 61, 76–78, 80, 96–99, 103, 197–199
Belgravia 167, 169
Benjamin, Walter 57
Bentley, John Francis 169, 175, 182
Berggren, Henrik 109
Berlin 18, 29, 32–37, 168
Białostocki, Jan 69–70
Birdstane 181–182
Birmingham 40, 162
Blees Luxemburg, Rut 180, 182
Blundell-Jones, Peter 112
body 4–5, 9, 20, 22, 42–44, 49, 52, 56, 58–61, 70, 78, 96–97, 100, 122, 151, 154, 164, 178, 183
Borromini, Francesco 12, 20, 46–47, 72, 131
Botticelli, Sandro 130
bricks 112, 119–121
bricolage 23, 27

Briggs, Asa 162
Brunnenstern 97, 99–103
Bruno, Giordano 69
Burnet, Sir John James 165, 167
Burnet, Tait & Partners 165, 169, 176

C

Calais 16–17
    the Jungle 16
Calvin, Calvinist 106, 111, 113, 115
capital 56, 100, 102, 109
Cardinal Manning 175
Carl, Peter 5, 16, 20–21, 30, 42, 48–49, 52, 61–63, 66, 96, 98, 100, 139, 197–199
Caruso, Adam 111–112
Cathedra 124, 126, 133, 151
Catholic 15, 27, 40, 53, 106, 111–115, 126
Celsing, Peter 110–111, 115
Centre Pompidou 57
Chadwick, Sir Edwin 164
Chandigarh 30
Chartres 58–59, 78
Chillida, Eduardo 9, 72, 76–77, 79–85, 90, 92, 95–96, 103, 200
Church of Sweden 111, 113–114
civic gospel 162
civic pride 162–163
civic ritual 163
civic virtue 13, 18, 70, 163, 166
cloister 30, 47, 115, 118, 124, 141
cliff, the 110, 139
Collage City 23, 27
Cologne 40–42
Comito, Terry 12
commonitas 129
communication, communicate 18, 20–21, 33, 40, 42–43, 47, 49, 61–62, 78, 80, 92, 102, 106, 111, 129, 163–165, 196, 199
communicative movement 49, 58–62, 67, 79, 103, 106–107, 122, 168, 196, 199
concinnitas 26
contingent 48, 68, 92, 162
continuity of references 42–43, 59–60
Cooper Union 28
cosmic conditions 12, 58, 72, 196
cosmologists 15
creativity, creative 9, 14, 19, 21, 25, 29, 32, 42–43, 66, 103, 107, 112, 162, 196–197, 200
Crowther, Paul 76–77
crucifixion, crucifix 80, 82, 95, 124, 126, 129, 141, 151, 182
Cubitt brothers, the 167

D

dance 4, 19, 31, 43, 53, 72, 78, 96, 199
Dasein 62–63, 76, 99
Da Vinci, Leonardo 70, 100

death 30–31, 42, 52, 59, 78, 83, 99–100, 103, 133, 151, 162, 166
decoration 29, 52, 68–69, 199
decorum 12–13, 18, 20–21, 25–26, 28, 30, 40, 44–49, 52–53, 59, 61–62, 66–72, 78, 92, 97, 106–107, 131, 162–163, 166, 176, 196–197, 199
dialectic 27, 35, 52, 57–58, 62, 80, 90, 98, 141, 167, 197–198
dialogue 30, 58, 62, 80, 85, 98, 100, 129, 197–199
disclosure (of Being) 103
distance 4, 32, 35, 43, 47–48, 83, 100, 103, 131, 133, 196
Domus Dei 115
Domus Ecclesia 115
Dresden 54, 66
dwelling 16, 27, 76–77, 96–97, 99–100, 103

E

earth 9, 19, 28, 31, 35, 42, 52–53, 59–63, 77, 83, 96–98, 100, 102–103, 107, 115, 119, 126, 141, 151, 172, 198, 199
ecology 19, 28
Eisenman, Peter 18, 21, 23, 25–29, 32–37, 43, 48, 103, 162, 199
Eliot, TS 112, 166
emptiness 77, 165
EPR Architects 169, 175
equipment 37, 67, 97, 103, 106, 121, 133, 151
Erasmus 69
ethics 12–13, 46, 48, 62, 70, 98, 169, 200
ethos 12, 19, 69, 72, 106
Eucharist 79, 115, 122, 124–129, 154
Eulogy to the Horizon 82–83
eurhythmic 52–54
Evans, Robin 12

F

facade 19, 26, 40, 44–47, 56–57, 66–67, 69, 71, 78, 90, 118, 122, 124, 140, 151–153, 162, 166–168, 172, 174–179, 182–183, 199
Fawwar 21–22
festival 9, 12, 18–20, 41, 45, 53, 56, 58, 62, 67, 70, 78, 90, 95, 97, 103, 162, 197, 199, 200
Ficino, Marsilio 69–70
Florence 13, 16, 54, 69–72, 96, 163, 166
form 4–5, 14–16, 19, 21–31, 35, 40, 42, 44, 47–48, 56, 58, 67–68, 70, 78, 80, 83–85, 90, 92–97, 100, 102–103, 106, 111–112, 122, 129, 139, 166, 168–169, 175, 182, 197, 199–200
formalism 9, 13–15, 18, 20, 22–28, 32–39, 48–49, 61, 67–68, 70, 139, 168, 199
fourfold 99–101
fragment 9, 27–28, 35, 119, 121, 139, 169
fresco 30, 60–61

G

Gadamer, Hans-Georg 4, 13, 19, 52, 61–63, 66–69, 72, 95, 97–98, 106, 196–200
Ganchegui, Luis Peña 80, 85
geometry 12, 20, 25–26, 28, 30–31, 42–43, 57, 61, 78, 83, 85, 95, 97–98, 100, 102–103, 131, 196, 198–199
Gilbert Scott, Giles 163
Goethe, Johann Wolfgang von 97, 141
Golgotha 124
Guest, Clare Lapraik 70, 72
Guild 47, 162
Gunn, Simon 163

H

harmony 26, 30, 43, 53, 61, 66, 70, 72, 78, 97, 112, 121, 141, 200
Hassett, Gráinne 16–17
Hawksmoor, Nicholas 167
Heidegger, Martin 5, 9, 19, 37, 61–63, 66–67, 76–78, 83, 95–103, 112, 131, 133, 141, 198
Hellerau 52–55, 60
hermeneutic 9, 19, 48, 62, 67–68, 107, 121, 196–198
heuristic 67, 97
          heuristic landscape 139
High Church 112–115, 129
Hollis, Leo 164–165
Holy Sepulchre 124
Houses of Parliament, 40, 164, 166
Hütte, hut 98–103, 196
Hvattum, Mari 198

I

ideal city 200
idealism 23, 53, 103
imitation 21, 28, 35, 53, 62, 66–70, 72, 95, 101, 163–164, 167, 196–198
Italy 12, 14, 18, 53–54, 67, 70, 96, 109, 139, 167

J

Jaques-Dalcroze, Émile 52–54
Jordan 124
          River Jordan 141
Judd, Donald 23, 31–32, 49

K

Kant, Immanuel 25, 29, 66, 69, 97, 103, 106
kehre (turn) 76–77
Kings Gate 169–171, 178–183, 201
Kingsgate House 165, 171, 176, 178, 182
Klippan 72, 106, 110, 112–113, 115–122, 124, 126–141
Koob-Sassen, Hilary 172, 174–177
kosmos 66, 200

L

Land Securities 169, 175–176
Lasch, Christopher 12, 14
Last Supper 79, 124, 126

latent background 61
Le Corbusier 21, 24–26, 29–32, 62, 78–79, 102, 109, 115, 129, 199
Le poême de l'angle droit 30–31, 78
Leatherbarrow, David 37, 44, 48, 129, 133, 162, 199
Lefebvre, Henri 31, 56–58
Leku 80, 83
Lewerentz, Sigurd 9, 72, 106–113, 115–117, 119, 121–122, 124, 126, 129, 131, 139, 141, 199
Lindgren, Astrid 109
Liverpool 40, 48, 163–164, 168
logos 30, 98, 198
London 9, 14, 25, 27, 31, 40, 49, 67, 162, 164–166, 168–169, 174
Longstocking, Pippi 109
Lutheran 103, 106, 110, 112–113, 115, 122, 124, 126, 133
Lynch Architects 24, 168–169, 171–173, 175–177, 180, 183

M

Machiavelli, Niccolò 69
Mallinson, Helen 200
Malmö 107, 126
Mantegna, Andrea 70
Marion, Jean-Luc 131, 133
Matcham, Frank 169, 172, 174
Mathematics of the Ideal Villa 24–25, 30
Mattsson, Helena 107, 109–110
McGuirk, Justin 31, 49
Medici 13, 70, 72–73
Medieval 12, 16, 26, 40, 45–47, 49, 56–58, 69–70, 80, 107, 111, 114–115, 129, 149, 163, 166, 182
Meller-Marcovicz, Digne 99, 101–102
methexis 98, 200
metre 78
Michelangelo 12–13, 46, 83, 100
million programme, the 109
mimesis 9, 35, 62, 66, 69–70, 98, 196–198
Mitchell, Andrew J 76, 95–97
modernity, 53, 109–110, 116, 131, 163, 166
monasticum 47, 141
Moneo, Rafael 72, 80, 90, 92–93, 95, 103, 107, 199
Municipal Reform Act 162
music 4–5, 19, 26, 30, 42–43, 46–47, 52–54, 56, 68, 78, 90, 92, 95, 111, 151, 196, 200
myth 14, 19, 52–54, 61, 79, 98, 102, 106, 109, 112, 115, 131, 166–167, 196–198

N

narcissism 14
Natura Naturans, Natura Naturata 69, 178
nature 5, 12, 14, 18–19, 53, 58, 62, 66, 68–70, 72, 85, 95, 97, 100–101, 106–107, 115, 133, 165, 166, 178, 182, 196–198
          second nature 18–19, 178, 182
          third nature 166
Neo-Gothic 163, 167
Neumann, Balthasar 60

Newman, The Blessed John Henry 176
Nietzsche, Friedrich 109–110, 131

O

oikos 92
ontological 21, 32, 42, 48, 62, 66, 68–70, 76, 97, 198, 200
          ontological movement 60, 79, 95, 129, 135, 199
oratory 30, 70
          Roman Oratory (the Oratory of St Philip Neri) 20, 46–47, 131, 199
orientation, 13, 18–19, 31, 37, 40–42, 46, 52, 54, 59–61, 66, 69, 72, 79–80, 92, 96, 100, 106, 119, 121, 125, 155, 167, 176
ornament 12–13, 18, 26, 29–31, 45–46, 52, 61–62, 66, 68–70, 72, 97, 99–100, 106, 163, 165, 182, 196, 199
Oxford Movement 114, 163

P

Paiva, José de 129, 149
Palazzo Chiericati 26, 44
Palazzo Rucellai 72
Palladio, Andrea 24–27, 30, 32, 44–45, 162, 199
Palazzo della Ragione 44–45
Paris 15–16, 18, 56–57, 59, 168
Parousia 58
participation, participatory 9, 19, 30, 35, 37, 40, 49, 58, 60–67, 69–70, 77–79, 106–107, 121, 124, 129, 131, 197–200
pathos (passive) 19, 139
patriarchal values 163
patrimonial duty 163
pause 19, 78–79, 199
phenomenology 9, 18, 20, 23, 31, 99, 112
phronesis (practical wisdom) 46, 62, 76
physiognomy 13, 37, 40, 42, 58–59
physis 62–63
Plato 9, 25, 46, 62, 66, 78–79, 97–98, 100, 198–200
play 18, 22, 30, 43, 66–69, 76, 95–96, 102–103, 106, 174, 196–197, 199
poesis, poetics 9, 15, 19, 21, 23, 35, 37, 48, 61, 78, 98, 112, 183, 196–198, 200
polis 15, 62, 96, 98, 198
practical philosophy 62, 198
praxis 5, 9, 18–19, 32, 42–43, 48, 58, 61–62, 68, 70, 98, 106, 162, 197–198, 200
primary dialectic 62
Protestant 111–112, 115, 133

Q

Queen Victoria 164, 168

R

Rappe, Dean Axel 115
rationalism 103, 114
          neo-rationalism 14
Reformation 113, 126, 129, 175

renewal 9, 18, 37, 40, 103, 133, 199–200
resistance 35, 53, 58–59, 97, 114
rhetoric 12–13, 20, 30, 46, 70, 72, 98, 149, 196, 198–199
rhythm 4, 9, 12–14, 18–19, 21–22, 25, 30, 33, 37–40, 45, 47, 49, 53–54, 56–57, 59–62, 66–68, 70, 78–80, 83, 85, 90, 92, 95–96, 100–101, 103, 107, 119, 121–122, 124–126, 133, 139, 141, 149, 151, 155, 165, 175–179, 182–183, 197, 199
Riemenschneider, Tilman 79
Ridderstedt, Lars 106, 111–115, 124, 126, 129, 139
River Fleet 165–166
River Thames 40, 60, 164–165
Rococo 129, 149, 151
Romantics, Romanticism 25, 52–53, 85, 115, 198–199
          German Romantics 103
Rome 14, 23, 26–27, 46–47, 67, 72, 113, 164
Ronchamp 30–31, 62, 112, 115
Rowe, Colin 18, 23, 25–28, 30, 32, 37, 67, 199
Rowland, Ingrid 43
Ruskin, John 31, 115, 164
Rykwert, Joseph 14–15, 18, 44, 46, 79, 131, 178

S
Sacks, Oliver 5, 43
sacrifice 14, 40, 44, 62, 79, 103, 112, 124, 126, 129, 138
San Sebastián 72, 79–80, 83, 90, 92, 95, 107
Santiago de Compostela 28, 79
Schumacher, Patrik 20–21, 43, 48
Schwarz, Rudolf 106, 115, 124, 129
Scuole 47
seasonal time 43, 59, 92
Sennett, Richard 14
Serra, Richard 9, 23, 28–29, 31–33, 35, 37, 48–49, 68
Sharr, Adam 98–99
Shift 32, 35, 37
sign 21, 30, 53, 56, 67
silence 35, 58, 60, 78, 80, 85, 95, 112, 129, 131, 183, 196
Silver Forest 180–183
situation, situational 14, 19, 20–21, 25–26, 30, 32–33, 35, 37, 41–45, 47–49, 53, 57–61, 63, 66–69, 72, 77–78, 92, 96–98, 100–101, 103, 106–107, 109, 113, 115, 119, 121, 124–125, 129, 133, 139, 151, 162, 167, 169, 178, 182–183, 197–200
Siza, Álvaro 72, 147–159
Skåne 110, 116
Snow, John 164, 167
social reason 198
Socrates 62, 78, 100
Solà-Morales, Ignasi de 76
Somerset House 164–165
space 5, 9, 12, 16, 20–23, 28, 30, 33, 35, 37, 40–44, 48–49, 52–54, 56–61, 68, 76–80, 83, 85, 90, 95–97, 103, 106, 110, 112, 115, 119, 121–122, 124, 129, 133, 141, 151, 155, 168, 176, 196–200

spatiality 9, 18, 21, 33, 35, 37, 42–43, 49, 54, 58, 61–62, 68, 70, 76, 79–80, 83, 92, 96, 103, 106–107, 111–112, 151, 183, 196, 199
spectacle 14, 31, 42, 54, 56–58, 61, 95, 162–163
Spielraum 95, 103, 139
Santa Maria 26, 46–47, 54, 71–72, 80, 82, 95, 129, 149, 151, 154–155
St Peter's Church, Klippan 72, 106, 111–113, 116, 119, 121, 122, 124, 126, 129, 131, 133, 139, 141
St Philip Neri 46–47
stair 52, 57–58, 60, 83, 93, 151, 174–175
Stella Octangula 100
Stockholm 106–110, 115
Swedish model, Swedish way 107, 109–110, 114
symbol, symbolism 21, 25, 46–48, 63, 66–67, 83, 99, 103, 107, 129, 149, 151, 155–157
symetria, symmetry 32, 43, 44, 106, 200

T
Tafuri, Manfredo 12, 109
techne 19, 48, 62, 198
technology 13–14, 18, 27, 40, 48, 56, 62, 72, 76, 103, 107, 133, 141, 166–167, 169, 196, 199
          technological-scientific thinking 103
Temple, Nick 9, 112, 129, 131
temporal 4, 8–9, 12, 19, 42, 56–57, 59, 66–67, 79–80, 107, 129, 133, 175, 182–183, 199
Terragni, Giuseppe 23, 25–26
Texas 27, 31
"The Origin of the Work of Art" 9, 77, 96, 103
The Relevance of the Beautiful 13, 19, 66–67, 95, 197, 200
The Way of the Cross 106–107, 122
The Wind Comb 80, 83, 85, 92, 95
theatre 16–17, 23, 52–54, 56–57, 60, 68, 78, 96, 106, 126, 139, 169, 174
          Victoria Palace Theatre 169, 172, 174
theoria, theory 9, 15, 18–22, 26–28, 32, 42–43, 46, 48–49, 54, 62, 78, 112, 115, 162, 197–200
threshold 12–13, 19, 21, 46–48, 52–53, 67, 78–79, 90, 92, 95, 100, 102, 115, 129, 151, 153, 154, 162, 168, 176, 178, 182–183, 199
Tiepolo 60
Timæus 100
Timorous Beasties 181–182
Todtnauberg 97–100
Topics 98
topography, 9, 14, 18, 20, 26–28, 35, 40, 42, 44–45, 49, 52, 62, 80, 95–96, 106, 141, 148–149, 154, 157, 162, 164, 168, 178, 183, 200
topology 42, 98
topos 46, 53, 62, 76, 106, 141 162, 164, 174–175
Totenbaum 99
tradition 9, 15–16, 18–19, 21, 23, 26–27, 35, 52–53, 58, 61–62, 69–70, 72, 78, 83, 98, 103, 106–107, 109–113, 115, 122, 131, 139, 149, 162–163, 166–167, 169, 175, 196–199
"Tradition and the Individual Talent" 112
treppenhaus 60

Truth and Method 4, 19, 52, 66–69, 106, 197, 200
typology, 30, 42–44, 100, 167, 196

U
universal 9, 27, 43, 48, 61–62, 68–70, 79, 98, 103, 106, 113, 124, 126, 198
urban depth 16, 18, 35
urban rooms 168, 176, 200
utilitarianism 15, 164

V
Vattimo, Gianni 76
Venus 129–130, 151
Vesely, Dalibor 9, 25, 40, 42–43, 48–49, 54, 57–61, 66–68, 78, 96, 103, 133, 139, 183, 196–197, 199
Vicenza 44–45, 162
Victoria and Albert Museum 162–164
Victoria Embankment 164–165
Victoria Street 40, 72, 164, 167–169, 174–175, 178, 182–183
Vienna 33, 35
villa 25, 44, 47, 72, 100, 102, 115–116, 174
Virgin Mary, the 129, 149, 154–155
virtual body 42
Vitruvius 27, 30, 32, 43–44, 46, 52, 78

W
Wahlman, Lars Israel 115
Wallenstein, Sven-Olov 107, 109–110
Wang, Wilfred 111, 115
weather 19, 42, 58, 182
Webb, Aston 162
west gate (St Peter's Church, Klippan) 128–129, 138, 140
Westminster Abbey 40, 167–168, 175
Westminster Cathedral 169, 175–176, 178, 182
Whiteread, Rachel 32–33, 35
Wilson, Colin St John 25, 112
workroom 95, 100–103
Würzburg 60, 78

Z
Zig Zag Building, The 169, 171, 178–180, 182–183

Image Credits

Álvaro Siza: pp 148, 149
Andy Laurie: pp 152 (top and bottom left)
Annabel Gray: p 16
©Bernhard-Heiliger-Stiftung: p 76, 77 (bottom left)
Caroline Elam: p 13
Claudia Lynch: pp 31, 128 (middle right)
©David Grandorge: pp 170–171, 181 (bottom), 202–203
David Griffin: p 27
David Leatherbarrow: p 44
©Digne Meller Marcovicz: pp 99 (top right), 101
©Duccio Malagamba: pp 150, 152 (middle left), 153 (top and middle right), 154, 159, 160
Eric Parry: pp 52–53, 55 (top)
©Fondation Le Corbusier: p 78
Franz Oswald: p 25 (right)
©Gráinne Hassett, The Calais Builds Project: p 17
©Google Earth: p 117
Hans Kollhoff: p 27
©Hélène Binet: p 121 (right)
Hufton + Crow: p 182 (left)
Joseph Rykwert: pp 15, 37 (right)
Laura Evans: pp 108, 109, 152 (middle and bottom right)
Lynch Architects: pp 168–169, 172–173, 175, 176, 177 (top and bottom left), 179, 182 (right), 183
©Mike O'Dwyer: p 180 (top)
MIT Press: p 25 (left)
Museo Chillida-Leku: p 77
Nick Temple: p 131
Nikita Sheagill: p 181 (top)
Patrick Lynch: pp 8, 29, 32, 33, 35 (left), 37, 40, 41, 55, 71, 72, 81, 82, 83 (right), 84, 85, 92, 93, 94, 95, 96, 110, 111, 113, 118, 121 (left and middle), 124, 126, 127, 128, 130 (middle, bottom left and right), 133, 138, 141, 142–143, 143–144, 149 (top three), 153 (middle left and bottom right), 155, 156, 157, 158, 159, 163 (right), 166, 167, 172, 177 (bottom right), 181 (bottom), 183 (left)
Peter Carl: pp 62–63
Pär Hedefält: pp 139 (right), 140
Richard Serra: pp 8, 36
Ross Anderson: pp 99 (left and bottom right), 100 (right)
Roberto Sueiras Revuelta: p 83 (left)
Rory Gardiner: p 178, 179 (bottom right), 184, 185, 186, 189, 190
Sandra Martin: p 152 (top left)
Sigurd Lewerentz: p 139 (four on the left)
©Swedish Centre for Architecture and Design: pp 106, 107, 117, 119, 121 (right) and 122–123
©Sue Barr: pp 178, 180 (bottom), 182 (right), 183 (right), 187
©Tim Soar: pp 179 (bottom right), 184, 185, 188, 189
©The Alberti Group, Bath University, courtesy Robert Tavernor: pp 71 (top), 72 (right)
©Tom Rothery: pp 190–193, 201
Trevor Patt: p 130 (left)
Wikimedia Commons: p 151

Acknowledgements

This book is a version of my PhD dissertation (Practical Poetics, The Cass, 2015) and some ideas inspired by this research were published in *Mimesis* (Artifice books on architecture, 2015). This work began life before that as an M-Phil dissertation at Cambridge University written in 1996 (published as *The Theatricality of the Baroque City*, Verlag Dr Muller, 2011); the seeds of certain philosophical interests, in what has now become known as *Civic Ground*, originally germinated in my B-Arch dissertation at Liverpool University in 1993 (*Can Architecture be Poetry?*). I have to thank my supervisors Peter Carl, Helen Mallinson and Joseph Rykwert for their help with formulating many of the arguments that it presents. I am grateful also to the late and much missed Dalibor Vesely, for first introducing me to the architectural *decorum* of spatial situations. I am very grateful to Robert Mull who supported this work in many ways. John Glew introduced me to the work of many of the sculptors discussed in this dissertation. I also have to thank the artists Rut Blees Luxemburg, Joel Tomlin and Hilary Koob-Sassen for collaborating with me on the work presented in the final chapter, and David Chipperfield and Kieran Long for inviting us to develop this at the Venice Biennale in 2012. As well as all the people, organisations and institutions credited across the page, I have also to thank Andy Laurie, Álvaro Siza, Ross Anderson, Eric Parry, José de Paiva, Pär Hedefält, Wilfried Wang, Jürgen Teichmann, David Leatherbarrow, Gráinne Hassett, Kalle Söderman, Annabel Gray, David Grandorge, Hufton + Crow, Tim Soar, Sue Barr, Tom Rothery, Mike O'Dwyer, Hélène Binet, Frida Melin at the Swedish Centre for Architecture and Design, Trevor Patt, Laura Evans and Sandra Martin for the use of their images and for their critical advice and insight. I need also to thank Luis Chillida and his colleagues at Museo Chillida-Leku, and Rafael Moneo for his help in understanding the close relationships between sculpture, geography and architecture at San Sebastián. Nina Lundvall needs thanks for her translation for me of the most relevant parts of Lars Ridderstedt's doctoral dissertation on the architecture of Celsing and Lewerentz. I would not have been able to devote so much time to this work without the understanding and trust of my wife Claudia Lynch: as ever, she has been a wry, rigorous, critical friend. I would like to thank also our co-director at Lynch architects, David Evans for his wise counsel and for his appreciation of the importance of this work to me. I must also thank Maia Caiger-Smith, Clémence Monk, Mary Chapman and Jessica Hendey for their help in keeping Lynch Architects running over the past seven years and whilst I was writing this book. Finally I'd like to thank my children, Valentin and Lotte, for putting up with the various trips to see "architecture", and for repeatedly pointing out that there are many other interesting things to do as well.

Artifice books on architecture
10A Acton Street
London
WC1X 9NG

+44 (0)207 713 5097
sales@artificebooksonline.com
www.artificebooksonline.com

All opinions expressed within this publication are those of the authors and not necessarily of the publisher.

Designed by Emma Kalkhoven at Artifice books on architecture.

Cover image: *Silver Forest*, 2015 by Rut Blees-Luxemburg, made in collaboration with Lynch Architects. Photograph by David Grandorge.

Printed by KOPA, Lithuania.

British Library Cataloguing-in-Publication Data. A CIP record for this book is available from the British Library.

ISBN 978 1 908967 84 8

Artifice books on architecture is an environmentally responsible company. *Civic Ground: Rhythmic Spatiality and the Communicative Movement between Architecture, Sculpture and Site* is printed on sustainably sourced paper.